RETHINKING THE TRAUMA OF WAR

Rethinking the Trauma of War

EDITED BY

Patrick J. Bracken and Celia Petty

Save the Children

FREE ASSOCIATION BOOKS / LONDON / NEW YORK

Published in 1998 by
Free Association Books Ltd
57 Warren Street, London W1P 5PA
and 70 Washington Square South,
New York, NY 10012–1091

ISBN 1 85343 407 8 hbk; 1 85343 408 6 pbk.

A CIP record for this book is available from the British Library.

Produced for Free Association Books Ltd by
Chase Production Services, Chadlington, Oxon OX7 3LN
Printed in the EC by T.J. International, Padstow

Contents

Notes on Contributors

Editors

Patrick J. Bracken is a consultant psychiatrist and senior research fellow at the Department of Social and Economic Studies in the University of Bradford. He spent three years working for the Medical Foundation for the Care of Victims of Torture in Uganda, East Africa, and subsequently worked at the Foundation's centre in North London.

Celia Petty is a social policy adviser with Save the Children Fund (UK). She has a PhD in social policy and was previously based at the London School of Hygiene and Tropical Medicine. Since 1991 she has worked with SCF on overseas policy and has wide experience in the area of conflict, family separation and child rights.

Contributors

Joan Giller, a gynaecologist and medical anthropologist, worked for the Medical Foundation for the Care of Victims of Torture in Uganda, East Africa, for three years. Previously she worked as a doctor with Karen refugees on the Thai–Burmese border. She has researched and written about the subject of rape and sexual violence.

Elizabeth Jareg, a child psychiatrist, has been an adviser in child development and mental health with Redd Barna (SCF, Norway) since 1986. She has wide experience of work with children in conflict zones. Her publications include work on child development in cross-cultural contexts.

Margaret McCallin, formerly director of the Refugee Children's Programme, International Catholic Children's Bureau (ICCB), is currently working with UNHCR. Her academic background is in clinical psychology. She has been involved in programmes to promote the rehabilitation and social integration of former child combatants and street children affected by civil violence.

Krijn Peters, a rural sociologist, has collaborated with Paul Richards in his recent work on the impact of the conflict in Sierra Leone on young people.

Paul Richards is an anthropologist. He has twenty years experience working in rural areas of southern and eastern Sierra Leone and has written extensively on the causes and consequences of the war in that country.

Naomi Richman is a child psychiatrist and formerly senior lecturer in child psychiatry in London. She has worked with Save the Children Fund (UK) in Mozambique and as a consultant in other parts of the world. She has published extensively on the psychological effects of wartime violence on children and has also been involved in research into the needs of refugee children in London.

Annemiek Richters is a medial anthropologist and Professor of Women's Health Care at the University of Leiden in the Netherlands. She has worked as a consultant to Médecins Sans Frontières in the former Yugoslavia and has published widely on the subject of rape and sexual violence.

Derek Summerfield is a psychiatrist at the Medical Foundation for the Care of Victims of Torture and honorary senior lecturer in the Section of Community Psychiatry, St George's Hospital Medical School in London. He has worked as a consultant to Oxfam and is a research associate on the Refugees Study Programme, University of Oxford.

Acknowledgement

We are extremely grateful to Save the Children Fund which funded the conference at which many of the chapters in this book were first presented and for its continued support.

Introduction

At some point in the future, historians looking back at relief provided to civilian victims of war in the 1980s and 1990s will notice, towards the end of the 1980s, 'trauma' projects appearing alongside food, health and shelter interventions. They will see a steady increase in the budget allocated to these projects by the major international donors. They will see a peak in 1993–94, with simultaneous crises in the former Yugoslavia and Rwanda, then a levelling off – possibly – until the next major genocide or mass outrage filmed by the Western media. They will also notice that while spending on trauma projects has been rising, during the same period there has been a general decline in aid budgets and, in the first half of the 1990s, concern about spiralling emergency relief costs. The reasons behind the increasing concern and interest in trauma are complex; they involve an intricate web of relationships between science, public policy and the media. The fact that trauma projects are not capital intensive; that a high proportion of the costs are spent on expatriate consultancy fees; that sustainability need not be a problem, as the project stops with the counselling; and finally, that they have media appeal, all contribute to their popularity with donors.

Over the course of the past two decades, the language of trauma has become part of the vernacular – it is accessible and familiar in contemporary Western culture. Thus, whilst a mass audience may find modern warfare, waged against ordinary civilians, almost unimaginable in its scale and brutality, when that experience is translated into the everyday language of stress, anxiety and trauma, its character changes and it becomes less challenging.

In an article published ten years ago in the journal *Social Science and Medicine*, Higginbotham and Marsella pointed to the way in which psychiatric care varied little in the capital cities of Southeast Asia. This was in spite of large social, cultural and linguistic differences between the peoples of these cities. This 'homogenization of psychiatry' was brought about through the inputs of Western (largely British, American and Dutch) psychiatric experts. Via the mechanisms of international mental health education, consultation and collaboration these inputs had created a form of psychiatric practice in these different cities which looked to the West for its conceptual foundations and for ideas about innovation and progress. While the anticipated effect of these developments was a better standard of patient care, these authors pointed to the unanticipated and very negative consequences which meant, in practice, an actual deterioration in the care received by people with mental health problems. They presented evidence for serious deleterious 'after-shocks' within local cultural systems. For example:

> The inability of local centres to generate research and evaluate services, in combination with pervasive resource and personnel deficiencies, means that hospitals become custodial end-points for chronic cases. Drugs and electric shock treatment are overused and non-psychotic patients are drawn into hospital work forces.

In addition to this, they argued that the importation of Western concepts of healing had the effect of undermining indigenous health beliefs and discrediting the existing matrix of local healers. This, in turn, led to a decrease in 'local healing opportunities'. The authors came to the conclusion that:

> The net result of introducing a formal treatment system for psychological problems is less help for those in need. (Higgin-botham and Marsella 1988)

By providing trauma programmes, donor agencies and NGOs have an opportunity to intervene in a way that is perceived to be useful, without engaging with the broader political, economic and human rights abuses that have characterised recent conflicts. But whilst trauma projects may be intrinsically appealing to a mass public that catches glimpses of war through CNN and the BBC, and to politicians, aid officials and NGOs who need to let the public know they are doing something to help, do war-affected people derive any benefit from them? Our main concern is to reflect critically on theoretical and practical aspects of these projects and the social, political and cultural contexts in which they are applied. We wish to examine the suffering brought about by war and the forms of support and care which help people to pick up the pieces of their lives and move on. We argue that Western agencies need to substantially 'rethink' responses to the suffering of war and to reconsider the underlying assumptions from which these responses are derived. By questioning the scientific basis for trauma interventions, we challenge the orthodox view that informs officials in donor agencies and justifies the use of public money on these programmes.

Warfare in the Modern World

(In the period since the end of World War II, many countries in the developing world have witnessed large-scale destruction through both the direct and indirect consequences of warfare.)For example, between 1960 and 1987, no fewer than sixteen African countries were seriously affected by violence and political conflict (Ityavyar and Ogba, 1989), and since then many more countries on the continent have had direct experience of warfare. The extent of violent conflict in the developing world is reflected in statistics concerning refugees. The United Nations High Commissioner for Refugees (UNHCR) estimates that in 1960 there were 1.4 million refugees worldwide. By 1992 this figure had risen to 18.2 million (UNHCR, 1993). Most of these refugees are in the countries of Asia and Africa with less than 17 per cent of refugees residing in the richer countries of Western Europe, the US, Canada and Australia (Desjarlais et al., 1995).

While warfare has become located primarily in the countries of the developing world there has also been a shift in its nature. In recent years, low-intensity warfare, acted out in impoverished countries, has become the most frequent form of large-scale violent conflict:

> ... whereas 72% of the conflicts (analysed in 1987) were between a centralised political system, or 'state', and an ethnically distinct people, or 'nation', only 3% of the conflicts were between states (such as Iran and Iraq). In all, 82% of the conflicts involved politically marginal, 'fourth-world' peoples. Most of these conflicts pitted states against indigenous nations, and guerrilla insurgencies against state government. (Desjarlais et al., 1995)

In these conflicts civilians are no longer 'incidental' casualties but the direct targets of violence. Mass terror becomes a deliberate strategy. Destruction of schools, houses, religious buildings, fields and crops as well as torture, rape and internment, become commonplace. Modern warfare is concerned not only to destroy life, but also ways of life. It targets social and cultural institutions and deliberately aims to under-mine the means whereby people endure and recover from the suffering of war.

The Increasing Focus on Trauma

Many Western agencies working in these situations have begun to focus on the psychological aspects of endurance and recovery. They have initiated projects aimed at the 'psychological wounds' of war, and the notions of 'trauma' and 'trauma counselling' have become popular. This focus on the psychological effects of conflict is backed by a growing interest in the subject among psychiatrists, psychologists and indeed the lay public in Western countries. After both natural and man-made disasters, efforts to provide debriefing, counselling and therapy for survivors are widely seen as an essential part of the emergency response. In the context of conflict, children (particularly child soldiers) and women (particularly surivors of rape), are often the main targets for such interventions.

Much of the discourse on trauma has revolved around the concept of Post Traumatic Stress Disorder (PTSD). This concept was developed by psychiatrists in the US in the wake of the war in Vietnam and reflected their concern to recognise the suffering of many veterans of that war. The concept has achieved wide acceptance and has been used to describe reactions to trauma (or 'extreme events') in many different situations, including work with both civilian and military casualties of war. In the past twenty years it has become generally assumed that PTSD captures the fundamental psychological disturbance after any particular type of trauma/extreme event. Counselling and psycho-therapeutic techniques have been developed to respond to this entity.

However, there is a growing concern that the models developed in Western psychiatry with regard to the effects of trauma should not be exported uncritically. The explosion of interest in this area has happened so quickly and with such an urgency that there has been little critical reflection upon its relevance to non-Western societies. There is a concern that the export of this discourse has tended to deflect attention from the broader social, emotional and economic development of children and adults who have experienced extreme suffering and witnessed the destruction of their families and communities.

WHAT THIS BOOK IS ABOUT

In May 1996 a conference was organised in London under the auspices of the Save the Children Fund (UK). This two-day event brought together people from many different parts of the world who are involved in helping individuals and communities rebuild their lives after war and violence. The conference was the direct stimulus for this book. Many of its chapters are based on papers presented at the conference. The authors are doctors, NGO policy makers, and academics who have been involved, in different ways, with individuals and communities who have suffered the consequences of war. They have become increasingly sceptical about the benefits of the discourse on trauma and in particular its relevance to communities in the developing world. The chapters are divided into two groups. The first section is more theoretical and more general while the second deals with specific groups and has a more practical focus.

The first chapter, by Derek Summerfield, is a wide-ranging discussion of the collective experience of war and its social and cultural dimensions. It describes the methods and analyses the objectives of contemporary warfare and considers various aspects of the social response to this. Summerfield draws attention to the political and ideological significance of 'social memory' for people whose lives have been deeply affected by conflict and contrasts this with the pathological 'traumatic' memory which is used as a basis for expert interventions. Alternative principles for intervention which he outlines are developed and elaborated in many of the subsequent chapters; these include the importance of rebuilding informal networks for mutual social support, listening to local priorities and strengthening the family and community structures on which children depend for their security and development.

This is followed by Patrick Bracken's discussion of central themes in the current discourse on trauma. Bracken outlines the cultural assumptions involved in Western psychiatric approaches to madness, distress and healing. He argues that these assumptions also provide the basis for current approaches to trauma. He examines the importance of 'cognitivism' in this area and shows how this underscores the preoccupation with 'reliving the trauma', characteristic of many therapeutic approaches. Bracken suggests that because the concept of PTSD derives from a particular cultural orientation to suffering, its relevance to non-Western communities is very limited.

The next section focuses on affected populations: child soldiers, survivors of rape, refugees and children separated from their families and placed in institutional care. The first two categories, child soldiers and survivors of rape, have been singled out for particular attention in trauma programmes. Margaret McCallin reviews recent research on child soldiers, and presents findings on why children come to participate in conflict, what the consequences of involvement are for these children, and how their social reintegration can be supported. She concludes that programmes of psychological recovery are at best a distraction and that the real priorities for former child combatants are education, employment opportunities and economic security for their families. The anthropologist Paul Richards and rural sociologist Krijn Peters also deal with child combatants, but in this chapter young people involved in the conflict in Sierra Leone speak for themselves.

They describe the circumstances in which they became involved, their understanding of the war itself, and their analysis of their future prospects. The interviews reveal, in a compelling way, the complexity of the lives of these young people. They underscore the point that to regard child combatants as either evil bandits or traumatised victims is far too simplistic. This chapter contains a description of the development of the war in Sierra Leone from the early 1990s. As well as setting the scene for the interviews that follow, this also serves to illustrate the complex nature of many recent conflicts.

In his analysis of the tactics used to undermine the social fabric and cultural identity of adversaries in civil conflict, Summerfield draws attention to the particular significance of rape. Annemiek Richters develops the theme of sexual violence against women and draws on her experience working in an NGO mental health programme during the war in the former Yugoslavia. Her chapter includes an analysis of the social and political meanings and implications of rape in times of peace and war, and a critique of the many trauma interventions that took place in the former Yugoslavia – in particular the 'off the shelf' PTSD programmes, implemented by expatriates with little knowledge or understanding of the complex history and culture of the region. Although some programmes, notably those initiated by local women's organisations, addressed rape in the context of the many traumas and losses experience by women, these were the exception. Most programmes failed to respond to the needs and priorities as defined by the women themselves.

This theme is taken up by Joan Giller, who gives a personal account of her work in Uganda, shortly after the end of the civil war. Giller and another expatriate doctor (Patrick Bracken) were appointed by an agency based in the UK to set up a trauma counselling service in Kampala, the capital of Uganda. Recognising that this was not a local priority, she describes how she and a Ugandan colleague, Stella Kabaganda, set up a dialogue with women in the Luwero Triangle area, where killing, rape and 'scorched earth' tactics had been carried out on a massive scale during the war. These enquiries resulted in a women's health project that dealt with some of the survivors' immediate needs; but just as importantly, it laid the foundations for a local organisation through which women have been able to gain greater economic security for themselves and their children. However, Giller remains ambivalent about many aspects of the work and, by clearly pointing to the contradictions involved, questions the validity of such projects in general.

Media reports of mass rape and the use of children as fighters have contributed significantly to the current interest in psychological interventions. The social and emotional needs of children who have been left without the support of their families and communities as a result of conflict has provoked far less interest. There is, however, clear evidence that increasing numbers of children are being placed in institutions as a direct and indirect consequence of war. In their chapter on conflict, poverty and family separation, Celia Petty and Elizabeth Jareg analyse the specific problems that face children who are institutionalised during conflict, and review alternative approaches to their care. Rather than focus on a narrow range of psychological issues, they emphasise the need for policy coherence between governments, donors and NGOs that promotes the reintegration of children within families and communities. Their analysis highlights the importance of reconstructing education and health services in a way that ensures equitable access to all children, and of promoting the basic livelihood security of the most marginalised households.

Finally, Naomi Richman considers the experiences of asylum seekers in the West, whose experiences are often very different from those of refugees who are locally displaced, and remain with their compatriots in a more or less familiar culture. She analyses the unique set of challenges that face them as they confront an alien culture and draws inferences for policy and practice, for both governments and the non-government agencies that seek to support them.

Future Directions

This book represents just one perspective on the export of trauma programmes. All the contributors are from Western agencies or institutions. We have all been involved, in different ways, with the suffering brought about by war in the developing world and have all become sceptical about this export. We have had experience of the negative effects of such programmes and have witnessed at first hand the 'cultural aftershocks', which are never recorded in conventional trauma research. We offer a critique of the trauma discourse, from within. It is not part of our agenda to offer a 'new approach', or to argue that there is a better way of doing 'trauma work', although many contributions do discuss different aspects of 'useful work'. It is not our job to speak for the people of the developing world about what should, or should not, happen. We can only point to some of the harm that is being done, and how it can be avoided. We are, however, hopeful that our critique may now open a debate about this work, a debate in which *perspectives from the developing world* can be heard and shared. We see this as the way forward.

Allowing such voices their place is never easy or simple in a world of large donor and provider organisations. However, in our view, this is essential. If UN and Western NGOs are to avoid doing harm through trauma interventions, they will need to learn how to listen and be guided by the people they claim to serve. We hope that the publication of this book will help international organisations rethink their involvement in trauma work. We hope that it will contribute to a climate in which people in the developing world who have suffered the effects of war and violence are allowed to speak and where they are heard and understood by those who wish to assist them.

References

Desjarlais, R., Eisenberg, L., Good, B. and Kleinman, A. (1995). *World Mental Health. Problems and Priorities in Low-Income Countries.* New York: Oxford University Press, p. 117.

Higginbotham, N. and Marsella, A. (1988). International consultation and the homogenization of psychiatry in Southeast Asia. *Social Science and Medicine* 27, 553–61.

Ityavyar, D.A. and Ogba, L.O. (1989). Violence, conflicts and health in Africa. *Social Science and Medicine* 28, 649–57.

UNHCR (1993). *The State of the World's Refugees 1993: The Challenge of Protection.* New York: Penguin.

1 The Social Experience of War and Some Issues for the Humanitarian Field

DEREK SUMMERFIELD

This chapter is concerned with the role of social processes in shaping outcomes – for good or ill – of the experience of war, at the level of the individual, community and society. It has four sections. Firstly, there is a brief overview of the ways that modern war and violent conflict are waged, and thus experienced by those whom the humanitarian field seeks to assist. This includes mention of the impact on women, on health workers and services, and on cultural life and identity. Secondly, some aspects and examples of social responses to war, torture and exile are presented. Thirdly, there is a discussion of the role of memory and meaning in shaping social struggle. This social memory is contrasted with the 'traumatic' memory which trauma consultants see as a basis for their interventions and prognostications. Lastly, the issues which emerge for those planning and implementing programmes for war-affected populations are discussed.

MAJOR THEMES IN MODERN CONFLICT

There have been an estimated 160 wars and armed conflicts in the Third World since 1945, with 22 million deaths and 3 times as many injured (Zwi and Ugalde, 1989). There were on average 9 wars active in any year during the 1950s, 11 during the 1960s, 14 during the 1970s, and at least 50 currently. Torture is routine in over 90 countries. Of all casualties in World War I, 5 per cent were civilians, in World War II 50 per cent, over 80 per cent in the US war in Vietnam, and currently over 90 per cent (UNICEF, 1986). In their report *The State of the World's Children 1996* UNICEF says that in the last 10 years, 2 million children have died in war, 4–5 million have been wounded or disabled, 12 million made homeless and 1 million orphaned or separated from parents. At present the United Nations

High Commission for Refugees (UNHCR) counts 18 million refugees who have fled across an international border, a sixfold increase on 1970, but as many again are internally displaced and often no less destitute. This totals one person in 125 of the entire world population. Of all war refugees, 90 per cent are in Third World countries, many amongst the poorest on earth. Between 2.5 and 5 per cent of the refugee population are unaccompanied children.

During the 1980s and 1990s there was serious conflict in Mozambique, Angola, El Salvador, Guatemala, Nicaragua, South Africa, Peru, Colombia, Ethiopia, Sudan, Somalia, Sierre Leone, Algeria, Liberia, Zaire, Rwanda, Afghanistan, Iran, Iraq, Kuwait, Turkey, Azerbaijan, Russian Chechynia, Israeli Occupied Territories, Indian Kashmir, Sri Lanka, Indonesian East Timor, China, Philippines, the former Yugoslavia, Northern Ireland and other places. The two most publicised in the 1990s have been Rwanda, where up to 14 per cent of the total population – almost all Tutsis – were slaughtered in just three months in 1994, and Bosnia where 200,000 have died and 20,000 are still missing. Over 90 per cent of modern wars have not been conducted between sovereign states and are 'internal': the majority of those targeted come from the poorest sectors of society, and from ethnic minorities with few allies at home or abroad. In Africa, Asia and Latin America, such wars are frequently played out against a backdrop of subsistence economies, with rural dwellers bearing the brunt. Many do not have a clear-cut endpoint, may become endemic and thus a part of 'normal life', incorporated into the day-to-day decision making of whole populations.

A key element of modern political violence is the creation of states of terror to penetrate the entire fabric of economic, sociocultural and political relations as a means of social control. It is often what has been termed 'total' war at the grassroots level. In some cases, as in South Africa or Argentina, the oppressive state initially picks off only known activists but with time begins to use terror as a blunter, less discriminating instrument. In El Salvador it was said that the military wanted to kill anyone with a thought in his or her head. The targeting of ordinary people, politicised or not, and their ways of life is not incidental but central to the modus operandi of most modern conflict. In Bosnia the mass execution of men; the shelling of cities; the homes, factories and mosques dynamited after whole populations have been driven out were all meant to say that there would be no going back, no resumption of pre-war norms. In Guatemala or El Salvador the mutilated bodies of those abducted by security agents, dumped in a public place, were props in a political theatre meant to render whole communities a stunned audience.

Observers of these conflicts noted that the decapitation of children was particularly effective as a mechanism of social terror. Indeed, nowhere are children exempted from violence. In Brazil squads of off-duty policemen regard the elimination of street children as a form of social work. In (white) South Africa 24,000 children as young as twelve were detained in 1985–89 without access to parents and lawyers and some tortured. In the Occupied Territories 25 per cent of Palestinians shot dead on the streets by the Israeli army in 1988–93 were children. During the 1980s the infant mortality rate in Mozambique, where (white) South Africa-sponsored Renamo guerillas were propagating a ruinous war, was said to be the highest in the world. There were 320,000 extra child deaths between 1981 and 1986, as well as 200,000 left orphaned or separated from their parents. There was general hunger, epidemics of measles (400 times more lethal in malnourished children), cholera, malaria and diarrhoea (Cliff and Noormahomed, 1988).

An estimated 250,000 children under eighteen years of age are presently serving in government armies or armed opposition groups. During the first years of the war in Afghanistan 10 per cent of combatants were under sixteen and 17 per cent between sixteen and eighteen (total 27 per cent). In the latest stage, the estimated proportions are 19 per cent and 26 per cent respectively (total 45 per cent). Child soldiers often carry out dangerous tasks like spying and mine laying. Children volunteered, or were coerced, into active involvement in thrity-three conflicts during 1995–96. Many do not see themselves as victims (see other chapters in this book). However some are abused during military training, killed for trying to escape, or expected to commit atrocities alongside adult soldiers or guerillas, sometimes against their own communities.

It is depressingly clear that these forms of warfare do work well for those who deploy them. War is not 'irrational' or 'senseless', as the media often calls it: there are winners and losers and assets pass from one to the other (Duffield, 1995). The war in the former Yugoslavia was not the result of 'Balkan blood' or 'ancient hatreds', terms that were bandied about at its outset, but of rational calculation. Without atrocity and ethnic cleansing the Bosnian Serbs could not have achieved the political gains they hold today. Economic and military elites have always defended power and privilege by violent means when necessary. Guatemala, where 150,000 largely rural people have been murdered by the state in the past thirty years, has long had the most distorted land ownership patterns in Latin America: 75 per cent of all land is owned by 2 per cent of landowners. Landless peasants can thus be kept dependent on seasonal work, under feudal conditions, on the large estates. Wars also generate consequences which take on a life of their own, not least through the spillage of weapons from war zones to other social arenas. The cheap hand-held automatic rifle has become a potent force in the lives of millions of people. In many settings there is an increasingly fine line between political and criminal violence, with security forces involved in unbridled profiteering, blackmarketing and extortion.

A full account of the effects of war would need to include discussion of the damage to infrastructural elements like roads, bridges and factories as well as crops and livestock – all of which impose huge burdens on postwar recovery. However, here I wish to focus on descriptions of the impact of war on women, health services and cultural institutions.

Women in War

Sexual violation is an endemic yet poorly visible facet of violent conflict (Swiss and Giller, 1993). After the declaration of independence from Pakistan by Bangladesh in 1971, it is reliably estimated that between 200,000 and 400,000 Bengali women, 80 per cent of whom were Muslim, were raped by Pakistani soldiers sent to quell the rebellion. In Mozambique and elsewhere women have been abducted and effectively enslaved in large numbers. In Iran, detained teenagers executed for political reasons have first been raped, denying them the automatic entry to heaven granted to virgins (Parliamentary Human Rights Group, 1994). Cambodian and Somali women have faced sexual violation before and during flight, and in refugee camps in Thailand and Kenya respectively, sometimes by camp authorities or local police. In India, women community organisers and human rights workers appear to be prime targets for rape. An estimated 250,000 women and girls were raped in Rwanda between April 1994 and April 1995. In Iraq under Saddam Hussein, there are licenced rapists employed as civil servants by the state. Many prisons in Iraq are reported to have specially equipped rape rooms. In Arab/Islamic culture, the honour of a family is located in the bodies of the women of that family; in their virginity, the clothes they wear and the modesty with which they deport themselves. The rape of a woman is thus a way of penetrating to the inner sanctum of her entire family's honour (Makiya, 1993). Most recently, there were the well-publicised systematic rapes of Bosnian Muslim women by Serb militias (see chapter 5, this volume). Underreporting of rape by victims is probably universal because of the associated stigma, perhaps most pervasive in societies (as in Asia) in which virginity is regarded as a woman's single most important asset in securing happiness.

The role of women during war has been described almost exclusively in relation to victim status. This has tended to obscure the extent to which women made significant contributions to political struggles in countries like Eritrea, Ethiopia and Nicaragua. But the attempted genocide in Rwanda in 1994 has shown women taking up a rather darker role, that of perpetrator. Educated women of every category, as well as peasants, participated in the genocide. Women teachers, civil servants, doctors, nurses and nuns made lists of people to be killed, handed over patients or others sheltering in hospitals or churches, betrayed colleagues, sang and ululated the killers into action, wielded machetes themselves and stripped the dead or barely living of their jewellery, money and clothes (African Rights, 1995).

Targeting Health Workers and Services

Violations of medical neutrality are a consistent feature worldwide and follow predictably from the way modern war is premised and played out. In Mozambique, 1,113 primary health centres, 48 per cent of the national total, were destroyed and looted, leaving two million people without access to health care of any kind. Mines were laid around hospitals and in the massacre of 494 people at Homoine in 1987, pregnant women were bayoneted in the maternity unit and other patients kidnapped. In Nicaragua, destruction of rural health clinics and targeting of their staff by Contra guerillas was meant to demonstrate that central government could not protect what was valued by its citizens and 300,000 (15 per cent of the rural population) were left without any health care (Garfield and Williams, 1989). Many health workers were forced to operate in clandestine fashion in the countryside, burying their equipment and medicines at night; this impeded the effectiveness of primary health work, such as immunisation, which depended on advance publicity.

In El Salvador, the extra-judicial execution or 'disappearance' of more than twenty health professionals in the first six months of 1980 set the tone for much of the decade. Soldiers made incursions into hospitals and surgeons were assassinated in mid-operation on suspicion that they were prepared to treat 'subversives'. The practice of medicine or community health care in rural areas was regarded by the military as linked to subversion, since the health worker was a source of advice and support to the peasant population. The bodies of health workers were left for discovery in a mutilated state: decapitated,

castrated or with 'EM' (Spanish initials for 'death squad') carved in
their flesh. This was exemplary brutality. In the Philippines, 102
health workers were subjected to extrajudicial killing or arbitrary
detention in 1987–89 by the army or government agents. Nurses in
rural areas faced death threats, sometimes broadcast on local radio
stations; these were intended to 'politicise' the clinics they ran and
make local people afraid to attend (Summerfield, 1992). Hospitals in
Croatia and Bosnia were repeatedly mortared by Serb forces; at
Vukovar 261 staff and patients were taken away for execution. During
the intifada in the Occupied Territories, the Israeli army fired into
hospitals and arrested patients, refused to allow seriously ill Palestinians to reach hospitals during curfews, assaulted, detained and
tortured health workers and obstructed delivery of key medicines
(Physicians for Human Rights, 1993). The United Nations Relief and
Works Association reported that in 1990 alone, Israeli soldiers forcibly
entered its clinics and hospitals 159 times.

The Iraqi government responded mercilessly to an attempted
uprising in the Shiite south after the Gulf War. They paid special
attention to those who had kept their hospitals open during the
uprising. Fifteen doctors at the Jumhuri Hospital in Basra were
executed on the spot and artillery fired at the building, crammed with
4,000 civilians. At Saddam Hospital in Najaf, army troops molested
female doctors, murdered patients with knives or threw them out of
windows. Other doctors were executed in public by firing squads. In
Indian Kashmir, a persistent pattern of extrajudicial abuses, and
impunity for the perpetrators, strongly suggests official policy. In
February 1993, Dr Farooq Ahmed Ashir, Chief Orthopaedic Surgeon
at Srinagar's Bone and Joint Hospital, was shot dead at an Indian army
checkpoint. He had recorded numerous cases of torture and assault on
civilians, giving evidence to Asia Watch and Physicians for Human
Rights. Professionals who see health in its widest sense – concerned
not just with what makes an individual sick, but what makes a whole
society unhealthy – cannot but raise questions which oppressive
regimes find subversive.

Even international peacekeeping operations are not immune to
violations of the Geneva Convention regarding the neutrality of
medical services. On 17 March 1993, United Nations forces in
Somalia, in pursuit of the warlord General Aideed, deliberately
attacked Digfa hospital in Mogadishu. Nine patients were killed and
there was extensive destruction of scarcely replaceable equipment and
supplies. The hospital was immediately evacuated, decanting hundreds of patients into the wartorn city; it is not known how many
more died as a result.

Assaults on Culture and Identity

Another key dimension is the crushing of the social and cultural institutions which connect a particular people to their history, identity and lived values. This was the norm during the era of Empire and even slavery was justified in the name of Christianity and 'civilisation'. A West African chief in those times is reputed to have commented: 'When the White man arrived he had the bible and we had the land. Now we have the bible and he has the land.' Following the Chinese takeover of Tibet in 1959, the number of monasteries fell from 2,500 to 70 in two years, and the number of monks and nuns reduced by 93 per cent. Countless statues of Buddha were broken and scriptures burned. Since their invasion in 1977 the Indonesian authorities have murdered an estimated 200,000 East Timorese, an ethnically distinct people. This is nearly one-third of the total population. The Pol Pot regime in Cambodia murdered between 1.5 and 3 million people, 20–40 per cent of the total population, in only four years from 1975. In a deeply religious land, Buddhist monks were singled out for execution and more than 90 per cent succumbed. So too was anyone found to speak French or even those wearing spectacles, since these were considered marks of the educated and modern. In Guatemala 440 Mayan villages were wiped from the map during the 1980s in a campaign of terror intended to eliminate them as a distinct cultural entity. The Serbs did not invent ethnic cleansing! At least 1.5 million people died in the Sudanese civil war during the 1980s; repeated large massacres of Dinka civilians were poorly reported in the outside world.

It was protest against Afrikaans as the medium of education, regarded as the language of the oppressor, which sparked the Soweto riots of 1976 in which around 500 black children were shot dead by the authorities. In Turkey, the Kurdish culture and language has long been suppressed and children must speak Turkish in school, a persecution which has fostered violent revolt by Kurdish activists. In 1992, 109 civilians were killed while celebrating Kurdish New Year (Newroz). Since 1992, 27 journalists and editors have been murdered or disappeared, newspaper offices bombed or shut down, and in 1997, 421 journalists were arrested. The Turkish government has brought 'low intensity' war to the Kurdish South East, with around 25,000 dead in the past thirteen years and 3,000 villages systematically destroyed. The Kurds – comprising 26 million in Turkey, Iraq, Iran, Syria, Armenia and Azerbaijan – are the largest ethnic group in the world without a nation state.

Middle East Watch (1993) documented that the Iraqi government campaign against its Kurdish population in the 1990s amounted to genocide within the meaning of the Genocide Convention of 1951. This included the use of poison gas – a mixture of mustard and nerve gas – dropped by aircraft, most notoriously on the town of Halabja in 1988 in which 5,000 civilians died. Many villages, with every building razed by explosives, have ceased to exist. And at the other end of the country, Saddam Hussein mounted a devastating assault against cultural and religious life in the Shiite south in the immediate aftermath of the Gulf War. Within a few weeks some 5,000 religious scholars and students from Najaf alone had been arrested and all the religious schools shut down. Many were executed. Mosques and their ancient cemeteries were levelled, the Golden Dome of the Shrine of Ali was hit by artillery fire and the interior ravaged. The cultural offensive against holy sites, seminaries and libraries continued long after the fighting in the cities was over. Ancient treasures that had survived centuries were looted or transported to Baghdad, representing gifts accrued over a thousand years. The libraries of the religious schools and seminaries of Najaf, Kufa and Kerbala were burned with their ancient manuscripts. It is possible that the scale and organised character of the assault has ended a thousand-year-old tradition of religious scholarship and learning, with unpredictable future consequences (Makiya, 1993).

In Bosnia hundreds of mosques have been intentionally destroyed by Serb militias and the educated amongst their prisoners reportedly singled out for execution. So too in Rwanda. When the army took over in Argentina in 1976, their attacks on the progressive professional sector included the burning of books from the university. In Mozambique the Renamo guerillas also targeted education and 45 per cent of all primary schools were forced to close.

SOME ASPECTS OF THE SOCIAL RESPONSE TO WAR, TORTURE AND EXILE

In the face of this multi-layered attack, the struggle to survive takes place in the context of a damaged social fabric, which in a different or lesser crisis might have retained more of its capacity to help people adjust and endure. For example, in the Sudanese civil war, disruption of the traditional cycle of animal husbandry brought social breakdown to the pastoralist southerners. Cattle were crucial to them, being a form of currency not just in trading but in rituals and disputes. Tribal marriages could no longer be arranged because of dislocation and lack of cattle (the only traditional dowry). Because of the endemic killings and rape in the countryside, security conditions became prime determinants of social behaviour, to the extent that families with noisy children were pushed out. Substantial numbers were forced to abandon their rural traditions and way of life, seeking precarious safety in urban areas where their traditional skills were worthless. Under normal circumstances Dinka people practised a tradition that ensured the survival of a man's name and lineage if he died or disappeared. The family took responsibility for finding a suitable replacement, often one of his brothers or first cousins, to produce children with his wife. This practice, known as *lahot* (entering the hut), was valued for its role in maintaining networks between families and strengthening political relationships with other groups. But it was undermined by the damage done to the local economy by raids by government militias and the neighbouring Nuer. The rules which governed family ties and support mechanisms gave way to looser networks which did not offer the same protection. Thus many women with absent husbands received little help, and were liable to be unwillingly displaced to camps where only prostitution averted total destitution for them and their children (Jok, 1995).

Guatemalan Indians, hunted by 'low intensity' warfare, felt that their collective body had been wounded, one which included the ants, trees, earth, domestic animals and human beings gathered across generations. Mayan origin myths are linked to land and maize. To them the burning of crops by the army was not just an attack on their physical resources, but on the symbol which most fully represented the Mayan collective identity, the people of maize (Lykes, 1994). When they talked about 'sadness' they meant something experienced not just by humans but also by these other interconnected elements which had been violated. When you touched the earth you could feel its sadness, and you could taste it in the water (Smith, 1997). To them all this was genocide. For the internally displaced, the war played havoc with their traditions. It was hard to pray to a local deity when you no longer lived near the geographical feature associated with it. In the Philippines women raped by soldiers during 'low intensity' offensives can end up as prostitutes in Manila. The definitive injury rape has inflicted on them, a catastrophic one, is social, because there is now no place for them in their rural communities.

Local Understandings, Organisations, Identity

The repertoire of explanations available to a particular people at a time of crisis draws on diverse ideologies and identities, often more than one at a time, and in dynamic and shifting relationships to each other. The Guatemalan Mayans have drawn on animism, Catholicism and the politics of oppression, an amalgam of which is at the heart of what it means to be Mayan. These meaning systems may throw up alternative or competing understandings. Catholic teaching in Latin America has traditionally carried an ethic of acceptance opposed to activist struggle. The downtrodden were enjoined to accept their lot on this earth and to wait for their reward in the world to come. But many Mayans also interpreted the pitiless violence of the 1980s in terms of traditional concepts like malignant fate, ancestral punishment and malicious envy (Zur, 1994). Recently, US-based Protestant evangelical churches have been proselytising hard amongst the Mayans, and have probably been able to take advantage of the cultural disruption wrought by the war. They purport to support Mayan culture but in fact classify much of the work of priests and traditional practitioners as witchcraft. This too can be used against a political construction of events, since state violence and poverty can be construed as the result of dabbling with the forces of evil (Smith, 1997).

In Cambodia, the local word meaning torture derives from the Buddhist term for karma, an individual's thoughts and actions (often bad) in a prior existence, which affect life in the present. Thus survivors can feel somehow responsible for their suffering (Mollica and Caspi-Yavin, 1992). In Mozambique both the Renamo guerillas and government forces sought to heighten the impact of their military efforts by incorporating traditional sources of ritual power – ancestors' spirits and myths of male invincibility, including ceremonies conferring 'vaccination' against bullets. The rural peasantry did the same thing to bolster their capacity to resist Renamo violence. Thus a war driven by South Africa's destabilisation policies has been imbued by local understandings and world views, becoming in part a 'war of the spirits'. This spiritual vivification and other cultural shifts may outlast the war, with as yet unknown effects upon the social order.

It is simplistic to see those exposed to these events as merely helpless victims, unable to act on their environment. Society and culture are impacted on by war, but also engage with it. Despite the assault on their way of life, the Guatemalan Mayans have emerged with a strengthened cosmology. The upheavals saw many seek new refuge in the old traditions, shamans and deities. Communities in flight petitioned the mountain spirits for the right to pass through their domain, and to take on a guardian angel role. At the same time there was a growth in politically conscious grassroots organisation in exile, a preparedness to write, speak and campaign openly whilst remaining on a platform of 'Mayanness' (Wearne, 1994).

The aftermath of war in Uganda has seen an erosion in the power of traditional elders and their wisdom. The refugee experience has undermined their influence since they have not been in a position to negotiate bridewealth payments as of old. There has also been the appointment of ritually insignificant men as government chiefs. For example, amongst the Madi people of the Moyo district, one of the reasons why the explanations of affliction offered by the elders were taken less seriously is that the intervention of ancestors, for whom they were interlocutors, was no longer considered to be the problem. Surely the ancestors would not have left people to suffer so much for so long, to witness such atrocities and the death of their children. The ancestors induced suffering for moral purposes but surely there were malign forces at work here. This meant witchcraft, in the form of young women seen to be possessed by wild and new spirits, including the ghosts of those slaughtered and left to rot in the bush rather than buried in the ordained manner. Witch killing can be seen in terms of the basic social need to make sense of suffering, to enforce social accountability and the emergence of a sustainable mode of communal order. The advent of AIDS, accelerated by war, was another challenge too great for the capacity of the elders to regulate and explain events. New forms were needed, with AIDS viewed as a 'poison' encompassable by beliefs drawn from witchcraft, Christianity and biomedicine (Allen, 1996). From Somalia too come accounts of the waning influence of traditional sources of wisdom.

The Mursi tribe of Southwestern Ethiopia see warfare as a means by which the very notion of their separate political identity is kept alive. Warfare has traditionally been a pervasive feature of their social organisation, an underpinning of 'normal' political relations and not a breakdown. It is at the heart of the balance they have struck with neighbouring tribes over time. However, this reciprocity has more recently been damaged by the introduction of weapons originating from the Sudanese civil war (Turton, 1991).

The push and pull of social tensions around political crisis and war impact on the way people define their identity. During the years of the then Yugoslavia, its citizens did not routinely feel that their bottom-line identification was as 'Serb' or 'Croat' or 'Bosnian

Muslim'. There would have been other identities, based on occupation or political affiliation or other role, which were more relevant to daily life than ethnicity. A man might have seen himself as much as 'carpenter' or 'communist' as he did 'Catholic Croat', yet it was this last which came to define him after the civil war started, whether he liked it or not. In South Africa, Zulu identity, which had never before been an issue in the anti-apartheid struggle, was manipulated by Zulu politicians and by elements of the white political and military establishment; both parties feared a loss of influence in the transition to black democratic, and non-tribal, rule. Between 1990 and 1994, 14,000 died in the massacres that ensued. Enmities have not subsided with majority rule, and killings continue. It can be argued that seccessionist movements in many parts of Africa and Asia are attesting to a perceived failure of the nation state, defined by boundaries bequeathed it by departing colonial powers and too often organised around the interests of local elites, to deliver what its citizens expect from their citizenhood. Older identities – around ethnicity or religion – may re-emerge as seeming to offer a more viable and coherent framework for their lives. Some of this alienation arises from what is seen to be the failure of Westernisation to deliver at the grass roots.

Torture, Expressions of Illness, Exile

'Torture' has come to be reified as an exquisite and distinct variant of 'trauma', yet it has no distinctive psychological presentation or syndrome and is handled as a function of individual personality strengths, the meaning assigned to events, and of social factors operating for good or ill at home or in exile. Basoglu et al. (1994) studied Turkish activists with a history of torture and found that the secondary consequences – on family, social and economic life – were more important predictors of outcomes than the torture *per se*. In Iraqi asylum-seekers in London, poor social support had a closer relationship to depression than did a history of torture (Gorst-Unsworth and Goldenberg, 1998). A recent study of refugee Tibetan nuns and lay students tortured by the Chinese found higher anxiety levels than in a control group, and asylum-seekers in Australia with a history of exposure to traumatic events (including torture in some cases) seemed to have more PTSD and perceived more difficulties in dealing with officialdom (Holtz, 1998; Silove et al., 1997). But neither study found evidence that the health status and overall functioning of these subjects was significantly reduced, nor that they needed formal psychological help. Some torture survivors say that this is not the worst thing that has happened to them. They cite other experiences, like the ominous disappearance of a brother, witnessing the gruesome death of people they valued, the crushing of their community or cause, as having affected them more.

In Brazil, people have come to express their responses to violent oppression and poverty through a metaphor of mental disorder (nervos or nerves). It is safer to be ill than to name the political factors that have made their lives so distressing. More typically, survivors of war and its upheavals bring concerns or distress couched in a somatic idiom. These ailments are often culturally endorsed forms of expression, as well as reflecting the elements of illness considered relevant to present in a medical setting (Lin et al., 1985). They may also be the only available expressions of the collective distress of powerless and persecuted peoples denied a social validation of their suffering and humanity (Farias, 1991).

Those forced into exile experience a rupture in the narrative thread running through their lives and around which they have organised their actions and associations. They must negotiate disrupted life trajectories, loss of status, culture shock and the attitude of the host society – ranging from accepting to discriminatory. Some seek to hold tight to traditional values and take a conservative attitude to the new social milieu; others want to assimilate. Thus there may be pressure on ethical values which until then had been unquestioned. Traditional hierachies, in particular the relations between generations, are subject to new forces and persuasions. Many master this crisis but others continue to be plagued by the sense that they are living in a broken social world. The uprooted may lack the social and emotional support which is protective in bereavement: some cases of chronic ill-health and illness behaviour, or difficulty in engaging with new challenges, may reflect unresolved grief (Eisenbruch, 1984). Lack of jobs is arguably making adaptation to exile in a Western country rather harder than, say, twenty years ago. There is also the question of what exile means to the refugee (see chapter 8, this volume). Those who were social activists, who have a firm political view on why they were persecuted, may behave differently from others who see themselves more as unlucky bystanders. Iraqi Arab refugees in Western Europe have defined 'refugee' as someone who could not go home. In contrast Iraqi Assyrian refugees have seen 'refugee' as someone who had no home, and do not view themselves as having 'lost' Iraq. Because of this they have much more of the attitude of a settler in their new environment (Al-Rasheed, 1994).

Memory, Meaning and Social Struggle

Researchers conceptualise Post Traumatic Stress Disorder as a disease of memory, arising because what they call 'traumatic memory' has been incompletely processed by the brain. In fact an authoritative account by Young (1995) shows why 'traumatic memory' is not a found object but a socially constructed one, originating in the scientific and clinical debates of the nineteenth century. There has always been unhappiness and disturbing recollections but not traumatic memory, in the sense that it is defined and deployed today. Young points out that during this century professional definitions of memory have tended to its removal from the exclusive ownership of the person carrying it, handing it over to experts to pronounce on its meaning and significance. Given that war is a public and collective experience, leaving memories which can be described as social as much as personal, these biomedicalised and individualised concepts have limited explanatory power and application.

It is a fundamental premise that what victims of terror and the upheavals of war experience is a function of what these events mean to them, or come to mean. Social memory is a wellspring for such understandings and attributions since it provides the backdrop against which current events can be set. Social memory carries a view or views of history and identity, of past crises and tests, and paradigms of struggle, heroism and wisdom at such times. It can thus offer time-honoured modes of coping, adaptation and problem solving on a collective basis.

Social memory is tenacious. The major religion in Cuba is not Catholicism but Santeria, which is derived from the Yoruba traditions of West Africa carried by the slaves transported there from the sixteenth century onwards. Though the social memory of slavery itself has faded, it lives on in the descendants of slaves as an ancient cultural form flourishing in a new world. In South Africa, the social memory of the deaths, through disease, of around 25,000 Boer women and children interned by the British during the Boer war of 1899–1902 (the first known use of concentration camps) had an enduring effect on the Afrikander mindset, colouring attitudes to the outside world as well as internally. In 1989, a displaced Nicaraguan peasant Juana Jiron Romero, a victim of several horrific attacks by US-sponsored Contra guerrillas, told me: 'This war is just a continuation of the one which my ancestors had to fight with bows and arrows against the conquistadors.' In Guatemala, the capacity of the indigenous Mayans to withstand mass murder and displacement in the 1980s was founded on a similar sense of history, the knowledge accumulated through having weathered attempts over five hundred years to eliminate, diminish or change them as a people. In Northern Ireland, Protestant and Catholic communities each draw on and are sustained by their own social memory of the past three hundred years, two versions that are hard to reconcile to each other.

My research in Nicaragua with war-maimed young men revealed how much they had been fortified by the belief that they had made a worthwhile sacrifice for what was at stake in the war, which for them and their society was the chance to shake off the shackles of local elites allied to US imperialism. It was the chance to redefine what it meant to be a Nicaraguan, to reclaim the central ground of their own history (Hume and Summerfield, 1994). One of the most telling recent examples of this capacity to draw on social or political values, and on co-operative effort and solidarity, has come from evidence about a secret military prison, Tazmamart, in Morocco (Van Ginneken and Rijnders, 1993). For eighteen years, fifty-nine men found guilty of sedition after unfair trials were held incommunicado and in almost complete darkness in small single cells which they never left. Split between two separated wings of equal size, they were exposed to extremes of temperature, poor food, little water, no medical care and no contact with their families. In one wing, where prisoners had structured their time with joint activities from their cells, including recitations from the Koran, twenty-four survived. However, in the second wing, where this did not happen and there was always chaotic argument and tension, only four survived.

Children, too, are not just 'innocent' and passive victims, but also active citizens whose values and causes are connected to collective meanings and memories. In Gaza, strong identification with the aspirations of Palestinian nationhood seemed to offer psychological protection to children facing high levels of violence from the Israeli army. The more they were exposed to political hardship, the more they deployed active and courageous coping modes (Punamaki and Suleiman, 1990). This does not mean that they did not also have fears, grief, nightmares or bedwetting. Similar observations were made in South Africa about young black activists during the apartheid era (Dawes, 1990).

We should not of course imagine that social memory necessarily carries 'truth' in a pristine form. Remembering is a purposeful activity: as time throws up new circumstances and demands, the meaning we give to our memories may change, and perhaps the memories themselves. In this sense the past is always available to be rewritten, for good or for ill. In France, social memory of German occupation during World War II has tended to exaggerate the extent of active resistance, and to play down the fact that the vast majority of civilians simply wanted to survive and saw no point in doomed gestures of defiance. It might be argued that national self-esteem required a unifying myth after the war. With the passage of time this version has been gradually challenged, and a social memory of heroic resistance has had to accommodate some new and uncomfortable material: not just passive collaboration by civilians but also active collusion by officials in the deportation of French Jews. Triumph over adversity, as we have seen in Eritrea and South Africa, may serve to take the sting out of memories of the hardship along the way. Conversely, some of the Nicaraguan men mentioned above had later been sufficiently disappointed by the electoral defeat of the Sandinista government to lose the sense of having suffered in a good cause. They now feared that it had all been in vain and for a second time were having to come to terms, different terms, with physical disability and the other losses. The rise of a belligerent Serbian nationalism in Europe, and its expression in atrocity and ethnic cleansing in Bosnia and Croatia, is rooted in a self-justifying discourse in which Serbian history is characterised as a long period of unjust victimisation which only now can be redeemed. Israel justifies its place in the Middle East, and by implication its treatment of the Palestinians, in terms of a social memory of centuries of persecution in Europe.

A study of Sudanese teenagers displaced to Juba from rural villages regarded as ancestral places showed the resulting loss of social identity and memory: none could write a history of his or her clan and many did not even know the names of their grandparents or the village their clan came from. Not one could name any traditional social ceremonies (Panos, 1988). Frequently at stake are the cultural and social forms which for a particular people define the known world and its version of humanity. In Africa, Asia and Latin America there are subsistence people who may not be able to imagine personal survival if their way of life does not survive. Indeed there are no socially defined ways of mourning a lost way of life. A social group is in an extreme predicament when it finds that what has happened seems incomprehensible and that traditional recipes for handling crises are useless. If events seem meaningless people feel helpless and uncertain of what to do.

Milan Kundera wrote that the struggle between people and power was the struggle between remembering and forgetting. All over the world oppressive regimes seek to control and manipulate social memory, to force people to disown their own realities and swallow their own words. In Guatemala, silence has been an essential survival mode: to say aloud the names of victims, and even to be related to them, was to be a subversive and therefore a target. One of my anthropologist colleagues was told by widows that they had 'forgotten' the names of their murdered husbands. Even public utterance of terms like 'health' or 'organisation' was dangerous because the military regarded them as code words for resistance. Concepts of guilt and innocence lose their distinctiveness and it becomes hard to hold on to assumptions about a reasonably predictable world upon which a rationally planned life depends (Zur, 1995). In Guatemala, and also in Turkey, one of the most corrosive and bitterly resented elements of state oppression has been the forced enrolment of rural men into patrols to supposedly assist the army in maintaining 'security'. These patrols were forced to spy on their own communities, and frequently to harass, injure and kill fellow inhabitants. In Guatemala some communities were forcibly displaced to camps where the army sought to 're-educate' them that the state was their protector, not their persecutor. These conditions make it impossible to properly mourn and honour the murdered and disappeared, reinforce everyone's sense of isolation and mistrust, and interfere with long-held Mayan forms of organising. These include storytelling, which is a traditional psychological resource for them. In Mozambique, Renamo terrorism seemed intended to instill an incapacitating fear into the population by conjuring up a vision of inhumanity and maniacal devotion to the infliction of suffering which set them beyond comprehension, outside the realm of social beings and hence beyond social control or even resistance (Wilson, 1992).

In El Salvador, the collective memory of the massacre of 30,000 peasants in 1932 was effective in suppressing even verbal dissent for over a generation: as late as 1978 whenever peasants began to talk about their social grievances, others brought up 1932 again. Martin-Baro (1990) described how destructively polarised choices imposed themselves on the developmental processes of Salvadoran children who had to grow up in a society whose 'normal' output was exploitation and dehumanising oppression. It was a climate of unremitting state terror, militarised social life and institutionalised lying. The response of the Salvadoran military to this analysis, a confirmation of it, was to murder him in November, 1989. In countries like Chile, Argentina and Uruguay, ostensibly democratising, memories of recent decades of terror remain a force in society, an implicit reminder of the consequences of pushing the military sector too far. Thus citizens rein-in their expectations and feel that only limited and tentative social agendas are safe to promote.

Memory and 'Disappearance'

The same Juana Jiron Romero mentioned above told me about the
Contra guerilla attack on the remote hamlet of Quisilali in March
1987, in which several members of her family had been murdered in
front of her eyes. One of them was her two-year-old daughter Liset and
Juana said that even two years later she still seemed to hear Liset's
voice pleading with her for water before she died. Standing in her
almost bare shack she said: 'Now I have nothing of hers ... how can I
show that she lived?' Then she said that shortly before the attack
some foreign travellers passing through by chance had taken a
photograph of her family. Somewhere abroad, she said, there was proof
that Liset had existed. It was important for her to be able to
demonstrate that Liset was not her private delusion or hallucination,
not a ghost, but had definitely lived – until she was murdered because
the US State Department decreed a war in Nicaragua whose hallmark
was atrocity. In El Salvador people are worried that they have not
recorded all the names of the 60,000 murdered by the army during the
1980s. Many Iraqi Kurdish refugees in London believe that it is their
duty to speak for and represent the 200,000 Kurds who have
'disappeared' at the hands of the Baathist regime, a duty more urgent
because of what they see as a general indifference to their fate. In
Mozambique, survivors fleeing Renamo atrocities were haunted by the
spirits of their dead relatives, for whom the traditionally prescribed
burial rituals had not been enacted (Harrell-Bond and Wilson, 1990).
In Vietnam, the 300,000 still missing twenty years after the war ended
are considered wandering souls for the same reason. They have lost
their place in the order of things, in the social and historical fabric.
There are personal memories of them but no external evidence or sign
to embody these memories. Who can show that these people once
lived, had values and causes, and thus what their deaths mean?

When those in power refuse to own up to atrocious acts
committed by agents in their name, they seem still to be insisting
that the 'disappeared' either never existed or were not the victims
but the guilty ones. In all the examples above, people understood
that restoring the dead to the social fabric of their times was not
just a matter of private significance and grief. It was important in
connecting these lost lives to the causes of violent conflict and the
motivation of its major players, in measuring the true cost of the
violence and mending the holes in the fabric that had resulted. The
dead are lost but they may be redeemed to the extent that their
names and fates recover a place on the public stage and their stories

become part of contemporary history, on whose scales they have weighed something.

The campaigning of the Grandmothers of the Disappeared in the 1980s in Argentina set a groundbreaking example, and similar actions have followed in countries like Guatemala (where the term 'disappeared' was virtually patented). Perhaps, now, it is not quite so risky to name missing persons. The application of forensic techniques to the exhumation of mass graves here and in Bosnia is giving some families a chance of having their 'disappeared' relatives reappear. But elsewhere, for example Sri Lanka, the rights of the 'disappeared' have not been able to command much attention in the political arena.

One recent development, almost a fashion, has been of so-called Truth commissions in a number of Latin American countries – El Salvador, Argentina, Chile and now Guatemala. The Truth and Reconciliation Commission in South Africa, which has now wound to a close after a marathon of testimony-taking from victims and perpetrators, has been able to push rather harder than was possible in these other countries – where the political and military order implicated in the events under investigation was still essentially in power. Nonetheless in all these cases the official purpose has been to facilitate societal recognition of what was done to ordinary people and hopefully promote 'reconciliation'. This means an attempt to incorporate the social memory of events which have been previously denied and hidden into the official history of the nation. Unfortunately, full accountability has been withheld by granting the armed forces blanket immunity from prosecution and even in South Africa amnesties were given to perpetrators who agreed to testify. This ignores the way that social cohesion depends on shared ideas about justice and ethics, and these are diminished when major transgressors cannot be held to proper account. It is interesting to speculate on the role played after World War II by the Nuremberg trials, where the verdicts included capital punishment, in helping victims of Nazi Germany achieve some sense of closure after horrific events.

Memory and the Trauma Field

Some of the 200,000 Southeast Asian women who were abducted during World War II to provide sex for the Japanese Army (who called them 'comfort women') are still campaigning for official recognition of what was done to them, and for apology and restitution. So too are British ex-servicemen survivors of Japanese death camps in Indochina and it is interesting to see how this group are handling the contemporary trauma

debate. In a documentary I reviewed for the British Medical Journal
(Summerfield, 1994), one man said: 'Stress, trauma, these are new
words which only came out with the Gulf War hostages.' He was also
implying that however unpleasant it was to be under guard in Baghdad
for weeks as war loomed, it hardly compared with four years of slave
labour in a Burmese death camp. Another said: 'These days they give
you counselling for constipation.' None of these men felt that the war
had made no mark on them, but they were still ambivalent about
calling that mark a trauma. They spoke freely of grief and horror but
seemed to be attesting not to long-term psychological effects but to an
overriding concern to bear witness. They could still shed tears, but so
they should, they implied. Japanese atrocities were unforgettable, but so
they should be. Such acts were also nearly unforgivable and, again, so
they should be, or at least until the Japanese government finally offered
the formal and unconditional apology withheld for fifty years. Until
then, full justice would be denied. As the living, they felt a solemn duty
to remember and honour the dead and to remind us of the cause for
which they died. It was to these ends that they addressed the
imperatives of memory. They did not mean 'traumatic memory'.

The other assumption associated with 'traumatic memory' is in
relation to its supposed capacity to persist for life and thus be an entity
transmissible to the next generation. This has been most developed in
relation to the legacy of the Jewish Holocaust, and occupies an active
corner of the trauma field in America, Western Europe and Israel, with
therapists, patients and a literature to match. Many health professionals have come to take it as given that such effects exist and can be
delineated within the individual psychology of those concerned.
Reviewing the Holocaust literature, Solkoff (1992) noted that psycho-
analytically-orientated studies had tended to support the concept of
transgenerational transmission of traumatic effects, but that population studies did not bear it out.

We now witness an extrapolation to contemporary war, notably in
Bosnia and Rwanda. Consultants to the World Health Organisation,
European Community Humanitarian Office and UNICEF have
claimed that early intervention by trauma programmes could prevent
mental disorders, alcoholism, criminal and domestic violence in both
the current and subsequent generations, as well as prevent further
cycles of warfare by nipping 'brutalisation' in the bud (Agger et al.,
1995). These sources have portrayed 'post-traumatic stress' as likely to
be the most important public health problem in the former Yugoslavia
for a generation and beyond. Where empirical evidence is claimed, as
with the UNICEF survey of 3,030 Rwandan children in 1995, the
naive application of unvalidated checklists was used to sustain a prior

conviction that such children, en masse, simply had been damaged for life (UNICEF, 1996a). UNICEF (1996b) states, unequivocally, that ten million children worldwide have been psychologically traumatised by war and that addressing this must be a cornerstone of their rehabilitation because 'time does not heal trauma'. In Cambodia it is expatriate workers who believe that the trauma of the Pol Pot era of 1975–79 has not been processed and talk about a 'culture of silence' which blocks what they see as a necessary expression of painful feelings and memories (Boyden and Gibbs, 1996). Cambodians do not share these ideas about themselves and point instead to their socio-economic problems. Who should be deemed to know best?

How do we assess the claim that without trauma programmes there will be a postwar crop of psychiatric disorders? During World War II several million British civilians were exposed to events which, by the criteria used on Bosnians, would have attracted the label of post-traumatic stress. So where did it all go? In relation to the prevalence of psychiatric disorders in the general population since then, can anyone seriously argue for the war as an aetiological factor whose influence has consistently escaped patients, their doctors and epidemiologists alike? Northern Ireland, where there has been unremitting civil conflict and several thousand deaths since 1969, presents an interesting example since it is one war zone where comprehensive health records are available. Over this thirty-year period there is no evidence of a significant impact on referral rates to mental health services (Loughrey, 1997). It should be emphasised that this says nothing about the human pain or misery engendered during this time, except that this has been handled by the individual, family and society, and not brought into the realm of mental health professionals. World War II does still retain a vivid place in British social memory, carrying elements of tragedy, triumph over adversity and thus associations with national character and identity.

As a basis for interventions in the lives of war-ravaged peoples, these claims by the trauma field seem fanciful and self-serving. Indeed, as European ideas applied to the non-Western world where most of the wars are, they seem a modern echo of the age of Empire, when Christian missionaries set sail to cool the savagery of primitive people and to gather their souls which would otherwise be 'lost'. We do no justice to the uncounted millions of ordinary citizens who must somehow reassemble their lives when we assume that they are intrinsically damaged human beings who cannot but hand this on to their children. Nor can we lightly assume that the first-hand experiences of children in Mozambique or Cambodia or El Salvador, however extreme, have irrevocably damaged them so that they constitute what some have called a 'lost' generation.

People may indeed invoke memory when they take up arms, or when they are at the receiving end of them, but this is social and not 'traumatic' memory and it is ridiculous to prefer an individual psychological paradigm over a sociological one to capture this. The impact of war experienced as catastrophic or even genocidal might usefully be traced through shifts in the collective world view and group identity of survivor populations and their children, and in the social and political institutions which represent these. What does it mean to be an Armenian, a Jew or, most recently, an East Timorese, a Guatemalan Mayan or an Iraqi Kurd, after attempts to eliminate them as a people, each with its history, culture and place in the world? How does the way they now engage with the world reflect their bitter knowledge that there are no limits to what can be done to a people without power or allies, and their collective adjustments to minimise the chances of a repeat?

Some Issues for the Humanitarian Field

Trauma programmes costing millions of dollars have been imported into Bosnia, Rwanda and other war zones on the back of extravagant claims about 'post-traumatic stress' in exposed populations (often portrayed as a 'hidden' epidemic, meaning that experts are required to diagnose and deal with it). Post Traumatic Stress Disorder, and the checklists used to diagnose it, are held to be universally valid, as are the mental health technologies brought to address it. Moerover rape, torture and the experience of being a child soldier (some consultants extend this to any child in a war zone!) are all held to denote particular psychological vulnerability. These assumptions, and this is all they are, have roots in contemporary ideas, trends and fashions within Western societies (see chapter 2). They also demonstrate the danger of looking at war with a gaze borrowed from a psychiatric clinic, and the application of a paradigm that transforms the social into the biopsy-chomedical. This is a serious distortion serving neither the interests of survivors nor of funders (Summerfield, 1996).

Only in the tiny minority who do develop objective psychological dysfunction is it appropriate to see 'suffering' as having become an entity apart, and potentially requiring treatment. For everyone else the suffering or misery engendered by war is normal and understandable, and there is little case for detaching it from the person carrying it – as a trauma model does. What distinguishes the misery of war from, say, the misery of a broken marriage will not generally be captured by psychological categories or checklists. These two situations might share checklist items like poor sleep or painful memories or jumpiness, but for most people these things would be scarcely the point of what they were going through. These and other aspects of physiological arousal are common at a time of crisis or difficulty of one kind or another, but to see them as the core of the experience itself rather than merely a by-product of it suggests a rather impoverished view of human sensibility and functioning. What is distinctive about the experience of either of these events would lie in the meanings brought to bear upon them, meanings which shape what the sufferer thinks and does about the problem. It is fundamental to realise that human responses to war are not analogous to physical trauma: people do not passively register the impact of external forces (unlike, say, a leg hit by a bullet) but engage with them in an active and problem-solving way. Suffering arises from, and is resolved in, a social context which contains mediating factors for good or ill. For the vast majority 'post-traumatic stress' is a pseudo-condition, a label that not only pathologises but may dehumanise survivors by stripping them of the complexity of their living realities and associations.

Humanitarian interventions are not exempt from considerations of power and ideology, and may be at risk of an unwitting perpetuation of the colonial status of the non-Western mind (Berry et al., 1992). Western psychological concepts are a product of a globalising culture and increasingly present as definitive knowledge. But almost all violent conflicts are in non-Western settings, with differing norms and traditions, range of attributions and understandings, expressions of distress and help-seeking, and modes of coping. There is no such thing as a universal trauma response and we must take a relativistic approach. The Rwandan language, for example, does not possess terms comparable to 'stress' or 'trauma', nor was there an activity called 'counselling' until UNICEF-sponsored programmes introduced it. The possibility that the Western trauma discourse imported into communities socioculturally devitalised by war might impair their struggle to reconstitute a shared sense of reality, morality and dignity merits serious consideration.

This critique is about culture but also about context, and there seems no more evidence from Westernised Bosnia than elsewhere that trauma programmes were imported to satisfy an expressed demand for this kind of service. Indeed we should note that the unregulated growth of trauma counselling of one kind or another into every corner of life in Britain, the US and elsewhere is not uncontroversial. Raphael et al. (1995) conclude that to date there is no firm evidence that this work, which they call a social movement, delivers something that could not have been obtained from the personal networks of those affected. There has been little or no independent evaluation of the benefits of trauma programmes in war zones, whose momentum has been driven by the assumptions with which expatriate agencies and staff arrived. The key question in evaluating, say, counselling centres in Sarajevo, is to assess how much client satisfaction has been a function of the mental health technologies deployed there, and how much of a social setting that provided for people to gather, share their problems with each other and muster collective solidarity at a time when many other facilities lay in ruins. This can pose difficulties if the sponsoring agency has a medical identity and must pitch its work in health rather than social network terms.

To what extent are humanitarian agencies reproducing definitions of war that suit their institutional interests, and which seem attractive to donors and the Western public? There is too often a one-way transfer, generally north–south, and the question is who has the power to define the problem and make these definitions stick? The attractiveness of trauma programmes for donors may be because they offer a fashionable, time-limited and apparently politically neutral form of intervention that avoids the controversial questions wars throw up. Both Bosnia and Rwanda showed how Western governments could hide their mixed motives over confronting causes and aggressors behind a 'bread and counselling' model of aid which did not include physical protection or reparative justice.

As noted at the outset, 90 per cent of all political conflict is internal. Duffield (1995) reminds us that war is generally not an extraordinary and short-lived event to be seen as extrinsic to the way a society functions in 'normal' times. It becomes a permanent emergency whose social and political dynamics are complex and still poorly understood; the nature of humanitarian intervention is itself a contributor to this complexity. The effects of war cannot be separated off from those of other forces: throughout the non-Western world, structural poverty and injustice, falling commodity prices, unbridled environmental exploitation and landlessness are all linked to a withering away of traditional self-sufficient ways of life. In Cambodia, Mozambique and elsewhere, imposed structural adjustment packages reflecting Western neoliberal economic orthodoxies mean slashed budgets for health, education and social welfare (but not arms) on which the poorest depend. This may undermine the social fabric no less effectively than the wars there have done (Boyden and Gibbs, 1996). The WHO (1995) is warning of a health catastrophe by the year 2000, with life expectancy falling in the poorest nations and one-third of the world's children under-nourished. Was the suffering of the several hundred thousand children who have died in Iraq from Western embargo-related causes since 1990 less of a 'trauma' than that occasioned by bombs and bullets? The arguments that constructions of 'trauma' or 'torture' are basically decontextualised might, in many respects, apply to 'war' as well.

What is needed is a more sophisticated level of scholarship and understanding of the interplay of political, socio-economic and cultural forces operating in a particular war and in the locality where an intervention is planned. All over the world huge numbers of ordinary, unremarkable people demonstrate a capacity to tenaciously endure and adapt, an unspectacular process which largely goes on outside the gaze of humanitarian agencies. What are the time-honoured coping patterns mobilised during crisis, and what happens when these too are engulfed by the conflict? Social and cultural institutions are targeted by war, but also engage actively with it, with changes that may take on a life of their own. What new questions might this beg? There should be some understanding of the norms of bereavement in a particular setting, so that requests for assistance that would facilitate mourning might be better recognised for what they are. Further, what might occupy the space that in Western culture is occupied by the trauma discourse? If a particular population did recognise a distinct form of suffering or mental disorder in relation to war, would this impinge on health services? Is it possible to generate data to demonstrate whether not just peace but justice makes a difference to outcomes? As ever the aim must be to improve the chances of accurate empathy with those to be helped, and cut down unwanted and wasteful interventions.

A measured information-gathering process seems the antithesis of what happened in Rwanda, for example. The 1994 genocide was not an utterly unprecedented event, needing unprecedented means to address it – including trauma programmes. Aid organisations do not seem to have asked what place previous inter-ethnic massacres of recent decades had occupied in Hutu and Tutsi social memory. What did people remember of those? What did they do then and how do they think their damaged communities mended themselves? If 1994 was different, why? What seems fundamental is that the voices of those affected can properly be heard, and that their knowledge and priorities can be the basic frame of reference within which offers of assistance are shaped.

No general case has yet been made for mental health to be seen as an appropriate realm for humanitarian operations for war-affected populations, whether in the emergency phase or later. Naturally there will be exceptions, like plugging a hopefully short-term gap in a health service when this cannot be done locally and when what is wanted is clear-cut and familiar. An example was the provision of a psychiatrist by Médecins Sans Frontières to serve in the sizeable war-affected Bosnian town of Gorazde, which had no one after the pre-war incumbent fled the country.

Helping agencies have a duty to recognise suffering, but are there to attend to what the people carrying the suffering want to signal by it. War-affected populations are largely directing their attention not inwards, to 'trauma', but outwards, to their devastated social world. They know that they will stand or fall by what they do in and about that world. Interventions that ignore this are in danger of being experienced as irrelevant or imposed and will fail. Thus what is pivotal is the role of a social world, invariably targeted in today's 'total' war and yet still embodying the capacity of survivors to manage their suffering, adapt and recover on a collective basis. It must be remembered that the destructive impact of war is strongly linked to calculated assaults on those institutions and activities that are pre-eminent in maintaining the integrity of the social fabric. A venerable body of literature, not least from anthropology, has shown that uprooted peoples do well or not as a function of their capacity to rebuild these social networks and a sense of community (Ager, 1993). The humanitarian field should retain the social rehabilitation/development frameworks that already characterise good practice, starting with a reinforcement of damaged local capacities in line with local priorities. The fortunes of children cannot easily be separated from their context: whatever is pro-family and pro-community must address what the trauma of war has meant for them.

A key challenge is whether agencies are prepared to stake their reputation on an analysis which puts at centre stage survivors' concerns about rights and justice, which may crucially shape outcomes. How much are they prepared to commit themselves to real advocacy when this might attract hostility from governments or other major players, including the charge that this is 'political' and not what charity is about? In my view no intervention in a war zone should be or can be politics-free. There is a human need to justify manmade suffering and a nonpolitical view of war doesn't make much sense to war victims. This will rightly favour agencies interested in more than 'hit and run' operations.

References

African Rights (1995). *Rwanda Not So Innocent. When Women Become Killers.* London: African Rights.

Ager, A. (1993). *Mental Health Issues in Refugee Populations: A Review.* Boston: Harvard Centre for the Study of Culture and Medicine.

Agger, I., Vuk, S. and Mimica, J. (1995). *Theory and Practice of Psychosocial Projects Under War Conditions in Bosnia-Herzegovina and Croatia.* Zagreb: ECHO/ECTF.

Allen, T. (1996). A flight from refuge. In T. Allen (ed.) *In Search of Cool Ground. War Flight and Homecoming in Northeast Africa.* pp. 220–61. London: James Currey.

Al-Rasheed, M. (1994). The myth of return: Iraqi Arab and Assyrian refugees in London. *Journal of Refugee Studies* 7, 199–219.

Basoglu, M., Paker, M., Ozmen, E., Tasdemir, O. and Sahin, D. (1994). Factors related to long-term traumatic stress in survivors of torture in Turkey. *Journal of the American Medical Association* 272, 357–63.

Berry, J., Poortinga, Y., Segall, M. and Dasen, P. (1992). Psychology and the developing world. In *Cross-Cultural Psychology, Research and Applications*, pp. 378–91. New York: Cambridge University Press.

Boyden, J. and Gibbs, S. (1996). *Vulnerability and Resilience: Perceptions and Responses to Psycho-Social Distress in Cambodia.* Oxford: INTRAC.

Cliff, J. and Noormahomed, A. (1988). Health as a target: South Africa's destabilisation of Mozambique. *Social Science and Medicine* 27, 717–22.

Dawes, A. (1990). The effects of political violence on children: a consideration of South African and related studies. *International Journal of Psychology* 25, 13–31.

Duffield, M. (1995). The political economy of internal war: asset transfer, complex emergencies and international aid. In A. Zwi and J. Macrae (eds), *War and Hunger. Rethinking International Responses to Complex Emergencies*, pp. 50–69. London: Zed Books/Save the Children Fund.

Eisenbruch, M. (1984). Cross-cultural aspects of bereavement: a conceptual framework for comparative analysis. *Culture, Medicine and Psychiatry* 8, 283–309.

Farias, P. (1991). Emotional distress and its socio-political correlates in Salvadoran refugees: analysis of a clinical sample. *Culture, Medicine and Psychiatry* 118, 257–64.

Garfield, R. and Williams, G. (1989). *Health and Revolution. The Nicaraguan Experience*, pp. 63–80, Oxford: Oxfam.

Gorst-Unsworth, C. and Goldenberg, E. (1998). Psychological sequelae of torture and organised violence suffered by refugees from Iraq. Trauma-related factors compared to social factors in exile. *British Journal of Psychiatry* 172, 90–4.

Harrell-Bond, B. and Wilson, K. (1990). Dealing with dying: some anthropological reflections on the need for assistance by refugee relief programmes for bereavement and burial. *Journal of Refugee Studies* 3, 228–43.

Holtz, T. (1998). Refugee trauma versus torture trauma: a retrospective controlled cohort study of Tibetan refugees. *Journal of Nervous and Mental Disease* 186, 24–34.

Hume, F. and Summerfield, D. (1994). After the war in Nicaragua: a psychosocial study of war wounded ex-combatants. *Medicine and War* 10, 4–25.

Jok, M. (1995). Dinka women and the future of Dinka society. *Refugee Participation Network* 20 November, 31–2.

Lin, E., Carter, W. and Kleinman A. (1985). An exploration of somatisation among Asian refugees and immigrants in primary care. *American Journal of Public Health* 75, 1080–4.

Loughrey, G. (1997). Civil violence. In D. Black, M. Newman, J. Harris-Hendriks, G. Mezey (eds) *Psychological Trauma. A Developmental Approach* pp. 156–60. London: Gaskell.

Lykes, M.B. (1994). Terror, silencing and children: international multidisciplinary collaboration with Guatemalan Mayan communities. *Social Science and Medicine* 38, 543–52.

Makiya, K. (1993). *Cruelty and Silence: War, Tyranny, Uprising and the Arab World*. London: Jonathan Cape.

Martin-Baro, I. (1990). War and the Psychosocial Trauma of Salvadoran Children. Posthumous Presentation to the Annual Meeting of the American Psychological Association, Boston.

Middle East Watch and Physicians for Human Rights (1993). *The Anfal Campaign in Iraqi Kurdistan. The Destruction of Koreme*. New York: Human Rights Watch.

Mollica, R. and Caspi-Yavin, Y. (1992). Overview: the assessment and diagnosis of torture events and symptoms. In M. Basoglu (ed.) *Torture and its Consequences*, pp. 253–74. Cambridge: Cambridge University Press.

Panos Institute (1988). *War Wounds. Development Costs of Conflict in Southern Sudan*. London: Panos.

Parliamentary Human Rights Group (1994). *Iran. The Subjugation of Women*. London: Parliamentary Human Rights Group.

Physicians for Human Rights (1993). *Human Rights on Hold: A Report on Emergency Measures and Access to Health Care in the Occupied Territories*. Boston: Physicians for Human Rights.

Punamaki, R.L. and Suleiman, R. (1990). Predictors and effectiveness of coping with political violence among Palestinian children. *British Journal of Social Psychology* 29, 67–77.

Raphael, B., Meldrum, L. and McFarlane, A. (1995). Does debriefing after psychological trauma work? *British Medical Journal* 310, 1479–80.

Silove, D., Sinnerbrink, I., Field, A., Manicavasgar, V. and Steel, Z. (1997). Anxiety, depression and PTSD in asylum-seekers: associations with pre-migration trauma and post-migration stressors. *British Journal of Psychiatry* 170, 351–7.

Smith, K. (1997). Clash of two worlds: coping mechanisms, culture and conflict. Unpublished Masters thesis, University of Bristol.

Solkoff, N. (1992). The holocaust: survivors and their children. In M. Basoglu (ed.) *Torture and its Consequences*, pp. 136–48. Cambridge: Cambridge University Press.

Summerfield, D. (1992). Philippines: health, human rights and 'low-intensity' war. *Lancet* 339, 173.

Summerfield, D. (1994). Freshly remembered. *British Medical Journal* 309, 1309.

Summerfield, D. (1996). *The Impact of War and Atrocity on Civilian Populations: Basic Principles for NGO Interventions and a Critique of Psychosocial Trauma Projects*. Relief and Rehabilitation Network Paper 14. London: Overseas Development Institute.

Swiss, S. and Giller, J. (1993). Rape as a crime of war: a medical perspective. *Journal of American Medical Association* 270, 612–15.

Turton, D. (1991). Warfare, vulnerability and survival: a case from southwestern Ethiopia. *Disasters* 15, 254–64.

UNICEF (1986). *Children in Situations of Armed Conflict.* E/ICEF.CRP.2. New York: UNICEF.

UNICEF (1996a). *Unicef Survey Documents: Horrors Experienced by Rwandan Children During the 1994 Genocide.* CF/DOI/PR/1996-08. New York: UNICEF.

UNICEF (1996b). *The State of The World's Children.* Oxford: Oxford University Press.

Van Ginneken, E. and Rijnders, R. (1993). *Tazmamart: Fort-Militaire Secret du Maroc. Consequences d'un Internement du 18 Années.* Amersfoort: Johannes Wier Foundation for Health and Human Rights.

Wearne, P. (1994). *The Maya of Guatemala.* London: Minority Rights Group International.

Wilson, K. (1992). Cults of violence and counter-violence in Mozambique. *Journal of Southern African Studies* 18, 527–82.

World Health Organisation (1995). *Bridging the Gaps.* Geneva: WHO.

Young, A. (1995). *The Harmony of Illusions. Inventing Post Traumatic Stress Disorder.* New Jersey: Princeton University Press.

Zur, J. (1994). Making sense of violent experiences: the reconstruction of meaning of la violencia among Guatemalan war widows. *Refugee Participation Network 16,* March, 10–12.

Zur, J. (1995). The psychological impact of impunity. *Anthropology Today* 10, 12–17.

Zwi, A. and Ugalde, A. (1989). Towards an epidemiology of political violence in the Third World. *Social Science and Medicine* 28, 633–42.

2   Hidden Agendas: Deconstructing Post Traumatic Stress Disorder

PATRICK J. BRACKEN

In the previous chapter Derek Summerfield presented substantial evidence in favour of a 'social' analysis of modern warfare. Contemporary wars increasingly involve destruction of communities, cultures and ways of life. Yet the way in which individuals and communities experience and cope with the suffering of war depends on social, cultural and political aspects of their situation. The current discourse on trauma has systematically sidelined this social dimension of suffering; instead it promotes a strongly individualistic focus, presenting trauma as something that happens inside individual minds. In this chapter I present a critique of this discourse. I explore the concepts underpinning individual therapeutic interventions: their origins, their incorporation in current cognitive approaches in psychology and their application in therapies for PTSD.

INTRODUCTION

In recent years, and mainly in Western countries, a new discourse has emerged concerning trauma and its psychological sequelae. At the heart of this discourse lies the diagnosis of Post Traumatic Stress Disorder (PTSD), which was first given full recognition in the Diagnostic and Statistical Manual – Version Three (DSM-III) of the American Psychiatric Association in 1980 (APA, 1980). A diagnosis of PTSD is made if the person exhibits a certain combination of symptoms. These symptoms fall into three groups:

(a) symptoms of intrusion; such as recurrent thoughts about the trauma, nightmares, flashbacks and exaggerated reactions upon exposure to reminders of the trauma;

(b) symptoms of constriction and avoidance, such as efforts to avoid thoughts about the trauma, efforts to avoid places or activities which remind of the trauma and evidence of more general withdrawal from the world;

(c) symptoms of increased arousal, such as irritability, insomnia, poor concentration and hypervigilance.

These groups of symptoms are now presented as defining the essential elements of human reactions to trauma. Within the discourse there is continuing debate about specific symptoms, and the DSM description of PTSD will no doubt continue to be revised. However, there appears to be a consensus about the formulation of post-traumatic reactions in terms of intrusive, constrictive and hyperarousal symptoms. These symptoms are held to be universal and it is argued that they can be seen in children as well as adults. It is assumed that they are expressive of conflicts and disturbances happening within individual minds.

PTSD is often presented as though it was something 'discovered' by psychiatrists, something, which since being discovered, throws light on other unexplained areas of psychological functioning. In fact, PTSD is something created by psychiatry at a particular historical and cultural moment. This is not to say that the suffering, which the PTSD concept attempts to capture, is in any way fictional or unreal. It is not to say that in the past people did not suffer in the wake of life threatening, terrifying or deeply distressing events. It is to assert that PTSD is one particular way of approaching and understanding the sequelae of such events.

The creation of PTSD is explored by the medical anthropologist Allan Young in his 1995 book: *The Harmony of Illusions. Inventing Post-Traumatic Stress Disorder*. In this work, Young traces the emergence of PTSD as a diagnostic category and a focus of psychiatric interest. He locates the origins of the trauma discourse in the late nineteenth century, when the word trauma, previously understood in terms of bodily damage, was extended to cover psychogenic sequelae of distressing experiences. From this emerged the notion of the traumatic memory as something locked in the mind and a continuing cause of distress. Young argues that recent accounts of psychological trauma have inherited this conception but have also been substantially shaped by a number of theoretical developments within American psychiatry, developments embodied in the publication of the DSM-III in 1980:

The adoption of the DSM-III was part of a sweeping transformation in psychiatric knowledge-making that had begun in the 1950s. These changes profoundly altered clinical practice in the United

States and prepared the way for a new science of psychiatry, based on research technologies adopted from medicine (experimentation), epidemiology (biostatistics), and clinical psychology (psychometrics). In the course of these developments, the traumatic memory, up to this point a clinically marginal and heterogenous phenomenon, was transformed into a standard and obligatory classification, post-traumatic stress disorder. (Young, 1995, p. 7)

Young's point is that the concept of PTSD has been constructed over time; it has a history. According to him, the disorder has not always existed, waiting to be discovered by psychiatry:

The disorder is not timeless, nor does it possess an intrinsic unity. Rather, it is glued together by the practices, technologies, and narratives with which it is diagnosed, studied, treated, and represented and by the various interests, institutions, and moral arguments that mobilized these efforts and resources. (p. 5)

In this book, as a whole, we are examining the export of the current discourse on trauma from centres and institutions of learning in the West to locations in different parts of the world experiencing violent conflict of immense brutality and destruction. The central question that concerns us is whether the assumptions about suffering and healing, incorporated into this discourse, are valid in the diverse situations in which they are applied. As a first step we need to identify and analyse these assumptions. I will argue that Western psychiatry is, itself, an ethnopsychiatry: a particular, culturally based, way of thinking about and responding to states of madness and distress. As Atwood Gaines writes:

Psychiatric systems, like religions, kinship systems, or political systems, are culturally constructed. Each mirrors a culturally constructed reality ... As such, folk and professional psychiatries are equally cultural, or ethnopsychiatries, the psychiatric edifices expressive of particular cultures. (Gaines, 1992, p. 3)

More specifically, the chapter explores some of the underlying assumptions of contemporary Western psychiatry, with particular reference to current conceptual and therapeutic approaches to trauma. In an article written a few years ago, Joan Giller, Derek Summerfield and myself (Bracken et al., 1995) identified and challenged three fundamental suppositions within the discourse on trauma. Firstly: *this discourse works on the basis of a strongly individualist approach to human life*, in which the intrapsychic world is emphasised, and society is understood to be a collection of separate individuals. We pointed out that this assumption is simply not valid in many non-Western cultures where very different notions of the self and its relationship to others and to the outside world exist. A further supposition is that *the forms of mental disorder that have been found in the West, and described by Western psychiatry, are basically the same as those found elsewhere.* This has been a guiding assumption within mainstream cross-cultural psychiatry for many years but has been substantially challenged of late (Bracken, 1993). Arthur Kleinman has argued that much psychiatric universalism is based on a confusion of issues of validity with those of reliability. In other words, just because we can identify a particular symptom in different cultures does not indicate that it has the same meaning in these different cultures. For example, most peoples report the experience of nightmares. However the meaning of nightmares varies greatly. In the West, these are generally understood to be inconsequential and have little effect on waking life, but in many non-Western cultures, where dreams are understood to be a bridge to the spiritual world, nightmares mean something very different and can have major effects on waking life. Kleinman introduced the concept of a 'category fallacy' to describe this problem. He defines this as:

> the reification of a nosological category developed for a particular cultural group that is then applied to members of another culture for whom it lacks coherence and its validity has not been established. (Kleinman, 1987, p. 452)

The third assumption, which emerges from the first two, concerns the *relevance of Western forms of therapy, and in particular psychotherapy, to non-Western societies.* As White and Marsella write:

> the use of 'talk therapy' aimed at altering individual behaviour through the individual's 'insight' into his or her own personality is firmly rooted in a conception of the person as a distinct and independent individual, capable of self-transformation in relative isolation from particular social contexts. (White and Marsella, 1982, p. 28)

It is possible to extend this examination of the assumptive framework of the discourse on trauma by looking closely at one particular set of ideas, which have played an important role in shaping its development. PTSD has become popular at a time when a particular set of ideas and practices, known collectively as 'cognitivism', have become dominant within psychology and, increasingly, in psychiatry. While there have been contributions from psychodynamic and behaviourist approaches, the discourse on trauma has been largely shaped by cognitivism. A central tenet of this approach, the need for successful 'processing' of a traumatic experience, is now widely accepted. As we shall see, cognitivism involves all of the assumptions mentioned above: a strongly individualistic approach, universality of the forms of mental disorder and the relevance of Western therapy in non-Western societies.

The Need to Deconstruct PTSD

The term 'deconstructing' is used in the title of this chapter. The notion of deconstruction has a number of sources, most notably the work of French philosophers such as Michel Foucault and Jacques Derrida and involves an unravelling of the background presuppositions in any particular discourse. Ideas and concepts which appear to be obvious and common-sense reflections of 'the world as it really is' are revealed as having been constructed over time. Deconstruction involves a destabilisation of such dominant, common-sense ideas. The ultimate aim of deconstruction is to give voice to alternative perspectives, to allow ways of seeing the world which have been hidden under the weight of 'common sense', to have their say.

Discourses, such as psychology and psychiatry, which in Western societies have assumed a pre-eminent role in explaining human behaviour only in the past century, have often done so by silencing other approaches. By showing them as not containing any necessary truth, deconstruction works to promote alternative approaches. It is only at night when the bright light of the sun has diminished that we can see the stars in our sky. However these stars are also present, but invisible, during the day. The point is that bright sunlight can serve to conceal as well as reveal the nature of reality. By demonstrating the origins and limitations of dominant discourses, deconstruction seeks to reveal and promote less powerful perspectives on life and reality. In the context of healing the suffering generated by war, the dominance of the PTSD model can cut off our view of other approaches. It can blind us to other ways of helping and can work to silence local perspectives on what is helpful and important in the wake of disaster. By showing how the discourse on trauma has been organised around certain assumptions I hope to show how it is also *limited* by these assumptions.

In the first section I will examine the cognitivist approach in psychology and psychiatry and then argue that this approach is underscored by fundamental assumptions which have dominated Western cultures since the time of the European Enlightenment. In the following section I will turn to the discourse on trauma and show how this has been influenced by cognitivism. In the last section I will question the universal relevance of this discourse by showing how the cognitivist approach to the self and therapy are culturally specific.

What is the Cognitivist Approach to Mind and its Disorders?

In many ways, cognitive approaches in psychology and psychotherapy are a crystallisation of a number of themes which are themselves the legacy of the *Enlightenment project* dating from seventeenth century European thought. A central concern of this project was the importance of reason and its place in human affairs. Finding a path to true knowledge and certainty became the major issue for thinkers during the European Enlightenment, and epistemology became the central concern of philosophy. A guiding theme was the replacement of religious revelation and the pronouncements of the ancients with reason and science as the paths to truth. This relegation of spiritual and ancestral knowledge has meant that in the past two hundred years European thought and culture have progressed in very different directions from most other cultures in the world.

The other major theme in European thought emerging from the Enlightenment, particularly on the European continent, was a concern with the human self and its depths. European thinkers became preoccupied with the 'inner voice' and the structures of subjectivity. This is particularly seen in the philosophy of Kant, later in the phenomenology of Husserl, and of course, in the psychoanalysis of Freud. In his work, Foucault has pointed out that the disciplines of psychology and psychiatry only became possible in a cultural framework substantially influenced by these Enlightenment and post-Enlightenment preoccupations. These disciplines represented a search for causal, scientific accounts of the mind and its disorders. They needed theories of the self and behaviour that would *explain* human action and so allow for technical interventions to be made.

Cognitive models and therapies involve the clearest expression of this cultural quest to use reason and scientific techniques in an exploration of the subjective realm. There are many reasons for the emergence of the 'cognitive revolution' in psychology (Harre and Gillett, 1994). As well as a growing dissatisfaction with the limitations of behaviourism, the emergence of the computer as a cultural icon in the West has been an important factor. In the past twenty years it has become possible not only to think of the mind as being *like* a computer, but also to propose that the mind *is* a computer. As psychology became concerned to understand the mind in terms of causal mechanisms and various versions of rule-following formulae, it found a natural ally in the developing world of artificial intelligence (AI). In fact, the assumptions underlying AI and cognitivist psychology are essentially the same. If it is possible, in principle, to account for different aspects of human thought and behaviour in terms of rule-following formulae, then, also in principle, it should be possible to build machines which would operate on the basis of these formulae and so replicate human intelligence and behaviour. Both developments assume that the human mind works in the same way as a computer.

Cognitivism in Psychology and Psychiatry

The basic premise of cognitivism is that there are underlying structures involved in human thought. These structures are based on the biological organisation of the brain and are thus universal, regardless of linguistic or cultural differences. However these structures cannot be fully characterised in biological terms alone, but need a separate set of non-biological concepts. In this model the brain is akin to computer hardware; the mind, or mental activity, is the software, the programmes which run on the basis of the hardware. In this framework it is logical to treat the brain and the mind as separate realms, and the project of cognitivism is the exploration of the structures and the underlying basic elements of the software: the mind. A fundamental assumption is that the structures and mechanisms of psychological life can be grasped in causal terms, and thus causal hypotheses can be generated which can then be used to produce predictions of variations in behaviour under certain sets of circumstances.

As cognitivism has become increasingly influential, more and more areas of psychology have come to adopt the paradigm. In developmental psychology, under the influence of Piaget, there has been a preoccupation with the kinds of operations that can be performed by the developing subject at different stages and with the underlying structures which underpin these. In personality theory there has been a shift towards an examination of the cognitive framework of the subject. Personal Construct Theory emerged in the 1960s and has become increasingly popular. In social psychology the idea that human beings operate personally and socially on the basis of unconscious models and rules has become something of an orthodoxy. These models and rules have been formulated differently and the terminology has also differed but the basic proposition has remained the same. As we shall see later, the notion that human beings operate on the basis of theories or schemata concerning themselves and the nature of the world has been particularly important in the area of trauma.

In contrast to psychodynamic approaches, therapy based on cognitive theory does not involve any deep exploration of childhood experience. It is very much focused on the 'here and now'. It does not theorise about the relationship between patient and therapist in terms of unconscious forces, or in terms of transference and countertransference. It involves the therapist in 'training' the patient to look inwards and examine his or her thoughts in a systematic and 'non-distorted' way. The patient, in turn, is involved in 'homework' exercises, which are carried out between sessions. The therapist's job is to help the patient confront his or her cognitive distortions, and, largely through blunt persuasion, provide much of the motivation for the patient to carry out the homework. At the heart of cognitive therapy is a belief in the importance of, and the benefits of, systematic reflection upon the contents of consciousness. By turning 'inwards' the patient is urged to bring reason to bear upon the internal workings of the mind. In the cognitivist framework the meaning of the patient's world is determined by the internal schemata in his or her own mind, which must be altered in order to change the patient's reality. In post-traumatic reactions it is assumed that the traumatic experience has disturbed these schemata. To progress beyond the trauma it is essential, in this framework, for the patient to process the traumatic experience and modify their schemata. 'Denial' and 'avoidance' must be confronted and, although sometimes very painful, the trauma must be examined and relived until it has been processed and neutralised. In the case of children and adults caught up in the atrocities of contemporary war, this can mean reliving, in minute detail, the suffering they have witnessed, or in some cases, have been forced to perpetrate on others.

Cognitivism and Current Conceptualisations of PTSD

Descriptions of post-traumatic states have been available in the medical literature for many years. Recently psychiatry has fixed upon the symptoms of intrusion, constriction and hyperarousal, defined them as the central and essential sequelae of traumatic experiences and reinterpreted the post-traumatic literature in the light of these. A number of clinicians have attempted to probe the ways in which traumatic events actually bring about such symptoms. Symptoms of constriction and avoidance have generally been understood in terms of a generalisation of fear stemming from the traumatic experience. PTSD has been presented as a form of phobic reaction and modelled in terms of classical learning theory (Keane et al., 1985). However the intrusive symptoms of PTSD, which are often presented as the *cardinal* symptoms of the disorder, are difficult to understand in these terms alone and most theorists have turned to cognitivism for explanations. A recurrent theme in this context is the idea that extremely frightening events have the effect of profoundly challenging the background assumptions of the individual with regard to him- or herself and with regard to the order of the outside world. The individual then has difficulty 'processing' the new experience as it conflicts with his or her deepest assumptions. The psychologist Ronnie Janoff-Bulman has developed this thesis at some length and her work is now widely quoted. She argues that the immediate effect of a traumatic experience is the production of terror and also disillusionment in the individual, and proposes that the symptoms of PTSD are best understood as being produced as part of the individual's innate attempt to cope with these feelings of terror and disillusionment. She writes:

> The confrontation with real or potential injury or death breaks the barrier of complacency and resistance in our assumptive worlds, and a profound psychological crisis is induced. (Janoff-Bulman, 1992, p. 61)

This 'psychological crisis' is experienced as a sense of inner turmoil. The assumptions about the self and about the meaning of the world, which had provided the background framework for the victim, are shattered:

> Suddenly, the self- and worldviews they had taken for granted are unreliable. They can no longer assume that the world is a good

place or that other people are kind and trustworthy. They can no longer assume that the world is meaningful or what happens makes sense. They can no longer assume that they have control over negative outcomes or will reap benefits because they are good people. The very nature of the world and self seems to have changed; neither can be trusted, neither guarantees security. (p. 62)

Janoff-Bulman's position is consistent with other 'cognitivist' approaches to trauma. From this perspective individuals develop theories about the world as they grow up. These theories orient the individual towards life and new experiences which, in turn, can challenge and change the theories held. While different words have been used to describe these theories the notion of internal 'schemata' is currently popular. Janoff-Bulman defines the term in the following quotations:

> Yet, in all instances, whether the organised knowledge is about a common object or a broad class of people, the relevant schema is essentially a theory that goes beyond the data given. A schema is not simply a straightforward accumulation of specific original instances and encounters but rather a generalisation or abstraction involving organised knowledge about a stimulus or concept.

> Our fundamental assumptions about the world are essentially our grandest schemas, our most abstract, generalised knowledge structures.

> Schema research demonstrates the theory-driven (rather than data-driven) nature of our perceptual and cognitive processes. (p. 29)

She quotes Daniel Goleman:

> ... Schemas embody the rules and categories that order raw experience into coherent meaning. All knowledge and experience is packaged in schemas. Schemas are the ghost in the machine, the intelligence that guides information as it flows through the mind. (Goleman, 1985, p. 75)

Schemata are thus held to be similar to the programs running on a computer. Such programs encounter new 'information' from a particular perspective and process it in particular ways. This 'information' is then incorporated by the program, which either changes elements of itself in response to the new 'information' or remains the same. Traumatic experience is held to contradict our 'grandest schemata' and overwhelm our ability to process and incorporate new experiences. As the traumatic experience remains unincorporated it continually presents itself to consciousness in the form of intrusive symptoms. As Bolton and Hill formulate it:

> There is in post-traumatic stress reaction a failure to integrate the trauma into the system of belief about the self and reality. (Bolton and Hill, 1996, p. 359)

Perhaps the most influential model of Post Traumatic Stress Disorder is the one developed by Mardi Horowitz in California in the late 1970s. It combines both psychodynamic and cognitivist theories. Horowitz proposed in his book, *Stress Response Syndromes* (1986), that traumatic experiences disrupt an individual's life by producing a block in cognitive and emotional processing. Horowitz, echoing Freud, assumes the presence of a 'completion tendency' in which the

> mind continues to process important new information until the situation changes or the cognitive models change, and reality and models reach accord. (Horowitz, 1986, p. 95)

Horowitz elaborates his theory in terms of 'cognitive processing' and suggests that there are natural and protective limits to the rate of such processing:

> The recurrence of a familiar nonstressful event is likely to be quickly and automatically assimilated. The cognitive processing will be completed, and the information in active memory storage will be rapidly terminated. The information in novel and stressful events, however, cannot be processed rapidly. Thus the point of relative completion is not achieved, and the active memory retention is not terminated, with relevant codings of information remaining in active storage.
>
> Assuming a limited capacity for processing, such codings will remain stored in active memory even when other programs have greater priority in the hierarchy of claims for channels. These actively stored contents, however, will generally be repeatedly represented. Each episode of representation will trigger a resumption of processing. Thus, whenever this set of information achieves a high-enough priority, representation and processing will resume.

If the contents are interrupted by controls that regulate priorities, they will remain in coded form in active memory. (p. 95)

For Horowitz, this process is conceptualised as a purely internal phenomenon located entirely within the confines of the individual self. It is a process that can be understood scientifically and can be helped by a series of technical interventions, which encourage the processing of the traumatic material. While Horowitz acknowledges that there are social, cultural and somatic aspects to the reaction to trauma, his approach is to separate out the cognitive–emotional phenomena and focus upon these.   Processing the trauma is essential if the person is going to be able to move on. This requires reliving the experience in one way or another and the therapist is required to help the patient face the trauma. Processing also involves work on the patient's beliefs and models or in cognitivist terms: their schemata. The psychologists Hodgkinson and Stewart write:

> One of the major goals of emotional processing after trauma may be to achieve 'cognitive completion', to integrate the stressful experience with enduring models of the world and one's relation to it ... The experience of being victimised causes a rupture in the person's personal, family and community identity; if unprocessed, the rupture continues, severing the meaning of all that happened in the past from the present and the future. A continuity needs to be re-established between past and present, and the experience integrated. (Hodgkinson and Stewart, 1991)

A basic assumption in the cognitivist framework is that the meaningful nature of reality is something 'conferred' on it by the schemata, or programs, running in individual minds. Trauma disrupts the meaning of the world through its impact on these schemata. Trauma is thus conceived of as acting on individuals, and therapy is oriented towards restoring or renewing the schemata in discrete individuals. Therapeutic strategies have involved a number of measures aimed at helping the individual adult, or child, to process and assimilate the traumatic experience. Numerous descriptions of these measures are available (see Meichenbaum (1994) for a comprehensive review). With adults, 'cognitive restructuring' is usually performed through talking about the trauma on numerous occasions. With children, drawing, painting and storytelling are often used with the same aim that the trauma should be relived. This approach has become so widespread that it now appears as 'common-sense' to many people living in Western societies. However as I have attempted to show above, this orientation towards self and the associated assumptions about where the meaning of reality is located, have their origins in specific developments in Western thought and culture.

The Problematic Export of PTSD

In the twentieth century there have been a number of substantial intellectual challenges to this Enlightenment-based orientation. From different directions the philosophers Wittgenstein and Heidegger have questioned the idea that meaning is something generated within individual minds. They point to the fact that meaning is actually located in a public and social realm of language and practice. They stress the embodied and encultured nature of our experience and shift attention away from the contents of individual minds to the cultural background in which people work out the meaning of their lives and actions. Furthermore they argue against the idea that this background can be grasped as any kind of model, schema or theory. Meanings are grounded in practices, many of which simply cannot be grasped in a theoretical frame. In other words, aspects of background culture will always be resistant to formalisation. Our understanding of our world and ourselves is not generated by a set of particular internal schemata but is instead incorporated in our social practices. As Hubert Dreyfus puts it:

> the understanding of being human in an individual's activity is the result of being socialised into practices that contain an interpretation not exhaustively contained in the mental states of individuals. (Dreyfus, 1991, pp. 16–17)

Dreyfus uses the example of child rearing to illustrate this point (as Dreyfus notes, it actually does not matter for the sake of this example if the description is fully accurate or not):

> A Japanese baby seems passive .... He lies quietly ... while his mother, in her care, does (a great deal of) lifting, carrying, and rocking of her baby. She seems to try to soothe and quiet the child, and to communicate with him physically rather than verbally. On the other hand, the American infant is more active ... and exploring of his environment, and his mother, in her care, does more looking at and chatting to her baby. She seems to stimulate the baby to

activity and vocal response. It is as if the American mother wanted to have a vocal, active baby, and the Japanese mother wanted to have a quiet, contented baby. In terms of styles of care-taking of the mothers in the two cultures, they get what they apparently want ... A great deal of cultural learning has taken place by three to four months of age ... babies have learned by this time to be Japanese and American babies. (p. 17)

In other words, much of our orientation to ourselves as persons and to the world around is not developed as a set of beliefs. This non-mental understanding is incorporated in our bodily experiences and our practices in ways which cannot be articulated in discourse. The meaningful nature of our lives and relationships is not something held together in a set of schemata. If this is the case then the potential for transformation of our reality through systematic introspection is limited. In addition, the belief that the meaning of our lives is held in schemata is seen to be just this: a belief, and not a representation of the world 'as it really is'.

The philosopher Charles Taylor draws on the thought of Wittgenstein and Heidegger and argues that the Enlightenment project has a moral or ethical dimension, which has often been invisible. When this dimension is brought to light, the limitations of the cognitivist paradigm, which, as argued above, is part of this project, become even more obvious. Taylor has argued that modern Western notions of self, individuality and agency are historically contingent. This is in spite of the fact that they often appear, to those of us who have lived and grown within Western modernity, as self-evident facts about being human. It is hard for us to imagine other ways of thinking about our *selves* apart from the ways we have been given by this culture. In his book *Sources of the Self. The Making of the Modern Identity* (1989) Taylor traces the origins of these notions about self. Furthermore he traces the particular sense of a moral order which has been established around them. Modern ideas about good and bad, right and wrong are often predicated upon a certain concept of the individual self and how this self is related to the wider order of the natural world and the universe at large.

He explains the ease with which computer models of thinking have become established in Western societies by pointing to this connection. Empirically, such models have had only limited success. AI has not lived up to its original aspirations and yet the computer model of thought is still widely accepted. It has already been noted that cognitivism is of growing importance in psychology and psychiatry. This contradiction leads Taylor to assert that:

... the great difficulties that the computer simulations have encountered ... don't seem to have dimmed the enthusiasm of real believers in the model. It is as though they had been vouchsafed some revelation a priori that it *must* all be done by formal calculi. Now this revelation, I submit, comes from the depth of our modern culture and the epistemological model anchored in it, whose strength is based not just on its affinity to mechanistic science but also on its congruence to the powerful ideal of reflexive, self-given certainty. For this has to be understood as something like a moral ideal. (Taylor, 1997, p. 6)

In other words our acceptance of cognitivism and computer models of mind and thinking cannot be explained by the empirical success of these approaches alone. This acceptance appears to be driven by other cultural aspirations and ideals as well. The moral ideal Taylor refers to relates to our cultural concern with autonomy and freedom. In the modern sense a free agent is one who is able to rely on his or her own judgements, able to look inside at his or her own needs and desires and who is able to seek fulfilment of these inner needs and desires in the outside world. A free agent is one who can stand back from the world and be responsible according to his or her own agenda. Thus our very notion of freedom involves both a separation between inside and outside and a calculating self-reflexivity. According to Taylor there are three aspects of the modern view of the self which are particularly bound up with the Cartesian, or epistemological, tradition:

The first is the picture of the subject as ideally disengaged, that is free and rational to the extent that he has fully distinguished himself from the natural and social worlds, so that his identity is no longer to be defined in terms of what lies outside him in these worlds. The second, which flows from this, is a punctual view of the self, ideally ready as free and rational to treat these worlds – and even some features of his own character – instrumentally, as subject to change and reorganising in order the better to secure the welfare of himself and others. The third is the social consequence of the first two: an atomistic construal of society as constituted by, or ultimately to be explained in terms of, individual purposes. (p. 7)

Taylor makes the point that to challenge one tradition automatically brings us into conflict with the other. The epistemological tradition gives support to the moral order of modernity and its ideals of disengaged rationalistic agency. In turn this order gives support to the apparent clarity and naturalness of cognitivist accounts of self and thought. These traditions stand together in 'a complex relation of mutual support'.

In the modern world of psychiatry and psychotherapy this mutuality becomes explicit in the credence Western culture gives to analysis of the self. Reflecting upon oneself in a detached and 'objective' manner has become something of a moral imperative. Analysing one's desires, motives and aspirations through one form of therapy or another is generally accepted as a 'good' way to deal with anxiety, depression and, more recently, psychosis.

However, it is cognitive therapy that has the particular agenda of bringing a rational ordering to the world of unconscious 'scripts' and 'schemata'. In this paradigm the idea is to rid ourselves of anxiety and despair through the Cartesian ideal of self-reflexivity. The end result of therapy is a self which is more self-aware and detached; a self which can monitor itself in a rational way and detect emerging difficulties; a self which has loosened the bonds of dependency; a self which is more 'free', in every way.

The question to be asked is: 'do different societies operate with fundamentally different notions of self and agency?' This question can only be answered by reference to the literature of social anthropology. My treatment of the issue here will not be intensive, but I shall give a few examples to illustrate my point. The anthropologist Clifford Geertz defines the issue at stake in characteristic terms:

> the Western conception of the person as a bounded, unique, more or less integrated motivational and cognitive universe, a dynamic centre of awareness, emotion, judgement, and action organised into a distinctive whole and set contrastively both against other such wholes and against a social and natural background is, however incorrigible it may seem to us, a rather peculiar idea within the context of the world's cultures. (Geertz, 1975, p. 48)

Arthur Kleinman has conducted extensive research on the problem of depression in Chinese and American patients. In his book *Rethinking Psychiatry. From Cultural Category to Personal Experience* he writes:

> Psychiatry in the West is strongly influenced by implicit Western cultural values about the nature of the self and its pathologies which emphasize a deep, hidden private self. In contrast, both classical Chinese texts and the contemporary common-sense viewpoint among Chinese, both laymen and psychiatrists, affirm

that the self is chiefly interpersonal. The Chinese view the self, to a large degree, as consensual – a sociocentrically oriented personality that is much more attentive to the demands of a particular situation and key relationships than to what is deeply private ... Social context, not personal depth, is the indigenous measure of validity. (Kleinman, 1988, p. 98)

Laurence Kirmayer (1988) points out that in Japan autonomy in interpersonal relationships is much less valued than in the West. He notes that for the Japanese the moral value of the self is expressed through an idiom of social connectedness rather than personal achievement:

The moral value of the self is expressed through social connectedness and endurance rather than through mastery or control of the physical or social environment. This supports a sociosomatic theory of the origins of distress, in which the self endures bodily suffering as a consequence of inescapable social conditions. Japanese sociosomatics emphasizes inborn constitution and the stress of fulfilling social roles as causes of disease. Morally upright behaviour may lead to illness when the person overextends himself ... this contrasts with Western psychosomatics, in which the intrapsychic self mediates the body's suffering and the person is morally culpable not only because of how he acts toward others but because of how he acts toward himself. (Kirmayer, 1988, p. 79)

Schweder and Bourne (1982) also distinguish two different approaches to the individual–social relationship. They characterise these as the 'egocentric contractual' and the 'sociocentric organic'. Societies which endorse the former as an ideal tend to emphasise the intrapsychic and promote reflection upon the self and its desires and cognitions. In sociocentric societies there is much less focus on the psychological realm and instead there is an orientation towards integration of the individual with the natural, supernatural and social worlds. This differentiation is now generally accepted in social anthropology and is increasingly accepted by mainstream transcultural psychiatrists (e.g. Leff 1988). It would appear that the disengaged self, idealised in modern Western culture, is not a notion that is 'at home' in many other parts of the world. Of necessity therefore, psychological theories and therapies which are based on this tradition, and which promote this orientation to the self will have major difficulties cross-culturally.

CONCLUSION

It is my contention that very serious problems arise if the trauma discourse is used in non-Western societies, or with refugees from such societies, without due regard to the problems involved. Within Western societies there is at least a shared background set of beliefs and assumptions within which this discourse makes some sense. In non-Western settings, idioms of distress are likely to be quite different. Because psychiatry understands itself as scientific and thus culturally neutral, it fails to grasp the cultural specificity of its concepts and interventions. Because, in general, psychiatry lacks a critical understanding of its own origins, it fails to see that the realm of the psyche is a constructed realm and not simply 'how the world is'. Psychiatry thus assumes that the models it produces are universally applicable and valid.

However, there is now a substantial literature and experience which would call into question this assumption. What clearly emerges from work in a number of areas is the importance of contextual factors in shaping the experience of and response to trauma. Issues of context are not secondary factors that merely impinge on the progress of a universal psychological or biological process. Rather, issues of context in terms of social, political and cultural reality should be seen as central to this experience and response. Social reality refers to such things as family circumstances, available social networks, economic position and employment status. Political reality refers to the individual's engagement, or otherwise, in a political movement. It also refers to their social position as determined by gender, class and ethnic factors and whether they are the victims of state repression or other forms of organised violence. Cultural reality refers to such things as linguistic position, spiritual or religious involvement, basic ontological beliefs (i.e. about what does and does not exist) and concepts of self, community and illness. There is obviously much overlap between these aspects of reality, and the terms are used here simply to provide a framework. These realities structure the individual's response to violence by determining the practical context in which violence occurs and in which the individual recovers. They also structure and determine the meaning of the event for the individual and the community involved. In turn these factors will determine what therapeutic efforts will be relevant, will be available and will be successful.

My argument is not that the Western discourse on trauma is fallacious or mistaken but that it makes sense only in the context of a particular cultural and moral framework. Its focus upon the intrapsychic and its proposals for technical solutions are at least meaningful, even if disputed, within a Western context. However, when exported to non-Western societies the discourse becomes confusing and problematic. I would emphasise that I am not questioning the motivation of most of the people who are involved in applying these ideas and techniques. Such workers are confronted by the outrage of violence and suffering in situations of war and seek whatever knowledge is available to guide their responses. However, because of the devastation brought by war, many countries are increasingly dependent on the support of Western NGOs and UN agencies to run health and social welfare programmes and are not in a position to question their interventions. When insufficient attention is paid to the sort of issues raised here, much damage can be done.

Nick Higginbotham and Anthony Marsella (1988) in their examination of the impact of Western psychiatry in Southeast Asia, point to the indirect, unanticipated and negative effects of the diffusion of psychiatric knowledge and technology in the region. They demonstrate how this diffusion has promoted professional elitism, institutionalised responses to distress and undermined local indigenous healing systems and practices:

Modern psychiatry's purely secular discourse ... forces a kind of epistemological break with traditional formulations embodied in many non-Western cosmologies. Psychiatry's reasoning and classification is intended to replace indigenous conceptions of disorder. (pp. 557–9)

They argue that the diffusion of psychiatric knowledge and technology occurs through education, consultation and collaboration and that this renders Third World psychiatry homogenous with:

[A] Common language uniting international and local levels [deriving] from shared assumptions about the shared nature of psychopathology, the use of standardised assessment, and the efficacy of scientifically derived bio-medical or bio-behavioural interventions. (p. 553)

When it comes to the discourse on trauma, which psychiatry presents as being universally valid, we can see very clearly the potential for the negative effects outlined by Higginbotham and Marsella. Thus, there is already a body of Western psychiatrists and psychologists involved in consultation and 'education' in the Third World and in Eastern Europe regarding 'trauma psychology'. This promotes a uniform language centred on the concept of PTSD, treats victims of violence with certain counselling techniques and 'educates' local people in the 'recognition' and measurement of the effects of trauma. A number of messages are implicit in the promotion of such a discourse in the Third World:

1   The individual trauma discourse is presented as the 'truth' concerning the effects of violence. This is clearly a distortion of the actual state of knowledge as presented in the relevant literature.

2   Because this knowledge involves a focus on the intrapsychic, there is a tendency to conceptualise recovery in terms of individual counselling and therapy.

3   Because this knowledge is not indigenous to the countries of the non-Western world there is a reliance on experts from Western universities and institutions to develop 'projects' for victims of violence and to train local people.

4   Because this knowledge is promoted as the 'truth', local concepts of suffering, misfortune and illness are ignored. The underlying cosmology of such local concepts, which may be extremely important in helping a community recover from the destruction of war, may subsequently be undermined.

In a previous century white missionaries from European countries brought another 'truth' to the Third World. These Christian missionaries assumed the superiority of their world vision and travelled abroad with a genuine motivation to improve the spiritual life of various peoples around the world. We now know how destructive and undermining the export of this religious world vision turned out to be for many native people.

It was in an attempt to undo some of this damage that Steve Biko and others formed the Black Consciousness Movement in South Africa. In a paper delivered at a conference of black ministers of religion, held in Natal in 1972, Biko said:

it has always been the pattern throughout history that who so ever brings the new order knows it best and is therefore the perpetual teacher of those to whom the new order is being brought. If the white missionaries were right about their God in the eyes of the people, then the African people could only accept whatever these new know-all tutors had to say about life. (Biko, 1988, p. 70)

In many ways science and technology have replaced Christianity in Western countries as the dominant way of ordering our thoughts about the world, about life and about death and suffering. The emerging discourse on trauma is clearly derived from this scientific and technological orientation. The challenge to Western NGOs and other agencies dealing with refugees and other victims of violence around the world is to establish ways of supporting people through times of suffering by listening and hearing their different voices in a way that does not impose an alien order. It is a challenge which demands that we work with a spirit of humility about what we can offer and an acceptance that there is no quick fix or magic bullet that will rid people every where of the suffering brought about by violence.

References

American Psychiatric Association (1980). *Diagnostic and Statistical Manual of Mental Disorders*. 3rd edition. Washington, DC: American Psychiatric Association.

Biko, S. (1988). *I Write What I Like*. London: Penguin Books.

Bolton, D. and Hill, J. (1996). *Mind, Meaning and Mental Disorder. The Nature of Causal Explanation in Psychology and Psychiatry*. Oxford: Oxford University Press.

Bracken, P. (1993). Post-empiricism and psychiatry: meaning and methodology in cross-cultural research. *Social Science and Medicine* 36, 265.

Bracken, P., Giller, J. and Summerfield, D. (1995). Psychological responses to war and atrocity: the limitations of current concepts. *Social Science and Medicine* 40, 1073–82.

Dreyfus, H. (1991). *Being-in-the-World. A Commentary on Heidegger's Being and Time*. Cambridge, MA: MIT Press, pp. 16–17.

Gaines, A. (1992). Ethnopsychiatry: the cultural construction of psychiatries. In Gaines, A. (ed.) *Ethnopsychiatry. The Cultural Construction of Professional and Folk Psychiatries*. Albany, New York: State University of New York Press.

Geertz, C. (1975). On the nature of anthropological understanding. *American Scientist* 63, 48.

Goleman, D. (1985). *Vital Lies, Simple Truths: The Psychology of Self-deception*. New York: Simon and Schuster.

Harre, R. and Gillett, G. (1994). *The Discursive Mind*. Thousand Oaks: Sage Publications.

Higginbotham, N. and Marsella, A. (1988). International consultation and the homogenization of psychiatry in Southeast Asia. *Social Science and Medicine* 27, 553–61.

Hodgkinson, P.E. and Stewart, M. (1991). *Coping with Catastrophe. A Handbook of Disaster Management*. London: Routledge.

Horowitz, M. (1986). *Stress Response Syndromes*. North Vale, NJ: Jason Aronson.

Janoff-Bulman, R. (1992). *Shattered Assumptions. Towards a New Psychology of Trauma*. New York: The Free Press.

Keane, T.M., Zimmerling, R.T. and Caddell, J.M. (1985). A behavioral formulation of post-traumatic stress disorder in Vietnam veterans. *The Behavior Therapist* 8, 9–12.

Kirmayer, L.J. (1988). Mind and body as metaphors: hidden values in biomedicine. In M. Lock, and D. Gordon (eds) *Biomedicine Examined.* Dordrecht: Kluwer Academic Publishers.

Kleinman, A. (1987). Anthropology and psychiatry. The role of culture in cross-cultural research on illness. *British Journal of Psychiatry* 151, 447.

Kleinman, A. (1988). *Rethinking Psychiatry. From Cultural Category to Personal Experience.* New York: The Free Press.

Leff, J. (1988). *Psychiatry Around the Globe.* London: Royal College of Psychiatrists.

Meichenbaum, D. (1994). *Treating Post-Traumatic Stress Disorder. A Handbook and Practice Manual for Therapy.* Ontario: Wiley.

Schweder, R.A. and Bourne, E.J. (1982). Does the concept of the person vary cross-culturally? In A.J. Marsella and G.M. White (eds) *Cultural Conceptions of Mental Health and Therapy.* Dorderecht: Reidal Publishing Company.

Taylor, C. (1989). *Sources of the Self. The Making of the Modern Identity.* Cambridge, MA: Harvard University Press.

Taylor, C. (1997). *Philosophical Arguments.* Cambridge, MA: Harvard University Press.

White, G.M. and Marsella, A.J. (1982). Introduction. In A.J. Marsella and G.M. White (eds) *Cultural Conceptions of Mental Health and Therapy,* p. 23. Dordrecht: Reidal Publishing Company.

Young, A. (1995). *The Harmony of Illusions. Inventing Post-Traumatic Stress Disorder.* Princeton: Princeton University Press.

3 Community Involvement in the Social Reintegration of Child Soldiers

MARGARET McCALLIN

INTRODUCTION

Increased media attention to the problem of child soldiers in recent years has tended to focus on the more sensational aspects of their experience: the atrocities they have committed, the abuse of alcohol and drugs, the sexual abuse many are subjected to.

This focus has also influenced the external response to their situation, which has emphasised *psychological* aspects of their well-being, with a related concern to implement programmes of psychological rehabilitation and recovery. In planning for the children's social reintegration, the factors that both influence their recruitment and participation in armed conflict and mediate their social reintegration, have largely been ignored.

Lack of information is partly to blame for this. However, the Child Soldiers Research Project, recently conducted for the UN Study on the Impact of Armed Conflict on Children (UN, 1996), has given us a much broader information base than we formerly had. The research was conducted using a case study methodology, and information was obtained from twenty-four countries where children are, or have recently been, actively involved in conflict. The results of this enquiry enable us to understand better the circumstances that lead to the children's participation in armed conflict and the consequences of their involvement. This information is crucial both to promote their social reintegration and to prevent re-recruitment.

The information from the research project indicates that it is children from already impoverished and marginalised backgrounds

* This chapter draws extensively on Brett, R., McCallin, M. and O'Shea, R. (1996), *Children: The Invisible Soldiers* prepared for the UN Study on the Impact of Armed Conflict on Children.

who are most likely to become soldiers at an early age. Their involvement in armed conflict can be directly related to the economic, social, political and cultural conditions which define the circumstances of their families and communities, and which almost always deteriorate as the conflict continues. It is therefore not only their experiences as soldiers that affect the chances of reintegration and future well-being of ex-combatant children, but also the fact that many will be returning to a situation that is even more precarious in social and economic terms than before. Programmes of psychological recovery and rehabilitation may assist some of these children in the short term, but their needs can neither be fully understood nor adequately addressed, within a purely medical model. A focus on the mental health aspects of their situation may in fact divert attention away from other concerns which, from the perspective of the children and their families, are equally if not more important, and which can have a significant influence on their reintegration into civil society. It is therefore important to understand the circumstances of the families and communities to which the children are returning, so that they can be involved in finding appropriate solutions for the social reintegration of their children.

WHO ARE THE CHILD SOLDIERS?

> ... the boys mainly came from poor peasant families in isolated rural areas or from the conflict zones. The poverty of their homes bordered on destitution to judge by the clothing, type of house, environmental conditions and educational level of the families. The child soldiers from urban areas came from homes where the head of the family was a woman, they were the sons of cooks, fruit sellers, small traders. These families had had numerous children and were obviously poor, to judge by the materials of which the house was made, their clothing and the marginal areas they lived in ... (Brett et al., 1996: Nicaragua case study)

Understanding which children in any society become involved in armed conflict is essential for their successful social reintegration. Firstly, it is evident that children are not recruited primarily for their fighting qualities but rather because of manpower shortages. In fact, the longer a conflict continues, the more likely it is that children will be recruited, and in increasing numbers. Regardless of geographical location, what emerged from the Child Soldiers Research Project was a remarkably similar picture indicating that, due to their economic, social, political or cultural circumstances, certain children are more vulnerable to recruitment than others. From the information given in the case studies, three broad categories were defined, although these merge and overlap in many instances.

1. The Poor and Disadvantaged

Children from the poorer sectors of society are vulnerable to forced recruitment, particularly when this is accomplished through recruiting raids which target gatherings of the poor and disadvantaged. This may be because government recruiters target those they see as a threat – e.g. potential recruits to an armed opposition group – or because they are members of specific ethnic, racial, indigenous or religious groups. Such recruitment can be part of a general campaign of repression and intimidation designed to break down the resistance of particular groups. Certainly the evidence indicates that the wealthier and more educated sectors of society are left undisturbed, and some may in fact send their children out of the country to a place of safety. Possibilities exist in some cases to buy the release of a child, but for those with few economic resources this is very difficult.

> E. was abandoned at a very young age. With no family, and no nationality, he lived off charity from the people in the area where he was born, and found a point of anchorage, an identity and a family in the militia. His weapon was a means of asserting himself at a crucial age (14 years) ... He controlled the road to Beirut for several years before becoming disillusioned: it was neither a family nor an identity. 'I was just a pawn in an internal, endless struggle.' He decided to leave, and was put into the care of a community which will help him to become more stable and to set up a little business. (Brett et al., 1996: Lebanon case study)

An almost automatic consequence of impoverishment is educational deprivation. This constitutes a strong push factor for children from poor and disadvantaged groups to volunteer for military service, as it can be seen as a route out of destitution. Settlements for refugees and displaced persons also provide a fruitful source of child soldiers. Displaced people often regroup themselves according to religion or ethnicity, thus providing a ready recruiting ground for any armed opposition groups who are similarly based.

2. The Inhabitants of the Conflict Zones

Where the conflict has persisted for many years, economic and social life will have suffered, education will be limited or non-existent and children in the conflict zones will be amongst the poorest and most disadvantaged. Children in these areas often become the main income earners, because so many family members have died or been disabled as a result of the conflict. In a situation of destitution, they may look to the only growth industry available to them – the armed forces or opposition groups.

Poverty is not the only risk factor in such situations, however. The very fact of where they live means that some children will have witnessed the abusive treatment of their families at the hands of government forces, and will join armed opposition groups as a means of achieving future security and stability. In some cases government armies and opposition forces will pick up unaccompanied children for humanitarian reasons – to protect the children – but these children may well end up fighting, particularly if their association is prolonged, and they identify with the group as their protector or new family.

A.A. is a fourteen-year-old child who, as a young boy, lived with his parents. Prior to the outbreak of the rebel war he was a primary pupil in class IV. When the rebels struck his home, A.A. became separated from his family. He lost contact with his parents and became his own caretaker. Several attempts to look for his family were futile. He became disinterested in all children's activities as a result of the loss of contact with his parents. He was often hungry and lacked any sense of direction. As a means of associating himself with some group and attaching himself to an elder, he voluntarily gave himself up to the Army Commander and was recruited as a 'vigilante' at a military check point. He served as a check-point attendant for two months. When the rebel war intensified in that part of the country, the army embarked on recruiting more personnel to fight the enemy. Vigilantes and check-point attendants became the army's first target. A.A., together with other children, was given an emergency training in weaponry and was handed an AK 47 to fight alongside the army. For several months, A.A. was engaged in active combat and earned himself the nickname 'Nasty Killer', on account of the ways he murdered and mutilated rebels captured by his troop. (McCallin, 1995: Sierra Leone case study)

3. Separated Children

This leads to the final category of vulnerable children – those who for whatever reason are not living with their families. There will inevitably be a high proportion of such children within the conflict zone itself, but also children from unstable or disrupted backgrounds: for example, children living in situations where the father has been killed or detained, where the mother is the head of household or where the child for whatever reason is living on the streets. These children are more likely to become child soldiers than others living in a stable, if poor, situation.

> K.W., the eldest of four children, lived with his family who had an adequate standard of living and were well able to provide for his needs. His father died when K.W. was seven years old, and the family circumstances changed drastically. The mother could no longer afford school fees, and the children had to discontinue their education. The mother remarried in an effort to find security for herself and her children. Her second husband, however, was violent and abusive. As a result K.W. abandoned his home and settled on the streets. He was poor, uneducated and lonely, and sought attention and an identity. With nothing else to turn to, he was attracted by the military, was recruited, and by the age of twelve had completed weapons training and was an active combatant. (McCallin, 1995: Sierra Leone case study)

Principally, these children are without the protection that the family can provide to prevent recruitment. There is no one to send them into safety, and at a physical level they cannot resist as well as adults. Without the family to guide them, they are also prey to militarist cultures and peer pressure, and cannot conceive of a life outside the conflict that may have characterised all their experience. All these factors can lead a child to seek a substitute or replacement family within the military.

TYPE OF RECRUITMENT

The manner in which children are recruited ranges from compulsory to voluntary recruitment, although in practice these categories often merge into one another. The most distinct category is *compulsory recruitment by conscription* which is, by its nature, a government prerogative. Many children, however, are conscripted under age, even where there is a legal minimum age of eighteen. This may be because the children lack documentation such as birth or identity records; they may enlist voluntarily for compulsory conscription whilst under age (sometimes a convenient loophole to mask conscription of children); they may be caught up in 'quota' enlistment carried out by government agents, village headmen, local militias etc., who are concerned to make up required numbers and therefore pay little heed to the ages of the conscripts; or the conscription system may be flawed or simply ignored by the military, particularly where there is a need for more manpower, or the military is targeting certain groups. Here conscription fades into forced recruitment.

Forced recruitment is also practised by armed opposition groups – when, for example, all members of an ethnic group may be required to join the armed struggle. In this situation, shortfalls in numbers of recruits may also result in the imposition of quotas on the populations in the areas under their control. A typical method, practised by both government and opposition forces, is press-ganging.

> A group of armed militia, police or party cadres would roam the streets and marketplaces, picking up any individual or rounding up any groups they came across. Alternatively, they would surround an area and force every man and boy to sit down or stand up against a wall, using a threat of opening fire. All those eligible would then be forced on to a truck and driven away. Young men were recruited while playing football, on side streets and alleyways, going to school or market places or attending religious festivals. Teenage boys who worked in the informal sector selling cigarettes, matches, sweets, chewing gum and lottery tickets were a particular target. (Brett et al., 1996: Ethiopia case study)

In rural areas, government and armed groups use similar methods of looting, killing, abducting children from home and school, and taking them by force or with threats and intimidation. This is not the case with all armed opposition groups, some of whom take great pains to justify their cause with the local population, and use persuasion rather than force. But when a heavily armed group enters a village and makes speeches calling for volunteers, how voluntary is the recruitment?

Some children do make a positive choice to join, or are led to volunteer by force of circumstances, or because the family makes a choice on the child's behalf. The causes of *voluntary recruitment* are varied, and a number of factors may operate simultaneously to influence the child's decision. They are here outlined only very briefly.

Cultural Reasons. Participation in military or warlike activities is glorified, and children are taught to revere military leaders. Value systems that endorse bearing arms as a mark of masculinity may draw or push youngsters into armed opposition groups, particularly where this is linked to a tradition of blood revenge. Some children may join as a result of peer pressure, particularly in urban areas or garrison towns, believing they will have fun and adventure.

Protection. The motive of revenge is cited less frequently by children themselves (Brett et al., 1996). Their primary motivation appears to be a sense of their own vulnerability, where enrolment in either government or armed opposition groups is a means of protecting themselves and their families from harassment. The single major reason for children volunteering to joint armed opposition groups is their own personal experience of harassment by government armed forces, including torture, loss of home or family members, or forced displacement or exile.

Ideological Reasons. Some children volunteer for armed opposition groups because they believe in what they are fighting for: a holy war, religious freedom, ethnic or political liberty, or a general desire for social justice. The children's commitment to the opposition cause may have been instilled in them throughout their upbringing and reinforced by the idealisation of a culture of violence.

Economic and Social Reasons. The motivation for volunteering may be to find a means of survival or support, particularly where the alternative to enlistment is unemployment. Here the family may in fact influence the child's recruitment, because it needs the income; in some cases the child's wages are paid to the family, or there are other incentives such as food or the provision of medicines. Economic motivation may be more than a matter of pure survival, as the army may represent the only route to influence, or upward social mobility. Girls were cited in some cases as joining an armed opposition group to escape early or imminent marriage, or conversely to be encouraged to join by their parents because they had poor marriage prospects.

THE CONSEQUENCES FOR CHILDREN
OF PARTICIPATION IN CONFLICT

With the exception of some armed opposition groups who make efforts to take account of the particular needs and abilities of children, child soldiers appear to receive the same training and treatment as adults. As this is frequently characterised by brutal and inhumane routines, it naturally falls hardest on the children. In armed opposition groups, the children may begin their service in support rather than combat functions, on guard duty, patrolling, manning check-points, as porters, spies or messengers. These latter functions can entail great risk and hardship for the children. They may be forced to carry very heavy supplies of food or ammunition, and may be beaten or killed if they become too weak to bear the load. As spies, the opposing side may kill them on capture. Whatever these support functions may be, there is little doubt that they are being prepared for more active involvement.

The consequences for children of their participation in armed conflict are considerable, and overwhelmingly negative; in only very few instances was it seen as a positive experience (Brett et al., 1996). As members of both government and armed opposition groups, their inexperience and frequent lack of training results in high casualty and death rates in active combat. Children are commonly used on the front lines, and their size and agility lead them to be given particularly hazardous assignments, such as laying or detecting mines. Suicide missions are considered the particular province of adolescents, because as one case-writer commented 'they are more physically suited for carrying out such operations and are better disposed to it mentally'. Many children who are injured in combat are left to die from their wounds, or are shot. Those who are too weak to keep up with the group, or who attempt to escape, either to avoid recruitment or desert the group, may also be executed. Children die from injuries incurred during beatings, whether as a punishment or to break the spirit of new recruits. Some children commit suicide following these events. They are also more prone to die from starvation and preventable diseases contracted in the unhygienic conditions in which they live.

With the exception of those armed opposition groups who treat children in a more humane manner, the treatment and training of child soldiers involves a high degree of risk for their physical well-being, especially for the youngest amongst them. Their bodies are still developing and they are thus at greater risk of injury and disability from the privations that are common in military life. These include poor diet, insanitary conditions and inadequate health care, and the rigours of harsh training routines and excessive punishments that can leave them weakened and debilitated.

There are numerous instances of the routine administration of drugs and alcohol, particularly before a battle. Sexual abuse of both boys and girls is not infrequently reported, entailing for many the risk of sexually transmitted diseases, HIV/AIDS, and pregnancy for the girls. Where the pregnancy is terminated in insanitary conditions, this can put the girls at additional risk. There is an apparent tendency amongst certain opposition groups to forcibly recruit very young girls, as it is considered that their young age means they will be free from HIV infection. As they are forced to render sexual services to the adult male combatants, their freedom from infection will be short-lived.

> At the age of thirteen I joined the student movement. I had a dream: to contribute to make things change, so that children would not be hungry, so that people could be the owners of their dreams, there would be no more differences between rich and poor and then ... we would have a just society ... A few years later I applied to join the armed struggle ... When I joined I was fifteen, with the inexperience and the fears of a little girl ... Through some girlfriends I found out that in organisations similar to mine, there were girls who were obliged to have sexual relations with the combatants ... The women among other things had to 'alleviate the sadness of the combatants'. And who alleviated our sadness after going with someone we hardly knew? ... At my young age I experienced abortion. It was not my decision, I could not decide on that. They decided, in any case. Hadn't I handed over my entire life? Had I not undertaken a commitment to permanent obedience and discipline? ... There is a great pain in my being when I recall all these things, principally because with time I have come to understand that to be a woman in any group was always a disadvantage. *In spite of my commitment, they abused me, they trampled my human dignity. And above all, they did not understand that I was a child and that I had rights.* (Brett et al., 1996: Honduras case study)

The most frequent injuries suffered by child soldiers are loss of limbs, loss of hearing and blindness. These disabilities will impose additional hardships in the future, compromising their chances of taking advantage of educational and vocational programmes, and impeding their social reintegration, as they become an additional burden for an already impoverished family. The situation of young amputees is especially distressing and precarious as, following amputation of the limb, the bone of a child continues to grow, and at a faster rate than the surrounding tissue. The child is therefore subject to great pain, and will require new prostheses (which the family is unlikely to be able to afford) more frequently than an adult.

Over and above these consequences of participation in conflict, some children are also subjected to regular beatings, and to degrading and humiliating treatment to subordinate them to authority. The degree of violence and degradation involved not infrequently leads to death (including suicide), disablement or emotional damage. One former child soldier described his experiences:

> Once they had shaved our heads, they forced us to support ourselves with our heads on the ground, the stones encrusted themselves in our skulls; another punishment was to support ourselves with our fists on the ground which caused lacerations; they also used to put us on our knees on the asphalt and make us walk like that. So that we could 'show our fibre' they beat us on the legs with sticks, they also beat us on the fingers until they were all bruises. These punishments were imposed when a new soldier made a mistake in something, we all had to pay. (Brett et al., 1966: Honduras case study)

It must be remembered that children experience all these violent events whilst separated from their families. This separation is probably the single most important consequence for the vast majority of children who participate in armed conflict, occurring at a time when they have most need of the care and support that family life can provide. At the time of demobilisation, the children may be confused by their situation, or indeed reluctant to relinquish their identity as a soldier, particularly when they believe they have played a role in addressing the ills that their society has experienced. This can result in a sense of abandonment or rejection. Regardless of the circumstances, many of the children may have identified with the army or armed group that protected and provided for them. Demobilisation may represent yet another loss for the children, which may influence their behaviour. It is thus important that the next stage for the child – that of social reintegration – is based upon a process of re-attachment to their families and communities.

The consequences of children's participation in conflict cannot be explained in simple or straightforward terms. The picture that emerged from the case studies documented in the Child Soldiers Research Project was one of ever-increasing risk. The world they face is one where the social and cultural environment of family and community has been destroyed or severely disrupted; where their physical and emotional well-being has been affected; where their opportunities for education and vocational or skills training, and ultimately their chances for employment, are even more limited than when they were first recruited. In almost all instances, the case studies describe their experiences as child soldiers as having a negative effect on these varied aspects of childhood that would normally contribute to their healthy development. It is this multiplicity of developmental insults that compromises child soldiers' capacity to reintegrate with their families and communities.

RECOVERY AS A SOCIAL PROCESS

> [The army] comes every year. Their base is only half a day's walk from here. They take the boys and men as porters, rape some of the women, steal the chickens and pigs, steal the rice and burn what we have in the fields. We have to hide out in the jungle for over two months of every year when they come ... we are tired of the war ... we are tired of giving our sons to fight for the [armed group] ... but what choice do we have? (Brett et al., 1996: Burma case study)

Although family reunification, and re-attachment to family and community are considered important determinants of effective social reintegration, this issue must be balanced by a realistic assessment of the situation of the children's families who are physically and emotionally worn down by the conflict, and may face increased impoverishment. Why, then, in such circumstances is it so important to secure the involvement of the community in the social reintegration of ex-combatant children? One programme that has implemented a community-based approach to the social reintegration describes the need for family and community involvement as follows:

- the children's families and communities have a better understanding of the underlying causes that lead to children participating in conflict;

- families and communities know their children better than programme staff;

- what is essential is not the needs of the children from an outsider's point of view, but the needs of the children from the point of view of the family and community, and more importantly that of the children themselves;

• any response to the real needs of the children can be better articulated and conceptualised by their families and communities;

• programmes for child soldiers can make only a limited, short-term contribution to the welfare and well-being of child soldiers. It is their families and communities who remain the primary agents in the development of the children.

• Families/communities know what can work or not work given their past, present and future situations. Their involvement therefore is vital. (McCallin, 1995: Children After War (CAW), Sierra Leone)

This project does not claim that such a process is straightforward. On the contrary, the development of the project involved a considerable effort to educate and sensitise people about the consequences of their children's participation in the conflict. This was 'a slow process which entailed an open ended dialogue through group meetings, workshops, focus group discussion with families and community members to try to understand the risk factors (root causes) within the family and community culminating in children being militarized' (McCallin, 1995). In our concern to support and prepare for this process, we should not forget the children themselves. They know all too well the complexity of factors that will influence their social reintegration, and as members of their communities should be encouraged to participate in the definition of solutions to promote their well-being.

Understanding the situation of child soldiers as a continuum that includes their experience before and after recruitment, *not only* their experiences as soldiers, shifts the focus of concern so that interventions to address the psychological consequences of their 'traumatic' experiences are an aspect of, and not central to, efforts to address their situation.

If, according to the best interests of the child, children and their families are positioned at the center of all strategies to close the gap between reality and the optimum environment for full development, then a model that treats symptoms rather than empowers whole human beings may be inadequate and counterproductive ... [T]he medical model ... tends to universalize a Western notion of child development which, even by using the term trauma, pathologizes children's invisible wounds and views them only as passive victims rather than active survivors. (Reichenberg and Friedman 1996)

Whilst not minimising the impact of traumatic events, it must be recognised that children's responses may be influenced as much, if not more, by their experiences of family loss and separation, and the precarious nature of family life that results from conflict (Jareg and Jareg, 1994). Recognition that the family and community is the best setting for the recovery of children who have experienced deeply distressing events is essential, therefore, but not sufficient in itself. It must be matched by interventions that address the needs of the children through dialogue, partnership and advocacy with affected communities, in order that the 'spirit' of the Convention on the Rights of the Child is translated into practical interventions that promote the well-being of the children.

For the people most concerned – the children themselves, their families and communities – sustainable initiatives that address the basic conditions of life that influenced the children's recruitment need to be seen as the best means of securing the social reintegration of child soldiers. One of the most striking aspects of the Child Soldiers Research Project was the fact that, prior to their recruitment, most of the children had limited or no education, schooling was disrupted or discontinued either as a direct result of the conflict or because the family could not afford it, or families needed the income the child could provide by leaving school and working. It is not surprising, therefore, that rather than detailing programmes of psychological recovery, the case studies made repeated reference to the linkage between education, employment opportunities, and the economic security of the children's families, as the factors that would determine successful social reintegration, and prevent re-recruitment. Similarly, the opportunity and willingness to work will facilitate the children's re-attachment to their families, as they will be 'valued for their contribution to the productive work of the family' (Gibbs, 1994) and in the process will be able to re-learn 'the values, practices, and norms that regulate and give reason to family and community life' (McCallin, 1995: Mozambique case study).

Without education, however, children's future prospects for employment are limited, and the army may remain the only available option to earn money and contribute to the family economy. For this reason, programmes of education and vocational training should be seen as a priority concern in the rehabilitation and social reintegration of child soldiers. But for the former child soldier, education is more than a route to employment – assuming that this is available. It is also the system within which children's lives can be normalised, and they can be helped to overcome their experiences and develop an identity separate from that of the soldier.

Given the large numbers of demobilised child soldiers in some situations, their varying ages, experiences and their own attitudes towards education, alternatives to traditional educational systems may be necessary, together with additional training for teachers. Opportunities for education and vocational training should also be appropriate to the circumstances of the communities, and not lead to unrealistic aspirations on the part of the children. For older children, or those who, due to long periods of time spent with the military have difficulty in returning to school, the creation of opportunities for self-employment together with basic skills training, should also be considered.

Whilst our concern in this chapter is the child soldier, we should also bear in mind that she or he will have brothers and sisters who have also suffered deprivation due to the war, and may be at risk of recruitment. Initiatives to assist the children's families and communities have implications, therefore, that go beyond the social reintegration of those who have already participated. They should also be seen as preventive strategies, to protect other children from becoming similarly involved, and even in some cases to limit the duration of the conflict. In one case, it was estimated that 45 per cent of combatants were aged eighteen and under. This was attributed to the fact that the conflict had proceeded for so long that the economy had been completely destroyed, together with almost all educational facilities; in these circumstances, military service was the only means of earning an income. Situations such as these pose questions about the prospects for peace, where children are growing up without education and trained in combat, and the meaning of their lives is derived from conflict. The extensive involvement of children as combatants may also, in itself, be a significant factor in prolonging the conflict, as there are always children available to meet the manpower needs.

In order to address this fundamental problem, there is clearly a need for strategies to prevent under-age recruitment. These range from political pressure on the part of the international community to encourage governments and non-government entities to recognise international standards and instruments, to recognising the crucial role communities can play in protecting the children. Priorities identified by participants at a symposium on child soldiers in Africa (Unicef, 1997) were:

- The establishment of eighteen as the minimum age for any participation in hostilities and for all forms of recruitment into all armed
forces and armed groups.

- The adoption and ratification of an Optional Protocol to the
Convention on the Rights of the Child raising the minimum ages
from fifteen to eighteen.

- The adoption by governments of national legislation on voluntary
and compulsory recruitment with a minimum age of eighteen
years; the establishment and enforcement of proper recruitment
procedures.

- Indictment and trial of those responsible for illegally recruiting
children.

Other practical measures that could make a significant difference
include:

- Development and support for community efforts to prevent recruitment.

- A focus in programmes of assistance to children on those most at
risk of recruitment: children in conflict zones, children (especially
adolescents) separated from or without families, including children
in institutions; other marginalized groups (e.g. street children, certain minorities, refugees and the internally displaced); economically
and socially deprived children.

- Finally, improving access to education, including secondary education and vocational training, for all children, including refugee and
internally displaced children.

If the international community is serious in its concern to assist
children affected by armed conflict, it should focus on these practical
measures to prevent recruitment, and on community-based initiatives
to reintegrate former child soldiers, rather than provide assistance
based on a medicalised trauma model.

References

Brett, R. and McCallin, M. (1996). *Children: The Invisible Soldiers*. Stockholm: Radda Barnen.
Gibbs, S. (1994). Post-war social reconstruction in Mozambique: reframing
children's experience of trauma and healing. *Disasters* 18, 3.

Jareg, E. and Jareg, P. (1994). *Reaching Children through Dialogue*. London: Macmillan Press.

McCallin, M. (1995). *The Reintegration of Young Ex-Combatants into Civilian Life*. Report for the International Labour Office. Geneva: ILO.

Reichenberg, D. and Friedman, S. (1996). Traumatised children. Healing the invisible wounds of children in war: a rights approach. In Danieli, Y., Rodley, N. and Weisaeth, L. (eds) *International Responses to Traumatic Stress*. New York: Baywood Publishing Inc.

Unicef (1997) *Symposium on the Prevention of Recruitment of Children into the Armed Forces and Demobilization and Social Reintegration of Child Soldiers in Africa*. Cape Town, April 1997. Report available from Unicef, New York.

4 Fighting With Open Eyes: Youth Combatants Talking About War in Sierra Leone

KRIJN PETERS and PAUL RICHARDS

YOUTH AND WAR IN AFRICA

Young people play a major part in most wars. However, in the African civil wars of the last twenty years recruitment has been extended to children, and girl fighters are increasingly common. In part this reflects demography. Africa is not only the world's poorest continent; it is also its youngest. In Europe and North America the age range five to twenty-four years accounts for only a quarter of the population, whilst in Asia the figure rises to 35 per cent and in Africa it comprises a staggering 45 per cent. In countries where poverty and numbers overwhelm education and job opportunities, militia enrolment is seen by many as a better option than starving on the street. But recruitment also reflects the discovery that children are good fighters. There are two main reasons for this. The first is technological: battle kit was once too heavy and expensive to be entrusted to children, but an AK-47, firing thirty bullets per trigger pull, is light enough for a ten-year-old to handle and costs no more than the price of a goat in some parts of Africa (Machel, 1996). The second is sociological: many children are single-minded in combat, free from the kinds of worries about dependents that instill battle-field caution into older combatants. With their own families scattered by war, children are often intensely loyal to their fighting group, the company of comrades-in-arms serving in some measure as a family substitute. Merging war with play, groups of youngsters in bush wars operate on their own initiative for long periods in remote terrain, making up rules of war as they go. Civilians bear the brunt of the resulting atrocities.

ADULT REACTIONS

Adult reactions to child combatants fall into two categories. Elites always fear 'unwashed' youth and Africa is no exception. Many under-age recruits are from remote rural regions and in countries such as Liberia and Sierra Leone, colonially-rooted attitudes to interior peoples reinforce stigmatisation of ultra-youthful rural combatants as 'bandits' and 'barbarians'.

The other reaction is to see young fighters exclusively as victims. There is a tendency, especially among humanitarian agencies, to see under-age combatants as children robbed of their innocence by undemocratic military regimes or brutally unscrupulous 'warlords' (Goodwin-Gill and Cohn, 1994; Human Rights Watch, 1994); this 'victim' view neatly dovetails with the capacity of many such agencies to provide trauma therapy. Our concern that the 'supply side' tends at times to take a lead in the analysis of needs leads us to flag alternative options for intervention in our conclusion.

The purpose of the present chapter is to let under-age African combatants explain themselves directly (cf. Cairns, 1996). It will become clear that many fight with their eyes open, and sometimes defend their actions with pride. Where war has destroyed families and schooling opportunities, opting for militia service allows them to reassert some control over their lives.

The important report by Graca Machel for the United Nations on children and war rightly cautions against seeing child soldiers solely as victims of war (Machel, 1996). The implication is that we should pay more attention to under-age combatants as rational human actors. The work we report below confirms that young Africans are conscious of their agency in opting to fight, and often wise beyond their years in understanding their subsequent predicament and what must be done to extricate them from it.

WAR IN SIERRA LEONE

The civil war in Sierra Leone began on 23 March 1991. The Revolutionary United Front of Sierra Leone (henceforth RUF/SL) sought to mobilise unemployed youth to overthrow the one-party regime of President Joseph Momoh. The RUF/SL was led by a cashiered army corporal, Foday Saybana Sankoh, trained as a guerrilla in Benghazi, Libya. The RUF/SL chose to establish itself in an isolated border region (Kailahun and Pujehun Districts) that was politically

alienated from the Momoh regime. Initially a force of no more than a
hundred or so, the RUF/SL brought in hired Liberian fighters whose
atrocities against civilians lost the movement any local political
support.

Disowned by local civilians, the RUF/SL turned instead to training
young people abducted from border mining districts. Some of these
youngsters were hijacked from run-down and nearly defunct local
primary and secondary schools. Others were young hustlers rounded
up from alluvial mining pits where they worked for Lebanese and
Sierra Leonean merchant 'supporters'. Some young people joined the
RUF/SL solely to survive, but to others the movement spoke to many
of their problems and frustrations. Only those abductees with education were taken for guerilla training; other captives were used by the
movement as slave labour.

In oppostion to the RUF/SL was an ill-equipped government army,
the Republic of Sierra Leone Military Force (henceforth RSLMF).
Inexperienced war-front junior officers quickly began to copy RUF/SL
guerrilla tactics, including recruitment and training of under-age
irregulars. These local irregulars were less daunted than RSLMF troops
by determined under-age rebel fighters prepared for combat on
fear-inhibiting drugs.

In April 1992 a pay revolt by some war-front junior officers of the
RSLMF escalated into a full-blown coup against the Momoh pres-
idency. The young coup-makers formed the National Provisional
Ruling Council (NPRC). Believing it had helped shape the radical
youth-oriented programme of the NPRC, the RUF/SL expected to be
invited to share in some kind of government of national unity
(RUF/SL, 1995). However, civilian, and especially capital city political
elements, rallied to the personable young chairman of the NPRC,
Capt. Valentine Strasser, a Krio, persuading him against any negotiation with the discredited RUF/SL. The army was re-equipped and
transformed. Fighting strength was increased from about 2,500
rank-and-file combatants when the war began to an estimated 15,000
by 1994. Many of the new intake were from the socially disadvantaged
'underclass' courted by the RUF/SL.

The NPRC government quickly lost control of its enlarged but
hastily-trained army. Soldiers and NPRC officials engaged in mining
of alluvial diamonds – the country's main resource – in the war-zone.
Military officers would declare zones off-limits and drive out civilians
while undertaking 'sweeps' against the RUF/SL, but in reality digging
for diamonds. Some rogue officers seemingly conspired to buy
diamonds from RUF/SL groups in return for weapons. Other units
faked rebel attacks in order to loot (Keen, 1995). The irregulars

recruited at the war front, however, proved to be militarily effective, pinning the RUF/SL into a last redoubt in Nomo Chiefdom on the Liberian border by December 1993. Many of the locally-recruited irregulars were fighting to revenge family members killed by the Liberian Special Forces during the initial RUF/SL invasion of 1991.

With its line of retreat blocked by a change of fortunes in the Liberian civil war the RUF/SL faced the option of disbanding or maintaining a low-level struggle based in isolated camps in the resource-rich Gola Forest segment of the Liberian border. The war continued in a low key. Having little faith in the corrupt and enlarged government (NPRC) army, citizen civil defence groups began to mobilise to protect rural areas against *both* RUF/SL pockets and army renegade units. The civil defence groups frequently drew upon the skills, both practical and esoteric, of local hunters known (in the Mende language spoken in southern and eastern Sierra Leone) as *kamajo* (pl. *kamajoisia*).

Later in 1994, refreshed by diamond mining, raids and weapons deals (some involving government soldiers) the RUF/SL renewed its campaign, launching hit-and-run raids on all parts of the country from forward bases in forested districts. The aims were to dislocate the mining economy, advertise the RUF/SL political programme, and gain new recruits (willingly, or by abduction). A total of seventeen expatriate hostages were also abducted, bringing greater international attention to the war. By March 1995 Freetown was coming under pressure from units of the RUF/SL which had advanced as far as the outlying village of Waterloo.

Resolution of the international hostage crisis after several months brought the RUF/SL wider publicity and initiated the building of a peace process, leading to a provisional cease-fire in January 1996. The NPRC regime, bankrupt of support in the country, split over the peace process. Strasser was replaced by Capt. Julius Maada Bio in a palace coup, and Bio was steered, by diplomatic pressure and public protest, towards elections, even as the war raged. The parliamentary election was won by an alliance led by the Sierra Leone People's Party (SLPP). The SLPP candidate, Ahmad Tejan-Kabbah, a former United Nations bureaucrat, won the election for president. Kabbah continued the peace process initiated between Bio and Sankoh.

The new democratic government was suspicious of the army and sidelined it during protracted peace negotiations, concentrating efforts on building up a para-military force modelled on *kamajo*-led civil defence activities. This largely ethnically-based militia – later officially named the national Civil Defence Force (henceforth CDF) – had acquired an estimated 15–25,000 recruits by the end of 1996. CDF units never observed the cease-fire, and key RUF/SL bases – including Sankoh's Gola Forest headquarters – were overrun by *kamajo* fighters during negotiations. Weakened by the continued CDF militia action a reluctant Sankoh signed the peace agreement with the Kabbah government on 30 November 1996.

Under-age combatants from the government side began demobilisation in 1993–94, but demobilisation of RUF/SL and CDF units was still pending when the peace agreement was signed. Surviving RUF/SL units went to ground in the forest. CDF operations continued. In February 1997, Sankoh, visiting Nigeria, allegedly to buy arms for a resumption of hostilities, was detained by the Nigerian authorities. On 25 May 1997 disgruntled soldiers attacked the main prison in Freetown to release soldiers held by the Kabbah government for a coup attempt. The president fled to Guinea, and the RSLMF mutineers promptly invited the RUF/SL to join a new regime headed by Major Johnny-Paul Koroma. After consulting Sankoh in Nigeria the RUF/SL leadership agreed to the proposal, whereupon several thousand RUF/SL cadres were bussed into Freetown.

The RUF/SL and the Armed Forces Revolutionary Council (AFRC) thus forged a regime of the kind the RUF/SL had originally envisaged in the aftermath of the NPRC coup in 1992. The civil defence militia changed places with the RUF/SL in the diamond-rich forested margins of the country, pledged to fight to restore the Kabbah government. The AFRC/RUF junta was finally displaced in February 1998 when Nigerian-dominated peace-keeping forces attacked and captured Freetown and major provincial centres. Die-hard RUF/SL units, accompanied by some RSLMF soldiers and irregulars, went to ground in old haunts along the Liberian border, from where the war might yet revive.

COMBATANT VOICES

The material presented below derives from sets of interviews with self-demobilised RUF/SL and CDF conscripts and under-age RSLMF-linked irregulars undergoing rehabilitation in two programmes in Freetown in 1996. The purpose of the larger study (Peters and Richards, 1998a; 1998b; Richards, 1998) from which the present selection of material derives, is to enrich community and agency discussions about options for demobilisation and rehabilitation of young people affected by war. Richards is a British anthropologist with many years field experience in Sierra Leone, including, most recently, a study of the Gola Forest region prior to and during the war. Peters is a Dutch rural sociologist who has worked with young ex-combatants in Sierra Leone and Cambodia. He also has experience working with children's puppet theatre. Richards' knowledge of the wider context of social life in Sierra Leone and Peter's specific knowledge of how to build rapport with children and young people were both important factors in ensuring the adequate cross-checking and contextualisation of informants' accounts.

Inspired by the earlier example of a collection of 'street children's' accounts of life in Freetown published by the People's Education Association (*Greens, Bras and Ballheads*, PEA, 1989) we aspire to let young people tell their story in their own words. To this end we here reproduce complete, or long and largely uninterrupted, interview sequences. Peters' interviews were conducted in English with assistance of a Krio or Mende-speaking interpreter, but only after lengthy sessions to build rapport. Richards' interviews were conducted in Krio, the national *lingua franca*. Richards is responsible for all translation, and for editorial work on the texts. Most informants were explicit about wanting to see their words in print. Originally we hoped to confirm an agreed text with interviewees and supply their names. Changed circumstances subsequent to the coup of May 1997 – in which some informants rejoined their irregular units and resumed combat operations – means we have had to suppress, for the time being, any personal identifications.

From a 'bank' of over twenty interviews we have chosen here to present five shorter accounts representing all the major groups of under-age combatants in the war – RSLMF-linked irregulars, female under-age fighters, RUF/SL cadres, and *kamajo* (CDF) combatants (further material is published in Peters and Richards, 1998a and b). Ages of informants ranged from ten to eighteen at the time of recruitment.

VICTIMS AND AGENTS

The war began in 1991 with no more than a handful of insurgents ranged against government forces of under 3,000. Recent (1997) estimates of total numbers of combatants in Sierra Leone, including the *kamajo* militia, are plus/minus 50,000 – a fifteen-fold increase. It has been estimated that perhaps half of all combatants in the RUF/SL are in the age range eight to fourteen. There are also many under-eighteen combatants in army irregular units and the *kamajo* militia. Both RSLMF and RUF/SL have deployed some under-age female combatants.

Under-age irregulars are rated highly by their officers. They fight without inhibition (Interviews 1 and 4) and kill without compunction, sometimes casually (Interview 3), sometimes as an extension of play. Children are good in ambush situations, one of the main combat tactics (Interview 2), and – separated by war from kin – develop fierce loyalties to their *bra* (Krio – literally 'big brother'), i.e. the officer responsible for recruiting and training them (Interviews 1 and 3).

Combatants report drug abuse – regular use of marijuana, being prepared for battle with injections of amphetamines, and taking crack cocaine or a cocktail of local substances including gunpowder to deaden fear (Interviews 2 and 3). Atrocities are undoubtedly committed under the influence of drugs. Girl combatants regularly experience military rape (cf. Littlewood, 1997), sometimes as a 'punishment' for losing ground (Interview 2). Large numbers of children have been conscripted against their will, mainly by the RUF/SL (Interview 5). In all these respects a majority of participants in the Sierra Leone war are properly considered victims of military manipulation. However, many under-age combatants also joined up voluntarily (Interviews 1–4), some looking for revenge (Interviews 1 and 4), others to survive. Youngsters in a war zone find themselves 'on the street' (Interview 3 and 4). Joining a militia group is both meal ticket and substitute education (Interviews 1, 3 and 4). The pay may be derisory (Interview 1), but weapons training pays quick dividends; the AK-47 commands food, money, a warm bath, and instant adult respect (Interview 3). The combat group is an important substitute for lost family and friends (Interviews 1 and 2).

Interviewees repeatedly return to the theme of educational aspirations. Economic failure, political corruption and structural adjustment wreaked havoc on educational systems in Sierra Leone. Formal education prepares young people in Sierra Leone inadequately for the economic realities of modern life (Mokuwa, 1997), and both RSLMF and RUF/SL recruited extensively from the swollen ranks of educational drop-outs hustling for a living in border logging and mining camps (Richards, 1996; cf. Reno, 1995; Zack-Williams, 1995). Even so, loss of educational opportunity is seen as a major factor in the decision to fight (see especially Interviews 1, 3 and 4).

Combatant accounts repeatedly stress that it makes little sense to stand down voluntarily without real promise of social reintegration, education or training, and civilian jobs, and that failure to address these aspirations first caused, and now prolongs, the conflict. Frustrated by the failure of demobilisation several informants re-enlisted after the military coup of 25 May 1997.

THE INTERVIEWS

Interview 1. Male youth ex-combatant, RSLMF-linked irregular

This account might be considered typical of the experiences of many male under-age RSLMF-linked irregulars. The young man comes from a rural family in Kailahun, and was eighteen years old when interviewed in October 1996 but had begun to fight in 1991, aged about thirteen. His family had been scattered by the RUF invasion, a younger brother killed, and his education halted. He fought for about four years, responding to a demobilisation offer only when there was a cease-fire with the RUF. He is frank that revenge was one of his reasons for fighting.

The account is especially interesting in that the interviewee was recruited by Capt. Ben-Hirsch, one of the first RSLMF officers in the war zone to respond to RUF tactics by creating his own force of under-age irregulars. Ben-Hirsch was allegedly one of the architects of the NPRC takeover in 1992, though ambushed and killed (the interviewee was an eye-witness) before the coup took place. It is interesting to note Ben-Hirsch adapting indigenous ideas, associated with the men's 'secret society' Poro, about *hindo-hindo* (mobilisation of village young men for community defence).

The young man now wants vocational training, but would re-join an irregular unit tomorrow if required. When he speaks of defending his 'motherland' he is probably talking about Kailahun, and perhaps his mother's village in particular. He has not seen his family since the RUF invasion in 1991 and does not know if they are dead or alive.

What is your name, age and where do you come from?

I am [...], I am eighteen years old. I come from Kailahun district, it is in the east, close to the border. I lived in a village, a big village with more than a thousand people.

You lived with your family there?

Yes, I lived with my father, while my father took me to my uncle at S., near D., to go and attend school. I was at the age of ten, then I went for the first time to primary school. I was attending the M. Primary School in S. After primary school I attended W. Secondary School.

Do you have any brothers or sisters?

I have three brothers, all smaller and two smaller sisters. I am the only one that was attending school.

When you were with your uncle, did you visit your parents?

Oh, yes. Every holiday I went to visit my father.

What kind of occupation did your father and uncle have?

My father, he was a farmer. At that age I liked farming. By then I wanted to become a farmer. ... not any more. My uncle, he was a medical cashier, at the hospital ...

So when the war broke out, do you remember that?

Yes, we were very close to the border, where the rebels entered. There was a time they even kept my father and mother. One of my smaller brothers was killed by the rebels, that was in 1991. They were with the rebels for eight months. After that I never set an eye on them again. I don't know if they are still alive. So after that I tried to join the army as a matter of revenging. I wanted to revenge my people.

What was your first experience with the war?

The soldiers came to my village and they were telling that the rebels should come from the east and that they were trying to kill people. So they said that we had to move, and we went to Kenema. Me, my uncle and his family. I already had been to Kenema, so it was not my first time.

Where did you join the army?

I went back to S. I met the lieutenant there, Lt Ben-Hirsch. So he tried to form some kind of organisation we usually call the *hindo-hindo* squad. That is a Poro Society [idea] ... for the boys to defend the land. Normally the village chief takes the boys for the Poro, but now the lieutenant did. When we joined, he trained us and gave us some weapons to fight the rebels. The lieutenant died during 1992 in a rebel ambush. Before the lieutenant died, he was promoted to captain, Capt. Ben-Hirsch. We were on a mission, and on the way we were ambushed, and he died.

What did you learn in the army?

So many types of weapons, AK, RPG, grenade-launcher and how to use them. When we were in the jungle, I usually held an AK-47, 12 inch, because that is the lowest weapon. I was able to use the gun. I was with six friends in the army. We stayed together. Now some have died, some of them are in Kenema and some of them are in this programme ... Since I arrived here I haven't seen [the others] any more. I stayed for three years in the army.

How did you come here [to Freetown]?

When I came to Bo, I was coming to trace my mother. When I came, I heard the announcement over the radio, FM 104. When I heard the announcement I went to the brigade headquarters to register. The announcement was saying: 'if any child had taken part [in the war], whether with the army or with the rebels, we should go and register at the brigade-headquarters'. So I went there and registered. After that they brought us here, in a bus.

Were you happy to leave the army?

I was happy, because at that moment they already had told the rebels to lay down arms. So [when] they took us, I was so happy, because the rebels had laid down arms.

Did you like staying in the army?

Yes, I liked to be free in the country[side]. Besides this, when they took you to training, they also tell you [things], we were trained to save life and property. So I liked that, because I was saving life and property. That's why I loved the work. When we were in the army, every month the government paid us. They allowed us the amount of six thousand Leones [about US $12.00]. Not plenty. The actual pay was five thousand Leones. I bought drinks and smokes: cigarettes and snuff, beer and wine. Just to have some mind [determination] to go and fight. I didn't use other drugs. The food was supplied by the government. Sometimes the food was delicious, sometimes not ...

Did you actually take part in the fighting?

Yes.

Do you know if you killed somebody?

By then [i.e. at the time], I did not know if I killed somebody, because we were fighting and shooting and only after the fight we went out to search for the dead bodies.

So in 1996 the bus took you to this place. Do you like it here?

We are still managing it. I'd like to go back but if they say I should stay here: no problem. We wait for the order.

What would you like to do in the future?

I would like to attend school, after that I want to do motor-engineering. I want to become self-reliant. At the moment I have nobody in Freetown where I can stay with. [If] someone wants to take care of me, I [will be] glad to do my course here at the Technical Institute ...

Do you feel that you have taken revenge?

They have already demobilised me, so presently I have no power to hold arms. Unless they allow me back.

So when they say that they want you back, you will go?

Yes.

And fight again?

Yes.

You want to go back to the army?

Yes, to defend my motherland.

Interview 2. Female youth ex-combatant, RSLMF-linked irregular

Now aged twenty, this young woman was sixteen when she first became a combatant. Unusually, she had a strong and supportive family background and good educational prospects in Freetown when she volunteered. She followed a soldier-boyfriend to the front (an old story) and there became an irregular associate of the RSLMF in Daru. Intelligent and brave, she soon became a valued fighter. Her testimony speaks of the horror of war, the ingenuity of young people in surviving it, and specifically of the sexual harassment that is routine for young women in war zones. It is especially worth noting that being a combatant does not protect a young woman from the threat of military rape (cf. Littlewood 1997). The comments on tactics are interesting. Like many RSLMF-linked under-age irregulars and *kamajo* fighters she justifies her participation by saying 'I was defending my country'.

Where and when were you born and what is your work?

I was born Freetown 1976. I now work as a seamstress, but I want to study again.

Do you have children?

One child.

What were you doing at the time you joined?

I was at secondary school in Freetown (Form 2).

What made you join (as an RSLMF irregular)?

I had a boyfriend who was a soldier, and I followed him from Freetown to Daru. I was attracted by the uniform. Full combat looks smart. I sent my mother a picture of me in full combat [gear] ... that was the first she knew I had joined.

Is the combat gear what makes girls want to fight?

Lots of young women followed the rebels [RUF/SL] because they offered them items, and their regular men did nothing for them.

Did you take part in fighting?

Yes.

How did you prepare for battle?

I just prayed ... I did not take any drugs.

Where did you fight?

Daru, Manowa, Pendembu.

Did you kill rebels in battle?

Yes, plenty. Also, when soldiers came back to camp with rebel captives I would be ordered to 'wash' them.

What was that?

To kill them.

Why was that 'washing'? Did you spray bullets?

No, bullets are expensive. I would kill them one by one.

Did you ever feel it was wrong to fight?

I was defending my country.

Did you ever feel sorry for the dead rebels?

At first, when we advanced, and saw their dead bodies, I would feel sorry, but we had to kill them ... they would kill us first if they had the chance. Rebels kill and split open the bellies of pregnant women. Rebels rape any women soldiers they catch ... [Government] soldiers raped us sometimes in the forest, but they are more careful ... the rebels, they all join in.

Did you fear to become pregnant at the war front?

I swallowed gun powder as a contraceptive.

Who showed you that?

No one ... I discovered it for myself. But I first took it to become brave for battle. If you take gunpowder before you sleep you will wake with red [fierce] eyes.

How did you fight?

I know the ambush tactics. We have rations and a special belt, and use sign language. We can be in the bush at the ambush point for up to five days.

How did the rebels fight?

The rebels are no good at ambush. They are not disciplined. They cannot 'bear' [stand the suffering] ... they more commonly attack according to time; 14.00–16.00 hours is their time. They want to be off, and go with loot. But when the rebels ambush an army 'big man' they know that you must go back for the body, so they use that to trap you.

Did the soldiers attack civilians?

They fought among themselves. An army paymaster [D.] was ambushed by army units. There was jealousy [about the money]. Many soldiers attacked, and many died.

Why did you decide to leave the army?

The rank smell of blood. Also it was the sight of dead comrades, their arms and legs smashed by RPGs.

How are things now?

My heart is now cool. I don't want to fight again. I work as a seamstress and have my own machine. But I still hope to study. I want to learn languages ... French and Dutch ... and become an air hostess [KLM and Sabena are the two foreign airlines flying to Sierra Leone]. But I have this sickness [shows us large tumour on her leg]. It started before I joined up. I can't sleep at times because of the pain.

Interview 3. Male youth ex-combatant, RSLMF-linked irregular

This account can be considered typical of the experiences of a rather different class of youngster – an urbanised, part-educated son of a northern migrant to the diamond fields. Here is a teenage combatant with a tendency to a 'rarray' [street] life (he was on the street in 1993 immediately before becoming a combatant). The war for the economically crucial Kono diamond fields has always been much more manifestly a direct struggle to control material wealth. Politicians and illegal miners have long defended their interests in this region with armed gangs (Reno, 1995). With some prior youthful experience of diamond mining, the interviewee reveals a knowingly cynical attitude to war and its material benefits. There is no sense of 'defence of motherland' here. RUF/SL attack on Koidu disrupted schooling and family support, but note how the boy abandons the father in the bush because he can no longer feed his children, and joins up with a Boy Scout troop that has already become a gang of survival-oriented bandits. Later the boy, coached by his older brother, already a regular soldier, becomes a combatant irregular almost by accident. He freely admits that he and his friends enjoyed army life. They were free to lord it over civilians, loot, and rape women. Drugs were routine, cocaine supplied to the fighters by their officer. The casual way in which the boy shot dead an RUF prisoner for 'insulting his mother' is chilling. He wants to go back to school because he once showed great aptitude, but senses it may be too late. The performance of the democratic regime is assessed solely in terms of food handouts. Here are some of the problems of the war in a nutshell.

What is your name, age, religion and where do you come from?

My name is ..., I'm [now] seventeen years old. I'm a Muslim. My father came from K., from the north. We settled in Kono district. That is where I was born, I was born in Kono district.

What kind of work did your father do?

My father was working for one of the companies ... SLST [Sierra Leone Selection Trust], a diamond company.

Do you have brothers or sisters?

I have five brothers, one is in the army [RSLMF] up till now. He is a sergeant. And I have five sisters. My mother is in K ... they are not divorced, the war set them apart. I have contact with my father, the last time he wrote to me a letter about the family. I lived in a town, Yengema, it is a big town. We have an airport and a good social life.

What did you do when you were young?

The time I was young I used to go with friends to the beach, to the cinemas, after school. Just after school. Because that time I was young I didn't listen to what my elders said. I just did things on my own will.

Sometimes we went out just [to] make some fun, make up some devils, dress up like devils and then go dancing in the streets. It was a way to get small money. The time I was young, I also went out hunting. But I remember once me and my best friend went out to the bush and I had a sharp razor-blade and I cut off his ... his [foreskin]. After some time my father came and gave me a serious beating and then took the boy to the hospital.

But why did you do that, to make him a Muslim?

No, just to circumcise him. I said to him that I was a doctor.

And he believed that you were a doctor?

Yes, he was small and I too was not circumcised, so I took it and cut it off.

At what age did you go to school?

I was seven years old. When the war broke out, in 1991, I was in Form 1 [of Secondary School]. I was good at school. In primary school I had double promotion. I didn't do Class 2 and I didn't do Class 4. At that time I wanted to become a doctor.

Your town ... many people mined diamonds, but was it safe?

Yes, we had so much security, SSD and at times some special South Africans ... protecting the diamond fields. But the time my father was working for the company I was not yet born. But later I accompanied some workmen [diamond diggers]. So when the diamonds came out, they gave some to me and then I gave them to my father. So I did some small diamond work. But at present I want to become a nurse.

What was your first experience with the war?

I was in school when I heard a gunshot coming from the headquarters, where the soldiers stay. So I heard a gunshot from there and I was really scared. The rebels already had captured the place, so we never turned back. We went to the bush area, to escape to stay alive. We only stayed for a few hours in the bush. So after two days I went back to the town, but the township was [held by] the rebels. I entered the town at around 8.30 in the evening, the place was so dark. I entered my house and took some of my things away. I went to my father's room and took his clothes, leaving the place at night again. I went back to the bush.

Did your father survive the rebel attack?

My father managed to escape with my brothers and sisters. I met them at one village, one day after the rebel attack. After that, because my father had not enough to give us food, I left him and joined the scouts, the Boy Scouts. We then took property from people from the town. We took what belonged to them. I was already before the war with the Scouts. They gave me a knife, but I was not wearing a uniform, a scout uniform. I just had the knife. We met one man standing with luggage, containing clothes and other things. We pushed him into the bush and took his luggage. The leader of the scout boys was called H., he was an older boy. I stayed for five days with the scouts. Later I went to a checkpoint, the last checkpoint as you enter Kono. So I was sitting there and I saw my elder brother. He was with his lieutenant. He told the official that I was his smaller brother. So then I joined and became a soldier. So later when the rebels attacked us they gave me a rifle to fire.

So at the moment the rebels attacked they gave you a rifle?

I was having a rifle already. I had the weapon when we entered the bush. I was just behind my brother, because he knew how to fight. They taught me how to use the gun. So when the rebels attacked Kabala a message came to our officer that he had to go there. So the next [day] we moved for Kabala. We went with a truck. I was at that time sixteen plus, that was in 1994. In 1993 I was living a street life, I was not with my father or mother.

How was the first time you had to fight?

I was sitting next to the sergeant, down at the checkpoint. We heard some gunshots. I was afraid so I jumped down into the gutter. And then the soldiers said: 'What are you doing there?' and he laughed. So I came out and took my rifle. So two of my friends who were sitting at the checkpoint answered: 'Just fire where the rebels are.' I was glad that my brother stood behind me, because I didn't know how to fight. The second time I fought was in Kabala, then they shot me here, in my foot.

When you were with the army did you fall into ambushes?

Yes, there were ambushes I fell into, in Kono district. That was with Lt. K[...]. He is still alive, in Gandohun.

How many years did you stay in the army?

One year and six months. I liked it in the army because we could do anything we liked to do. When some civilian had something I liked, I just took it without him doing anything to me. We used to rape women. Anything I wanted to do [I did]. I was free.

Did the army pay you?

Yes, but I had no official number, so normally the lieutenant made sure that we got something. Sometimes I went to my mother, to buy some rice for her ... a bag of rice.

Were you not afraid to fight?

The first time I was really afraid, but later I got used to it and I was not afraid any more.

Do you remember the first time you killed somebody?

I remember. An officer captured a rebel. He told me to take care of him. He was tied with his hands on his back. So he was sitting and I had my rifle. But he was talking in a bad way to me, he even insulted my mother. And then I asked him: 'Are you talking to me?' He said: 'Yes.' So I shot him in the stomach and he fell and bled to death. Later, when the lieutenant came back, he took me to the captain, and I had to stay for seven days in a room. That was my first killing. But in the battle I also killed.

Did you at that time drink or smoke anything?

Oh yes, the lieutenant used to provide us cocaine. I put it here, on my nail, which is very long ... [the nail] of my thumb, and sniffed it. It was free, for us to fight. Just before the fight. We also used to smoke marijuana, it was common to us, every day we smoked it. And Totapak, a long packet, it is a rum. And Ramram, you smoke it. It is like a leaf, like marijuana.

How did you come here to this programme?

Well, our commanding officer called us and mentioned that those who are not at least seventeen or eighteen should leave the army. And that they should go to Freetown, where there was a place for us, where we could forget about all we had done in the army. I heard that before but I never listened to it. I always wanted to keep fighting. Until I was seriously shot. Then I went to the hospital, it was the headquarters hospital in Yengema. I was there for just two weeks, for my foot.

So after that you went to this place, in a bus?

Because I had not so much money I got a lift to the checkpoint. Someone told the soldiers about me. Most of my friend are still in the army. They will stay in the army till they die.

Were you happy to leave the army?

Yes, really happy. And the people here take us like we are their sons. So I hope I to continue my schooling, but now it is a long time since I was in a real class. After secondary school I want to learn nursing, here in Freetown. But when I qualify I want to go back to Kono to help my people ...

Interview 4. Male youth ex-combatant, *kamajo* fighter

This account by a young *kamajo* fighter provides a telling political analysis of the war, as well as evidence about the background of the CDF. Here is a young man who began to fight when he was sixteen because his schooling had been halted by RUF attacks. He returns to his village to 'represent' his father – owner of a hunting gun – in a *kamajo* unit raised by the local chief. All the time he dreams of returning to school. He is angry with the rebels for disrupting his education. And yet he has a remarkably clear understanding of what they are fighting for. RUF cadres are students like himself, a fact he gleans from letters they drop in villages, outlining their aims. He can well understand their bitterness against a corrupt patrimonial system that provides education and jobs for only a favoured few. But he is also clear about the movement's major strategic mistake – violence against impoverished civilians and not the oppressive one-party regime. He is very impatient with the demobilisation programme, because of delays in restarting his education. His hopes of becoming a scientist (mathematics is the key to all science, he tells us), travelling overseas to study, and returning to benefit his village, diminish by the day. He has some sharp comments about the educated elite who exploit the system and put nothing back. Yet he has gained something in Freetown. He has become a born-again

Christian. This gives him a new insight on the war. The magical techniques of the *kamajo* he now understands are from the devil (although insisting that they are as real as the mathematics he so admires). No war can be won by weapons. The fighting only escalates. So he has advice for the government. End the war by sitting down to find out what made the RUF/SL so bitter. (Throughout the account we use the anglicised plural 'kamajors' rather than the Mende plural *kamajoisia*.)

First I want to know your name, age and where you came from?

I am [...]. I am eighteen years old. I come from Kono district, in the east ...

When you were young what did you want to become?

The time I was small I desired to become a doctor, that was at the age of seven. The time I began to develop to an adolescent age my intention was to do physical science. While I was in school, during 1992, the rebels came and attacked the place, I decided to leave school and go back to my village, to my father.

Why did you go back to your father's place?

Well, my father was a hunter, he had a gun. There was a mandate signed by the paramount chief that every man with his own gun ... should go and defend his ground at the war front. So by then I was with my father during the war. And my father was now moving to an old age, so I went to represent my father with the gun. So this led me to take part in the war, but war was not my career. It is just because of problems and difficulties. But during my childhood it was not my desire. My desire is to be educated.

Tell me about your primary school.

My first year I took first position to go to the second class, the second year I took the second position to go to the third class. The third year my academic interest began to decline. But when I went to the fifth class I regained my power and began to study again ... and the subject I liked was maths. From there I started to score, even the last time, when the war approached Kono in 1992, I took the first position. I want to believe in studies, because when you study, when you work, you receive. If you do not study you do not get any result.

So in 1992 you went to your village?

At that time I was in the headquarters of the district, named Koidu town. I was there attending school. There was no school in our village, so I left the village, to go to the city to seek education.

And then the war came to the Koidu?

When the war came to the headquarters, it was ... let me see ... six to seven in the morning, when the rebels attacked. I was preparing to go to school. It was a Friday. But when I heard the gun then I decided to undress [get out of the school uniform]. After the enemy invaded the town, we managed to escape. I had to go to Guinea, as a refugee. I later decided to go back to the headquarters. By then the government soldiers had [re-taken] the place. They drove the rebels from the headquarters. When I heard about this I decided to go back. But back in Koidu I decided to go back to my village, only to return when education improved. But the war became worse. So eventually I decided to represent my father at civil defence: the kamajors. My father had bought a gun with his pocket money. There was an order that everyone with a gun should go to the front. You and your gun should go to the war front. When you had a gun you had to go by force [it was compulsory]. If you refused they would take the gun from you. So I decided, when that situation comes, to take part, to go. That was in 1994. I was sixteen.

Did you go alone to join the kamajors?

No, we were many from my village. There were more than fifteen from my village. They sent you by turns. You go for three months, after that you come back, and the next man goes for three months. They go by turns to the front. When you finished your time, you came back and started to work [on the farm, etc.]. You can be a hunter at the war front and at the same time a farmer or a commercial business man or whatever. You only go there for months, maybe two or three. That was the way we protect ourselves, because the government soldiers were then in certain situations maltreating our people. But we, the civil defence had the same right as the government soldiers in the battlefield. So when you became a civil defence man the soldiers would not disadvantage you. We were both fighting for the land.

Were there other boys with the kamajors?

There were small boys who were not even my rank. Fifteen, fourteen [years old] and even younger, small boys. They are more brave than the bigger boys. A person [not yet reaching] adolescence does not think much. What he desires to do, he will do it.

Were you not afraid?

I was not afraid, because what I think is when I have to die, I die. If God saves me then I will be saved. Whether you die or live, the rebels were maltreating us. They came and killed our people, they came and stole our properties. So as a man you have to stand for your right and fight for your property, fight for your land.

But were those your own ideas?

Yes.

Were you able to use a gun?

The gun was not heavy. You can take it with one hand.

Was there any training?

Yes, there was. The village leader goes for training. Because the skills – the tactics – of the hunters applied when going to kill an animal in the bush are the same tactics we should apply in the field to get rid of the rebels. So you don't need to go for training, because the skill is with you now. The idea to go and kill an animal in the bush is the same idea to go and kill the rebels. Because the animals stay in the bush there, you pick up an idea: you want to kill it, and so also with human beings. Maybe you will go around the people in the bush, examine them in what way you can get rid of the people. Because the kamajors are very, very wise. The wisdom they use to kill an animal is the same wisdom that they use to attack the rebels.

So they are good fighters?

Yes, they are very, very good. In fact the enemy has more fear of kamajors than of government soldiers. Yes, they say that the civil defence used to attack them unexpectedly. Because the place where you [do] not expect human beings to be, a *kamajo* can be possible [in] that place. So when the time reaches for the rebels to share their food, and they think nobody is around, there could be a *kamajo* around. And if the *kamajo* happens to fire, just a shot ... because the bullet we use in this civil defence gun, it is many in the shell ... so when you release one shot, that bullet will kill many, many people. The bullets are very, very tiny, but when you shoot, it spreads.

So it can kill three or four people at once?

Even more than ten.

But what are the big guns, the long ones?

You mean the ones the government soldiers use [RPG?]? They use them in combat areas. They use them in clearing an area. But in bush-fights that gun would you not be able to go. The rebels always like to go in the bush. The kamajors go and search in the bush and kill them. In the bush you are only able to take a light object with you. You are not able to take a heavy object with you in order to go and fight in the bush. You must take a lighter object in order to do the thing.

Did you also fight the rebels when you were with the kamajo militia?

Yes, at regular times.

And did you also kill somebody?

I am not sure if I have killed somebody because it is group fighting. So maybe you are pointing at one man and your neighbour also [is aiming] at the same man. So after the operation there will be a lot of dead bodies. But you will not be able to identify [which ones you killed] because there were many in the action.

You go out with a group of say for instance ten people?

Yes, yes, more than ten, even more than twenty. When you want to capture a large village ... we even go with more than forty. We go there and surround the place. We travel in the bush. We travel a lot and then surround the place. Then the operation takes place.

After a fight what do you do with the dead bodies?

We don't have anything to do with them.

You do not bury them?

No, we don't bury them because they are the enemy. They come to spoil our land. They come to disturb our future as well. They even kill our people, so that's why we kill. So we don't have any sympathetic feelings for them.

What happens to their guns?

If we happen to kill them we take their arms.

How long were you with the kamajors?

In 1994 I decided to go to represent my father. In 1995 I left to go back to Koidu, and from there I heard about this project.

Why did you leave?

Well, because my career is to go to school. And the situation had become [more] normal, [so I could leave] the village in order to ... follow my education. When I came I met some fellows and even a [Catholic] Brother and I discussed the issue with him. So I was in preparation to leave the war and go back to school. So eventually I heard about this project, and they told me that this project can assist you with school, and help you forget the war. So I was glad to come. But when I came and when I saw the situation, I [thought about going] back. But some of my friends encouraged me not to go back.

How did you hear about this programme?

Well, the way I heard about this programme, if I had known how it was [really] like, I would not have come from Kono. The way I heard about facilities, the way I heard about education. If I had known for sure I would not have left my land to come here. Because the motive I [had in leaving] Kono was to come and be educated. The Brother convinced us to come, [but] when we [arrived] we were discouraged, so we thought we would go back. Some of our friends, they just went. But...I [now] thank God because the first thing that happened was [that] I knew Jesus Christ. There was a time when I was in the provinces I didn't know Jesus, but then the missionaries came to teach us, to preach to us, to enlighten us, to teach us about the way of God.

Did you tell me that you wanted to go back home?

Even now, my desire, if it becomes real, is to leave here in order to go back to Kono ... yes, I will go ... because if I stay here I will just be at this ... It would give me no benefit. We just eat in the morning, in the day and in the evening. But if I can go back to Kono and attend school, because every day you sleep time goes out of you. So that is why I desire now to go back to Kono to [re-]start education. Because God knows it is a long time since I left school. The time I started to go to school I was just age five or six. I thank the Almighty, because I was brilliant in school. But then the war approached. But I said when this situation is normal I will go back to school. The reason why I took part in the war was because there was no education in our headquarters.

In future, as you once told me, you want to be a bio-chemist?

So I desire. Whether I become a bio-chemist, or an engineer. Because I want to study pure science, and I might be able to specialise. That is the reason why I always do mathematics, because mathematics is the key of science.

[Here we omit a section, to be found in full in Peters and Richards (1998a), on *kamajo* weapons and sorcery]

Now you are a Christian what do you think about kamajo sorcery?

[At that] time I didn't know Jesus Christ. I didn't know the life of Jesus Christ. But when I came to Freetown I received Jesus Christ as my Lord and personal saviour. So all what the kamajors are doing, their witchcraft, the wishes [charms] they use to fight, all is work of the Devil. When I came here I had the desire not to fight again, to be a real Christian. I don't want to be with these people again ... war is the work of the Devil. Because according to the Bible, if you are a soldier ... even in the Bible we have soldiers, isn't it so? ... we have Joshua, King David, they fight ... they fight with nothing. With nothing [except] the support of the Lord. Even the time when they killed Goliath, [David] picked up the stone and what he said was: 'I'm going to kill in the name of the Lord.' But now, these days, people fight with other forces, with other supernatural forces. Now, according to my own view, this is not the work of God. Because if you are fighting an enemy in that evil way ... I don't even believe now that arms can ... because since I was here in Freetown I discovered that ammunition cannot finish a war. Only the Lord God will bring war to an end through peace talking. But if we continue to use arms, we end up killing ourselves. In the end there will be nobody in the land. If I am asked by government officials, I will say 'stop using arms' [and] 'try to make peace'. The reason that made the war to come, let them search for that [reason]. And if they know the reason, or the problem, how the war came to the country, then you can make the situation become normal. But if we start to fight, eventually there will be no person left.

What are the reasons this war started and continues?

Well, according to my own view, [it started and continues] because when the rebels caught some of our brothers and sisters they took them along with them and told them the reason why they are fighting. Because of the past government, the APC government, the way the government maltreated people. No freedom of speech. When you emphasise on your rights, they take you to court or jail you. And the same bad thing with education. Most of the rebels are students, the majority are students.

How do you know?

They write on paper that they drop. After an attack, they write a message and drop it. These are the reasons why they are fighting, they say. The government doesn't give any encouragement to people to get land or to go to school. When you come from poor families, but with talent to be educated, there is no financial support. The government doesn't give a helping hand. They are only bothered about themselves. This was the reason this government made the war to come, according to my own view. When the [rebel] people attacked a place, the paper, the document they leave at that place, when you come and read the document, this [gives] the[ir] reason to fight. The other reason is assistance. If Mister A happens to be in the head-office [top position], and you, Mister Z, you don't know him, there is no political influence between you and him. So when you come with your problem to him, he will not assist you. Only if you are the man who [wishes?] by him, whether his son, his brother's son, or his brother's relation or his wife's sister's relation, or his relatives. But for you as a low man, when you come to that person, to that official in that place, he will not give you any assistance. Because he doesn't know you. This made the war to come.

But are these good reasons to fight?

Yes. But if the rebels had come peacefully, if they hadn't stolen our people, hadn't burnt our villages ... if they hadn't done anything that harmed us ... but if they had only gone to the government with blood ... If they had come trustfully [in a trusting way?] to the government, come and attended to the government [changed it?], we sure [would] have been glad. Because, according to their view they are fighting for their rights. That was the reason why the war came, the reason why I was against them. They are fighting for their rights, but during their fight for their rights, they go to the villages. They go to [persons] who don't know anything about the government. They go and kill [them] and steal [their] property. That was the reason why I was against them. But if the rebels [had come] down here [to Freetown] to this people ... because these are the people who created the war ... if the rebels would have come to them, plenty of Sierra Leoneans would have supported them. But because they went and [attacked] the poor, that's why I was against them. Because when you consider the rebels the way they think about [them] in the provinces, it is that they are just armed bandits. They are just thieves.

What do you think about the present government?

The government now? The government comes, [with] their mass media, to make things normal. Well, we are watching them. If they do as they say, OK. If they are not responsible for what they say, we are still with them.

If they are not doing what they promised, it is all right?

If they are not doing what they say, it is all right. All is all right. Because now it is a democratic state. Now what they promise to do, if they fail to do it, the next elections the people will not vote for them. But if they do the will of the people it is good.

A last question. If you had three wishes, what would you wish?

My first wish is to be educated. Because why? Because of the too much illiteracy, the way our brothers in Sierra Leone don't know their rights. Because when you are educated, you know your rights. This is the first wish in my life. I admire education above anything. I admire academic education above anything in my life, according to my own desire. Second, after I am educated, I wish to go to the Western world. To study ... and because when you travel you see changes. And when you are in those areas people are moving faster. When you [go] and you see people, how they move with their lives, how things are going ... when you come back to your country, [and] you apply the same method, then you become developed. But some of our brothers ... they get money to be educated. But instead of helping the poor they steal the money. They do things that are not beneficial to their country. If I happen to cross to the Western world and go and finish my course, I [must] come with a new improvement to develop the area where we live in the country. If I happen to study much I [will] go to study to serve my country.

And what is your third wish?

My last wish is that the war ... according to God ... that the Lord ... may it come to pass ... that the war finishes. Because when the war finishes, all these things I mentioned will be fulfilled. If still the war is existing, these things will not be fulfilled. Because after this project will be finished after two or three years, then I will be relying on the resources of my village. So from my parents, they make some money through their farm, the coffee farm, the cocoa farm. When they harvest they support us with education. But these past years they harvest nothing. But when the war will come to an end they can again support me to get education. So this is my last wish. I pray to the Lord that He brings peace to this country, because people are suffering. People are dying, the poor become homeless, people became fatherless. Yes, I want to stop the war.

Interview 5. Male youth ex-combatant, self-demobilised from RUF/SL.

This young man, now about twenty, was captured and forcibly inducted by the RUF/SL in a raid into north-western Sierra Leone in January 1995. Although he completed guerrilla training and served on operations he never gained any promotion in the movement, remaining ambivalent about the struggle. He is frank that his lack of conviction was more a question of the hardship than any political objection. He found the RUF's ideological teaching about the state of Sierra Leone made sense. When interviewed in October 1996 he had managed to escape four weeks previously, after nearly two years, and had been re-accepted in his home community, a town not badly affected by the war. Interviewed in a quiet domestic setting, and no longer under local suspicion, he provides a remarkable account of RUF/SL aims and operation, and life in one of their guerrilla camps. The account supports in some respects the picture the movement paints in its own propaganda document (RUF/SL, 1995). The Gurkhas referred to in the account were a mercenary force of ex-Gurkhas led by a Canadian (Col. Robert Mackenzie) hired by the NPRC government. They were withdrawn shortly after Mackenzie was killed, and replaced by the South African private security firm Executive Outcomes.

Tell me about how you were captured?

It was early morning. They came down the road as I was going to work. They pulled me and loaded properties on my head. They threatened to spray me with the gun if I didn't go. We walked day and night, with only snatches of sleep. We made food for them.

Where did you go?

We walked for seven days. Any town we reached we would get food from the people. After eight days we reached the Malal Hills ... on top of the hill.

What happened then?

We rested for one day, then they called us to a lecture. They said 'If we write about bad in the country nothing will happen, so we have brought you inside the revolution to act to make bad things stop.' They showed us plenty of things that had to happen ... they said there is no freedom, no medical attention, no better roads ... the system is rotten.

And after that what?

They came to scrape [shave] our heads. We were sent to base camp for training in the Malal Hills.

How long did that last?

Three months, for basic training. Then they were training us to fight. After three months government forces attacked us, so we had to evacuate the camp. The place is a long hill. The camp was shifted to the other end. So we had to advance to the other part. Then we completed training.

What sort of training?

We were trained in all kinds of war tactics.

Who were the people being trained?

All of us were Sierra Leonean boys [*Salong bobo dem*] ... from all tribes ... Temne, Mandingo, Kailahun [Up-Mende].

What did you do after training?

We advanced to Western Area, around Mile 38 [on the Freetown road]. We reached Waterloo [twenty miles to Freetown].

Did you really want to join them, since the RUF captured you?

I saw that what they were saying about the country was true, but I did not really want to join, mainly because of the strain ... one, the loads we had to carry, two, the walking, three the hunger ... we did not have good supplies, it was always a problem to get food ... and we were under rain day and night.

What about the fighting?

I did not feel happy about the killing and looting.

Some say the RUF is just different gangs with no overall leader. Can you comment about Foday Sankoh?

It is true that there are plenty in our group who have taken over one year in the movement without seeing Foday Sankoh. But he communicates commands to us by radio message, regularly. If one week goes by without getting radio messages then our commanders go to visit Sankoh. They use by-pass [footpaths in the bush], through the swamps and bolilands.

Did you ever see Sankoh?

Yes ... I went with the commanders to take leave of Sankoh before he went to Ivory Coast [for the peace negotiation, January 1996].

What route did you use?

We left Waterloo area and went through Yonibana and Moyamba. It took us four to five days [on foot] to reach Sankoh's camp [the Zogoda]. His base camp is on flat ground in thick forest.

What happened after Sankoh had left?

I joined another group to return to the Moyamba area. I was now assigned to a new 'forward defence' [camp]. I was there for six months after the cease-fire.

But then you ran away?

I was sent with a written message for another 'forward defence' [in our sector]. But I did not meet anyone in their camp. They had gone to look for food. Then I saw two people coming to check on me. I somersaulted into the bush [as trained] to hide. They passed by. I wondered what to do. Then I said to myself 'if I meet them again I will give them the letter, but if I do not meet them then I will give up [the struggle]'. This is what happened. I kept the letter.

How did you manage?

I reached a civilian zone behind our [RUF] line. I did nothing to them. I did not explain I was escaping [civilians in RUF 'ideology zones' were under strict orders to detain and return camp run-aways]. I just explained that I had a problem. I made up the story that I had [accidentally] shot my friend in the foot. Otherwise, they would have held me. One civilian said he would help me. I begged long trousers from him and a polo neck [sweater], so that I looked decent. Then I said 'you and I have made "society" [secret arrangement], if anyone asks don't say anything'.

How did you get back home?

I travelled as far as Sanda [chiefdom], sleeping in the bush at night. It was four days and nights before I met the road. I would sneak inside the empty farm huts at night to look for scraps of food. I did not dare approach anyone in the farms to ask for directions. But when I reached the road a driver helped me. I made it to [...], and reached the checkpoint after midnight. I knocked on the window [shutter] of my step-mother's room, but she was afraid [to open]. My dad was brave enough to peep out, and I called his name. Still, he could not believe, at first, it was me. I came with nothing, bare foot. It was September [last month].

What has happened to the other young people captured with you?

All the [...] people are still in the camp behind Moyamba, except for the Form 2 and 3 girls. They have gone to Foday Sankoh's base camp to resume their schooling.

Were you accepted after you reached home?

When I had arrived my big brother took me to the officer commanding to report. Later I went to the chief, and he then called the people to say it is me, one of the young people seized in January 1995. Crowds then came to our house to ask about their children [seized with me].

How are the other captives doing?

The load carrying brings some to the point of death. It is complete slavery. But plenty of others have turned to *agba* [become leaders] in the movement. The RUF promotes by ability, so some have really joined. But most now want peace, and to see their families.

Some say there is a drugs problem in the camps. Is this true?

There are no drugs in camp. The penalty for *jamba* [marijuana] smoking and rape is execution. There is no cocaine. Even for smoking a cigarette they beat you. If I had a headache they would give me aspirin from medicine they looted.

What else can you say about the camps?

There is church and mosque. You are free to be Muslim or Christian, but if you do not pray they punish you. In Malal Hills it is hard to get water. Every day we had to fetch water. You go at 5 a.m. It is one mile to climb back. There is a rope. Sometimes you go three or four times. The water is dirty, and sometimes you slip and drop the bucket before you reach. You do not return to camp before midday. Small boys can be promoted above you. Some were my juniors at school. A small boy can order you 'fuck you, go get water for me'. He is your superior.

But what about the atrocities, like amputation?

They cut hands in revenge for the attacks by the *kamajo* [hunter's militia].

What will the ones who have really joined want to do if the war ends?

What they really want is work. Some will want to learn trades, like carpentry. Even my own boss will want some as apprentices. But others will want to be in the army.

Will the combatants forget? Will there be tribal war?

The RUF people will forget. What has happened has happened. There is no tribalism. It is an armed struggle, but there is no pay. Many would change to national service in the army. Many want the war to end. They pray for it to end, but they do not yet have the chance to escape. Many want education ... to go back to school. But they are afraid of the army ... that the army will kill them. So they wait, for Foday Sankoh's last orders, to come out and lay down arms. They are very well disciplined.

What about looting?

They take things [only] when villagers run away.

What can you tell me about some of the attacks? For example, the one on R.[...] [in February 1996].

I wanted to take part in that attack, in case I got a chance to escape. But that was why they would not let me go. They brought others, not from this District.

Some people say some government soldiers join RUF attacks?

I never saw any government soldier in our camp. Maybe the big men have some arrangement. What I know is that there are a lot of captured government soldiers with Foday Sankoh. He holds them. Some fight for him. He says he won't kill them. They will accept him when they know what he is trying to do.

What about the attack at Magbosi [on a convoy, August 1995]?

That was the RUF. They know how to train for manoeuvres.

Do you know about the Gurkha attack on Malal Hills?

Yes. It was morning time. We were listening to a radio message, to announce promotions. Then we were called out of the base, and then ordered back in. Two jets came to bombard. But we knew the air raid was not the thing, that ground forces would come, so we were ready.

They told us they [Gurkhas] are coming. We fought seriously. It was not an ambush.

Did you see the Gurkha commander [Col. Mackenzie]?

There was one white man. He had compass, camera, gun. He was hit, and then killed. We dragged his body back to camp. We saw he had a tattoo on his arm. They cut the arm off, to show the tattoo to identify the person, to prove to the government that he had been killed. We buried Tarawali [RSLMF Major, aide-de-camp to NPRC Chairman Valentine Strasser]. After that attack the commanders decided to move the camp. After one week the jets came to bombard but we had left the camp site by then.

Did you listen to [broadcast] radio in camp?

They listen to FM and [BBC] Focus on Africa ... but don't blast this over FM or the ones who have been left behind will feel the pain. They know that some of us who escape talk.

Is there any training in camp [other than for combat]?

They have 'Dr Blood' [field medical orderlies]. They teach some of the women they have captured. They have some captured dispensers, who give them the ideas. Women 'with sense' [intelligent] learn the work. Some are now very skilled in treating wounds.

CONCLUSION

What do we learn more generally from the interviews above? The first major point is the clear evidence the interviews provide that young combatants have clear, rational reasons for joining a militia force. They fight with open eyes, to reverse educational disadvantage, to defend their communities, to take revenge, and to make a living from loot. Neither dupes nor victims, they seek to stay alive using their strength and ingenuity as best they can.

A second general feature is the similarity of viewpoint apparent among combatants from opposing groups. Despite their leaders' competing political aims, young fighters in Sierra Leone appreciate that they face a common set of difficulties arising from social exclusion and lack of educational opportunity. Bracketed by the Kabbah government as 'bandits' and 'rebels' large numbers of NPRC-recruited army irregulars ended the war as firmly ostracised as their former enemies; it is no surprise they reacted by joining hands with that former enemy after the coup of 1997. Further combinations and alliances of this kind will continue to erupt across Africa's war-torn political landscapes, and confound diplomatic opinion, so long as basic social grievances and educational deficiencies remain unaddressed.

Finally we return to the concern expressed earlier about viewing African under-age combatants as victims of traumatic experience. Undue focus on victim trauma risks masking the underlying social forces that, at the extreme, result in significant numbers of excluded young Africans ending up trapped in militia activity. One young man was scathing. 'Here' (in demobilisation camp), he told us, 'we are just hanging about talking about our problems to care givers and playing football. What we need to do is get back to school and start learning something. At very least let me learn how to make a cutlass blade so I can go and brush a farm.' Except for the small number of very disturbed individuals therapy without a clearly thought-out route to *social* reincorporation merely sugars the pill. A demobilisation programme for under-age combatants that is not also a major initiative in education, training, job creation and social rehabilitation is not worth the name.

References

Cairns, E. (1996). *Children and Political Violence.* Oxford: Blackwell.
Goodwin-Gill, G, and Cohn, I. (1994). *Child Soldiers: the Role of Children in Armed Conflicts.* Oxford: Clarendon Press.
Human Rights Watch/Africa Human Rights Watch Children's Rights Project. (1994). *Easy Prey: Child Soldiers in Liberia.* New York: Human Rights Watch.
Keen, D, (1995). 'Sell-game': the economics of conflict in Sierra Leone. *West Africa At War: Anarchy or Peace in Liberia and Sierra Leone?.* A one-day conference held at the Department of Anthropology, University College London, London WC1E 6BT, 21 October 1995.
Littlewood, R. (1997). Military rape. *Anthropology Today* 13, 1.
Machel, G. (1996). *Impact of Armed Conflict on Children.* Report of the expert of the Secretary-General pursuant to General Assembly resolution 48/157. New York: United Nations.
Mokuwa, S. (1997). Rice biodiversity education: a problem-based curriculum innovation for post-war recovery (Case Study of Kambia District and Freetown in Sierra Leone). MSc thesis, Management of Agricultural Knowledge Systems, Agricultural University, Wageningen, the Netherlands.
PEA (1989). *Bras, Greens and Ballheads: Interviews with Freetown 'Street Boys'.* Freetown: People's Educational Association of Sierra Leone.
Peters, K. and Richards P. (1998a). Why we fight: voices of youth combatants in Sierra Leone. *Africa* 68(2) (in press).

Peters, K. and Richards P. (1998b). When they call us rebels it's a lie: young irregulars talk about combat in Sierra Leone, *Cahier d'Etudes Africaine* (forthcoming).

Reno, W. (1995). *Corruption and State Politics in Sierra Leone.* Cambridge: Cambridge University Press.

Richards, P. (1996). *Fighting for the Rain Forest: War, Youth and Resources in Sierra Leone.* Oxford: James Currey.

Richards, P. (1998). Sur la nouvelle violence politique en Afrique: le sectarisme seculier au Sierra Leone, *Politique Africaine* (forthcoming, June 1998).

RUF/SL (1995). *Footpaths to Democracy: Toward a New Sierra Leone.* No stated place of publication: The Revolutionary United Front of Sierra Leone.

Zack-Williams, A.B. (1995). *Tributors, Supporters and Merchant Capital: Mining and Under-development in Sierra Leone.* Aldershot: Avebury Press.

5 Sexual Violence in Wartime. Psycho-Sociocultural Wounds and Healing Processes: the Example of the Former Yugoslavia

ANNEMIEK RICHTERS

You can't prevent the birds of sorrow
from flying over your head
but you can prevent them
from building nests in your hair. (Chinese proverb)

Western feminism has created a 'new language' that, in some parts of the world, is starting to change the way that sexual violence is perceived and understood by both victims and society as a whole. Drawing on feminist analysis, this chapter explores the global relevance of this language; it takes as its focus the social and political meanings of wartime rape in the former Yugoslavia. A critique of interventions for rape victims in Bosnia identifies problems of insensitive and inappropriate rape trauma work and highlights the need to understand the 'multiple' traumas women suffer in war. This insight is also relevant to wartime rape in the developing world. While there are substantial differences between the meaning and implications of rape in civilian contexts and rape in the midst of war, in all situations rape involves domination and silencing. These commonalities and differences are explored in this chapter. In both war and peace, rape needs to be recognised as a human rights infringement, as an assault on the humanity of the victim.

INTRODUCTION

The Need for a New Language

Historically, rape has been conceived as something inevitable in human society and not warranting moral comment, although there are now signs that the time has finally come to consider rape as a violation of the victim's humanity, as a human rights as well as a health and development issue (Richters, 1994). However, because rape as a major form of sexual violence against women has been silenced for so long, in Western societies we are just beginning to understand what it means for women to be raped, and to consider what its causes and consequences are in various sociocultural circumstances. This has led to a debate about how we should respond to rape in a curative as well as a preventive sense.

One of the first steps that is needed is a language to describe the social and symbolic aspects of rape, and the physical and psychological effects of rape for individual women. By deconstructing and rejecting sexist modes of speech, women in Western societies have, in the last few decades, started to develop such a language. For many women, this has been a matter of emancipation. However, in the case of rape this new language could be of importance for prevention as well as for therapy.

Whilst this analysis may be useful for peacetime societies, it is questionable whether in times of war the same language is appropriate for the understanding and treatment of sexual violence. And since language is a sociocultural product, it is also questionable whether that language is relevant in non-Western cultures. What, therefore, is the relevance of linguistically conventional Western approaches to rape-trauma in times of war, either in Western or in non-Western cultures and societies? These questions are dealt with in the second part of this paper.

Rape in Western Feminist Discourse

It is perhaps not surprising that the incidence and variety of sexual violence against women has been more reported and described than singled out for linguistic de- and re-construction. Of the various forms of sexual violence against women, rape is most commonly singled out by the media. From the relatively few studies of women's experience of sexual violence that have been carried out, it is clear that the victim's perception of the sociocultural environment in which this takes place is crucial for recovery. Without taking account of the linkages between the social, cultural, political, psychological and physical aspects, rape crime cannot be understood, still less treated. As far as I know, only a few support programmes for traumatised women address those linkages and as such contribute to the kind of context-specific healing processes I will advocate in this chapter.

Studies of various forms of trauma have tended to reveal that the reconstruction of meaning is one of the primary psychological processes organising the response of victims. For example, a study of the efforts of a sample of women in the US to make sense of their experience of being raped showed that this had made them aware of the 'little rapes' that plague women on a daily basis. 'Little rapes' are defined as encounters with phenomena such as sexist jokes and pornography, which were only interpreted as negative after the experience of actual rape. The rape experience made the women realise that their lifeworld and their language is full of symbols of objectification and degradation of women, out of which arises the potential for rape. A critical examination of their own sociocultural world and language, with its devaluing, degrading and often perverse constructions of women and sexuality enabled these women to stop blaming themselves, to acknowledge their victimisation and to become angry. This process was associated, by the women in the study, with steps towards some resolution of the trauma (Lebowitz and Roth, 1994).

The women in this study realised that they were not only victims of an individual perpetrator, but of male hegemony within society at large. This awareness has led many rape victims to work with and support other traumatised women and/or to engage in social action to address wrongs in the wider world. In the latter case, they transcend their personal tragedy and focus instead on the general public order. Emotions like anger and a wish for revenge are then often channelled into a desire for justice and human rights activities. Herman (1992) writes that participation in public truth-telling or testimony, has proved to be a great help in handling the personal psychological problems caused by sexual violence for women in the US. Her observations correspond with those of Zur (1993) in her study of Guatemalan Mayan Indian war widows. The widows who were best off were those who began to comprehend the violence in political terms, through participation in human rights agencies and women's groups.

However, although rape in peacetime is a terrible experience, most victims do not relate it to their position as women in society as such. Rape is generally perceived by individuals as an accidental event that disturbs the relative stability and predictability of their lives, but is unrelated to the structural nature of the world they inhabit. Therapy is based on this individualistic presupposition, and in many cases the sociocultural environment reinforces the view of rape as an 'accidental', and thus implicitly, a preventable occurrence. There is an assumption that this belief will support the victim in her efforts to readjust and 'recover'.

In peacetime, rape is a signifier of male power. It can signal to women that they are vulnerable, socially and physically not equal to men, and exist only by man's good graces. Even when rape is not an acute problem, the omnipresence of rape-fear can work factually and symbolically to maintain or restore the gender biased, hierarchical order of society. The motivation for rape is often to confirm women's place in the world as women, to corroborate female powerlessness and endorse male power (Zarkov, 1997). Marcus (1992: 397) defines rape therefore, as a sexualised and gendered attack which imposes difference along the lines of sexual violence. To her, rapists do not beat women at the game of violence, but aim to exclude them from playing most sociocultural games altogether by cornering them in a sexualised, gendered position of passivity. According to a number of sources consulted by Seifert (1995, 1996) psychological and socio-psychological studies carried out with rapists in civilian life come to the unanimous conclusion that the consumation of rape is not primarily a matter of sexual pleasure, but an act of aggression. In the perpetrator's psyche, rape does not fulfil a sexual function. It has little to do with sexuality in itself but very much to do with power. It is an act of extreme violence implemented, of course, by sexual means. The source of satisfaction for the perpetrator is the humiliation and degradation of the victim and the feeling of power and supremacy. Offenders hardly ever talk about rape in terms of sexual pleasure.

Recognition of Rape: from Personal to Public Discourse

During the last ten to twenty years, public testimony has contributed to a changing perception of sexual violence in North America, Western Europe and many other parts of the world; this is no longer seen simply as a private event, but also as a symptom of wider social dysfunction. As such rape has been placed on the political and the social science agenda. The paradigm switch has simultaneously generated new and improved knowledge of: (i) women's experiences of sexual violence; (ii) sexual violence as a private and a public issue; (iii) sexual violence as a psychological and a sociocultural phenomenon;

and (iv) appropriate counselling and therapeutic approaches. Despite these changes in understanding, responses at government level have been poor and differences remain in the interpretation of sexual violence, and how it can be prevented or reduced. Moreover, the impact and geographical spread of these changes remains limited, despite the growing body of knowledge, which is due largely to women's activism within the context of the international women's movement.

IS RAPE IN WAR DIFFERENT?

Although knowledge and understanding of peacetime rape in the developed world is growing, the history of rape and sexual violence in war remains unwritten; this is largely because military historians have shown little interest in harm done to civilian women. However, in the early 1990s, the mass rapes committed in the former Yugoslavia featured prominently in media coverage of the war, and in subsequent socio-political analysis of the war. As a direct result of the news coverage, an influx of rape trauma projects flooded into the former Yugoslavia. The assumptions on which many of these projects were based proved unfit to tackle the complexity of the problem: peacetime approaches, which were fixed on the individual psyche, captured neither the historical, social, cultural nor religious context of the violations. Furthermore, they often failed to acknowledge the 'multiple traumas', including loss of the basic means of survival, that faced these women in their everyday lives.

Although rape is always a matter of regulating power relations between the sexes and/or between competing groups, there are some differences between rape in peacetime and war that do make a difference. These differences can be found in (i) the motivation for rape; (ii) the execution of the rape; (iii) the consumation of the rape by the offender; and (iv) the consequences of the rape for the victim. These four aspects of rape have not yet, to my knowledge, been systematically studied, nor has there been a systematic analysis of the various types of war which can be distinguished in relation to rape violence.

Seifert (1994), Thomas and Ralph (1994), Card (1996) and others identify a number of functions and meanings of rape which can possibly allow for a differentiation between peacetime rape and rape in war:[1]

1. Orgies of rape originate in a culturally ingrained hatred of women that is acted out in extreme situations (rape as misogyny).

2. Rapes have always been part of the 'rules of the game of war'. It is a right mainly conceded to the victors (rape as reward).

3. In military conflicts the abuse of women is part of male communication. What counts is not the suffering of the women, but the effect it has on men (rape as terror).

4. Rape can be considered the final symbolic expression of the humiliation of the male opponents who are not able to protect 'their' women (rape as the messenger of defeat).

5. Rape is also a result of the construction of masculinity that armies offer their soldiers, and of the idolisation of masculinity that is a concomitant of war in Western cultures. In wars men graduate to manhood. Rape is used as a tool for initiation and social bonding (rape to boost morale).

6. Rapes committed in war are aimed at destroying the adversary's culture. Because of women's cultural position and their important role within the family structure they are a principal target if one intends to destroy a culture and community (rape as cultural warfare).

7. Rape is used in war propaganda to underline the bestial nature of the enemy. This kind of propaganda is used by the power-holders to stir up hatred of the enemy and thereby get support for their war from their own people (rape as propaganda).

These points show that the differences between peacetime and wartime rape are not simply a matter of degree. The fact that wartime rape is without significant social or judicial risk is in this context only a minor, but not unimportant, point. The differences between peacetime and wartime rape become particularly apparent in certain types of war. Rape does not, after all, occur on a massive scale in the service of an overarching strategic aim, in every war. However, this was undoubtedly a characteristic of the recent war in the former Yugoslavia. Sexual violence does indeed occur in 'regular' (declared) wars between nations – not only the Japanese army had 'comfort houses' – but most sex crimes are committed in civil or tribal wars.

This difference between 'declared' wars between states and civil and tribal wars is important. The aim of 'declared wars' is to destroy the political system of the enemy and its leaders (although civilian morale became a 'legitimate' target in World War II: *pace* London,

Rotterdam, Dresden and on an apocalyptic scale, Hiroshima). The aim of civil and tribal wars, however, is to destroy the culture and the identity of the population, and consequently the future of the enemy.

Just as the consequences of rape vary for individual women according to their culture, religion, ethnicity, age, social class and economic situation, so the motives, execution, and consumation of rape will also vary according to the type of war that is being fought. It is, for instance, important to consider which of the functions and meanings of wartime rape listed above apply in the particular case. This is not just a matter of academic interest; it has practical implications for the prevention of sexual violence in war (raising issues of preparedness and protection), the counselling of victims of rape, and the implementation of humanitarian and human rights law in the aftermath of war.

TRAUMA PROGRAMMES AS LEARNING EXPERIENCE

Rape in the Context of Multiple Traumas: the Recent War of the Former Yugoslavia

We still know relatively little about the traumatic consequences of wartime rape for women. That is partly due to the fact that in war, women often suffer from multiple traumatisation and rape trauma mixes with other traumas such as the loss of husbands, children, parents, relatives, homes, etc. What is experienced as the dominant trauma, and why that is the case, is often hard to detect and can vary in individuals and cultures.

These questions are particularly complicated in the context of the war in the former Yugoslavia. The conflict was a civil, ideological and religious war, and a revival of age-old tribal conflicts. Sexual crimes were therefore not only a matter of manipulation of social and symbolic gender marks of 'otherness', but of ideological, religious, ethnic, cultural and geographic marks as well. In such an atmosphere it is always relatively easy to draw ordinary citizens first into accepting atrocities and gradually taking part in them. As a consequence of the chaotic situation, any violent act, rape included, could come from any side: from a neighbour, an old friend, a co-worker, from the pubowner, the shopkeeper or the policeman.

Since the abuse of women in peace is rarely taken seriously, it is unsurprising that most descriptions and analyses of sexual violence in war portray rape as an inevitable and unremarkable by-product. However, because sex crimes were used on a large scale by all warring parties in the war in the former Yugoslavia to solicit support for their cause from the outside world, this attitude changed. In particular, news of the establishment of camps explicitly intended for sexual torture, raised worldwide indignation. The estimates given by the media, of women raped in and outside those camps, ranged from 10,000 to 100,000. It has been claimed that ethnic rape was an integral part of official policy in the genocidal campaign for political control and destruction of the other's culture.

Some members of the UN troops who were in Bosnia to protect the people were also guilty of misuse of women. There are reports of refugee women being forced to sexually service these troops to receive aid (MacKinnon, 1994: 185). In Sarajevo, it was an open secret that the UN troops had a brothel where young women would offer their services in exchange for food for their families.

Many authors now maintain that reports of sexual violence against women during the war were manipulated for political ends. The danger of this controversy is that purposive acts of disinformation may produce doubt about the credibility of women's individual testimonies, and distract our attention from the severity of the consequences of sexual violence for the abused women as individuals, and for their families.

We have of course no doubt that when forcible impregnation took place, it resulted in infections (ranging from ordinary infections to HIV/AIDS), in physical trauma, in induced abortion or childbirth, and in psychological distress. Many women considered the foetus conceived by rape as 'a thing', as an 'unnatural body', and children conceived by rape were frequently abandoned right after birth (Kozaric-Kovacic, 1993, 1995). Often the consequence of rape was that women (and what was left of their families) fled with the intention never to return.

Less attention is given in the international media to the fact that soldiers on leave or ex-soldiers sometimes raped the women of their own ethnic group in their home village or town. It is said that they sometimes 'excused' themselves to the victims. Their reasoning (as the stories go) went as follows: we as men have served our country and suffered at the front. Now we need some compensation at the homefront. Women should also contribute to the war by letting men who deserve some catharsis use them. Women seem to have been raped by their own husbands as well. These men, having come home from the front enraged, frustrated and often numb, sometimes sexually assaulted their wives as a means of working through their feelings of anger.

In sum, the collective anti-female violence during the war in the former Yugoslavia must not only be interpreted within the context of the destruction of the adversary's culture and future, but also within the context of the formation and strengthening of national identities and conservative gender arrangements.

When I mentioned in the introduction the need to develop a new language to describe the social and symbolic aspects of rape and the physical and psychological effects of rape, I asked whether the language as developed for peacetime rape would be appropriate for the understanding and treatment of sexual violence in cases of war. Does the situation, as described above, in the former Yugoslavia, challenge the validity of that 'new' language? In many ways the same ingredients are present, albeit in different proportions: dominance, humiliation, subjugation, control. The major difference would appear to be that in ethnic wars sexual violence is orchestrated to undermine women not as individuals but as the embodiment of the nation and its future, as opposed to individual women.

Trauma Programmes in the Former Yugoslavia

Inter-governmental agencies (IGOs) like WHO, UNICEF, UNDP and ECHO, and myriad NGOs (non-governmental organisations) came to the war theatre to provide therapy, like bees to a honey pot. They often came with preconceived notions of the nature of the problem, and pre-packaged solutions that were readily accepted by funding agencies. A cultural critique was the last thing these organisations had in mind.

The proliferation of psychosocial and trauma programmes during and after the war in the former Yugoslavia was an entirely new phenomenon in the emergency aid response to war. The assistance provided requires critical examination. Firstly, health professionals and the general population were only familiar with the medicalising and institutionalising approach to mental health problems that had been in place prior to the war. However, the appropriateness of the model that was on offer, namely psychotherapy and counselling as practiced in Western Europe and North America, was never questioned by the intervening agencies. Yet the issue is not which of these models was 'better' but whether either approach addressed the most pressing needs of the population in these circumstances.

As coordinator of one these programmes, the mental health training programme run by Médecins Sans Frontières (MSF) in Sarajevo, I noticed that most of the experts who were 'flown in' to offer psychological assistance were unfamiliar with the situation they had to face. They lacked knowledge of the history of the region, of its cultural, social, political and economic systems, its former and actual power structures, and the nature of its health care system. They were unfamiliar with the psychology of the people, differentiated by nationality, sex, age, religion, place of birth, and with the traditional ways of coping with many different kinds of loss. They were experts in peacetime calamities, with little or no knowledge of the understanding and experience gained in dealing with victims of World War II. They came full of confidence to put their (American) textbook wisdom into practice, in particular in relation to Post Traumatic Stress Disorder (PTSD). As part and parcel of a large-scale aid operation they perplexed the people they were meant to assist and, like the war itself (albeit in different ways), disrupted relations between them. They certainly would have much to tell their colleagues and acquaintances when they returned home, but it is to me still doubtful whether their presence really contributed to the well-being of their clients.

During my stay in Sarajevo in 1994, it was very difficult to share my doubts with other expatriates. They were doers with a mission to 'save lives' in an emergency situation. That left them no time for critical reflection about the relevance and possible negative implications of their deeds for the people and community concerned. I encountered a similar attitude among many of the acknowledged experts in mental health who came by the dozen for short visits to teach mainly the tricks of their trade – mostly involving PTSD – which were assumed to be universally valid. They did of course not 'save lives', and the generalised quick-fixes they had to offer could not withstand the specificity of the situation. One Dutch psychiatrist, head of the mental health emergency clinic of Holland's largest university hospital, was a laudable exception to this psycho-jetset. He rejected my invitation to take part in the MSF project. His explanation was that, since in times of peace there were many cases about which he did not know what to do, how then could he be of any use in a war situation?

Most expatriates, however, were not aware of the profound, often invisible gaps which exist in culture, religion, psychological make-up, historical background, gender identity, and moral outlook on life between themselves and the various groups they came to work with: gaps which, as products of the politics of history, already existed before the war, but may have deepened because of it. Academic psychiatry and psychology are, just like medicine, too often presumed to be sciences universally applicable, with the same results everywhere.

Women's Support from Within the Former Yugoslavia

Not all programmes were like this, and in particular, some of the women's support programmes had a broader view than the PTSD approach. Certain of these initiatives for women's projects were taken by local women – the Autonomous Women's centre discussed in this section is an example of a project started locally, which later received funding from outside agencies. Other projects, like Medica and Admira, also discussed in this section, were started by expatriates.

There were a number of women from the former Yugoslavia who because of their positions in politics, academia, science, and the media, and because of their connections with women's movements all over the world, were able to make rape in war a political issue and to question the established, marginalising explanations that had been offered. This happened at a time when women worldwide were preparing to put sexual violence against women on the agenda of the UN World Conference on Human Rights in June 1993 in Vienna.

A case in point were feminists in Belgrade, who not only admitted that all warring parties were guilty of rape, but who even had the courage to acknowledge that many more rapes were being committed by Serbian than by Croatian and Bosnian forces. They have maintained the position that all survivors of rape must be assisted. In December 1992 they started the Group for Women Raped in War and on International Human Rights Day, in December 1993, this group opened the doors of an Autonomous Women's Centre Against Sexual Violence.

Women of that Centre analysed and responded to rape at an individual, social and political level. Their goal was to meet the basic needs (including the emotional needs) of rape survivors, and to comprehend and condemn the use of sexual violence as a method of subordinating women, and as a political and military weapon of war and ethnic cleansing. The Centre organised women's counselling, worked on women's rights campaigns, networked with different women's groups in the country, and had an ongoing public campaign to 'make sexual violence against women socially visible'. An additional aim of the Centre was to maintain communication with feminists and activists contesting violence against women in Croatia and Bosnia-Herzegovina. These women refused to be victims, although some had been victimised. Instead of feeling powerlessness and despair they asked the 'why did it happen' question and pointed to nationalism, militarism, religious funda- mentalism and sexism. They resisted being silenced and separated from Croatian and Muslim women, and of perceiving them as 'others' (Hughes et al., 1995).

These women demonstrate the importance of solidarity and concord between organised groups of women. But they also teach that the response to rape should be comprehensive, and that rape trauma is only one aspect of a complex of traumas in war. They stressed that therapy should not merely be the soothing of individual psychic pains, but should at the same time be directed at the social and cultural destruction caused by the war. By doing so they protested against the instrumentalisation of women according to national interests – interests which were repeatedly redefined according to changing priorities. They opposed nationalist ideology which valued women primarily for their reproductive potential and 'reclaimed the rhetoric of motherhood' (Bracewell, 1996). As Bracewell points out, women in the peace movement used their status as symbols of the nation's future to protest for peaceful negotiation; they used this against the imperatives of state nationalism and militarism in a way that men could not. By doing so, they not only concerned themselves with the consequences of the war for women, but also with the ideologies which fuelled the war. As noted above, Lebowitz and Roth have pointed out that a critical examination of sociocultural context and language with their devaluating, degrading and often perverse constructions of women and sexuality can enable women to stop blaming themselves, to acknowledge their victimisation and to become angry.

Apart from local projects such as the Autonomous Women's Centre already described, many initiatives were funded and organised by external agencies. Indeed, the focus on rape by the international media resulted in an influx of international programmes. These could only operate on the scale and with the intensity they did due to the support of foreign women's organisations, and the financial and logistical backing of the European Community, Government agencies, IGOs, churches and public fund raising. For example, the initiative for one that has had a lasting impact, the Medica project in Zenica, was taken by the German gynaecologist, Monika Hauser, after she had seen reports in the international media of widespread rape in Bosnia-Herzegovina at the end of 1992. In Zenica she met committed women from the town who were already actively helping the refugees. They immediately took up her idea of creating a multi-disciplinary centre for gynaecological and psychological care. Hauser was rapidly able to raise the necessary funds in Germany, starting with donations from friends, and could therefore make a quick start with the realisation of her plans (Fischer, 1997).

Another programme, Admira, was founded in the Netherlands in 1993, to support individuals and organisations in the former Yugoslavia involved in aid to women who were victims of rape and other forms of sexual abuse. As domestic violence strongly increased due to social destabilisation resulting from the war, this was also included in the programme. Admira has a pool of women trainers (psychotherapists, social workers, organisation consultants, medical doctors and a gynaecologist), to train and support local people. This service was initially only offered to women's organisations in Croatia, Bosnia and Serbia. Among them are the Autonomous Women's Centre Against Sexual Violence in Belgrade and Medica Zenica. Gradually, however, Admira has extended her training programme to regular welfare and health care organisations and also many foreign IGOs and NGOs.

Because of a continuous evaluation in the Admira project of the training sessions, knowledge is being developed of the relevance and limitations of the approaches used and the repeated need for adjustments. This knowledge is by itself quite telling. What the women in the different women's organisations supported by Admira apparently appreciate most is the respect with which they are approached by Admira trainers and the working methods used. Instead of being told what they need and what they should do, they feel enabled to find their own solutions to issues they have themselves identified as problems.

CONCLUSION

It is too early to judge the impact of projects like those of Admira and Medica Zenica in the former Yugoslavia. Certainly, much has been learned in the process thus far and many women have benefited from those projects. However, it is regrettable that no in-depth multidisciplinary evaluations are available yet (and perhaps never will be) concerning what precisely has been learned and what has been overlooked. Based on the arguments presented in this chapter, it is clear that many questions remain to be answered. Without a participatory long-term assessment, it is difficult to discuss the relevance of the kind of psychosocial and trauma programmes developed in the former Yugoslavia within a European context, let alone their relevance for other parts of the world.

One reason for being cautious about generalising from the experience of sexual violence related to the war in the former Yugoslavia to other war-stricken parts of the world, is that little is known of the way in which rape is perceived and experienced in various parts of the world, and how women living in different sociocultural circumstances have coped with their rape experiences, both historically and in more recent conflicts. What we also know little about is how women have managed to resist or prevent assault. In order to develop this knowledge the one-sidedness of the victimology discourse needs to be challenged by survivorological enquiries. As far as the identification of physical, mental, sexual and reproductive health consequences of rape for women is concerned, we have to be aware of cross-cultural differences in, for instance: the perception of the human body; definitions of coercion and consent related to sexual behaviour; the place and meaning of sexuality in a particular society; idioms of distress; health seeking behaviour; power relations between the sexes; and obstacles to disclosure of information.

The trauma of wartime rape is often part of a mass of traumas with long-lasting consequences. What these consequences will be in the former Yugoslavia we can at present only guess. Mugyenyi (1997), in her study of Ugandan women who were teenagers during the last war, which ended in 1986, has found that their war experience included losing parents, becoming refugees, rape, forced early marriages, domestic work, slavery, participation in war as combatants, and dropping out of school. This meant that most of these girls had such a bad start in life that continuing experience of traumatic events persisted after the war. Not having family and/or kinship protection, for instance, made life difficult for those women, and stood in the way of their social reintegration. For them, the role of church and other organisations concerned with the practical reconstruction of war-torn communities, and their reintegration in such communities, may have more priority than support as envisioned in Western trauma therapy.

What case studies like that of the former Yugoslavia make clear, is that support by health workers to trauma victims, in particular after the emergency phase is over, should be integrated in more comprehensive, interdisciplinary projects aimed at sustainable civil development and the promotion of human rights. Listening to the victims of war and in-depth knowledge of the culture concerned is required for the establishment of priorities in psycho-social relief programmes (Richters, 1994, 1995).

General guidelines for intervention in the area of 'sexual violence and women' should be adapted to particular sociocultural contexts on the basis of long-term action and participatory research. In this action and research, the gender dimensions of the culture and society concerned before, during and after the war, must always be taken into account. While domination and violence appear to be universal aspects of rape, the ways in which these elements operate vary in different contexts. However, privileging gender as the unifying element of the community of all women should be avoided, since issues pertaining to class, nationality, race, ethnicity, religion, or sexuality usually intersect with those of gender. They all influence the role sexual violence plays in the different phases of conflict, and the experiences of women (and also men) of sexual violence.

Note

1. In these functions and meanings of wartime rape, women are depicted only as mere pawns in men's war games. However, a number of case studies from Latin America teach us that women can also be actively involved in fighting or opposing military regimes (Aron et al., 1981; Bunster-Burotto, 1986; Meertens, 1992). In these situations the motive of rape can just be to punish women for their own activities or for the sins of their (ideological) comrades. In this context state-sponsored sexual violence against women aims at restoring the traditional, non-political role of women in the (political) community of the nation state.

References

Aron, A. et al. (1981). The gender specific terror of El Salvador and Guatemala: post traumatic stress disorder in Central American refugee women. *Women's Studies International Forum* 14, 1/2, 37–47.
Bracewell, W. (1996). Women, motherhood and contemporary Serbian Nationalism. *Women's Studies International Forum* 19, 1/2, 25–33.
Bunster-Burotto, X. (1986). Surviving beyond fear. Women and torture in Latin America. In J.C. Nash and H.I. Safa, *Women and Change in Latin America*, pp. 297–317. South Hadley: Bergin and Garvey.
Card, C. (1996). Rape as a weapon of war, *Hypatia* 11, 4 5–19.
Fischer, E. (1997). Am Anfang war die Wut: Monika Hauser und Medica Mondial in *Ein Frauenprojekt im Krieg*: Köln: Kiepenheuer and Witsch.
Herman, J.L. (1992). *Trauma and Recovery: The Aftermath of Violence. From Domestic Abuse to Political Terror*. New York: Basic Books.
Hughes, D.M. et al. (1995). Feminist resistance in Serbia. *European Journal of Women's Studies* 2, 509–32.
Kozaric-Kovacic, D. et al. (1993). Systematic rape of women in Croatia and Bosnia and Herzegovina: A preliminary psychiatric report. *Croatian Medical Journal* 34, 86–7.
Kozaric-Kovacic, D. et al. (1995). Rape, torture, and traumatization of Bosnian and Croatian women. Psychological sequelae. *American Journal of Orthopsychiatry* 65, 3, 428–33.
Lebowitz, L. and Roth S. (1994). I felt like a slut – the cultural context of women's response to being raped. *Journal of Traumatic Stress* 7 3 363–91.
MacKinnon, C.A. (1994). Rape, genocide, and women's human rights. In A. Stiglmayer (ed.) *Mass Rape. The War Against Women in Bosnia Herzegovina*, pp. 183–97. Lincoln: University of Nebraska Press.

Marcus, S. (1992). Fighting bodies, fighting words – a theory and politics of rape prevention. In J. Butler and J. Scott (ed.) *Feminists Theorize the Political*, pp. 385–404. New York: Routledge.

Meertens, D. (1992). Gender and violence in Columbia. Reflections on a complex relationship. *VENA Journal* 4 2 31–6.

Mugyenyi, M. (1997). Teenage girls, war trauma, healing methods. The case of Uganda. PhD research in progress. Kampala, Uganda.

Richters, A. (1994). *Women, Culture and Violence – A Development, Health and Human Rights Issue*. Leiden: VENA.

Richters, A. (1995). Conflict and mental health in Bosnia–Herzegovina. Theoretical and practical reflections. Conference paper, International Conference on Mental Health in the State of Kuwait, 1–4 April 1995.

Seifert, R. (1994). War and rape – a preliminary analysis. In A. Stiglmayer (ed.) *Mass Rape. The War Against Women in Bosnia-Herzegovina*, pp. 54–73. Lincoln: University of Nebraska Press.

Seifert, R. (1995). The female body as a symbol and a sign. Gender specific violence and the cultural construction of war. In A. Gestrich (ed.) *Gewalt im Krieg: Ausgebung, Erfahrung and Verweigerung von Gewalt in Kriegen des 20. Jahrhunderts*. Jahrbuch for Historische Friedensforschung.

Seifert, R. (1996). The second front – the logic of sexual violence in wars. *Women's Studies International Forum* 19, 1/2, 35–43.

Thomas, D.Q. and Ralph R.E. (1994). Rape in war. Challenging the tradition of impunity. *SAIS Review* 14, 1, 81–100.

Zarkov, D. (1997). War rapes in Bosnia – on masculinity, femininity and power of the rape victim. *Tijdschrift voor Criminologie* 39, 2, 140–51.

Zur, J. (1993). The psychosocial effects of 'La Violencia' on widows of El Quich Guatemala. In H. O'Connell (ed.) *Women and Conflict*, pp. 27–31. Oxford: Oxfam.

6   Caring for 'Victims of Torture' in Uganda: Some Personal Reflections

JOAN GILLER

No people do so much harm as those who go about doing good.
(Mandell Creighton 1843–1901)

The plane swooped low, almost skimming the surface of Lake Victoria in the final breathtaking stages of its journey from Nairobi to Entebbe, Uganda's main airport. For the time being at least, the excitement I felt at arriving in such an enthralling country overcame my apprehension concerning the work on which I was about to embark.

The invitation to join the project in Uganda had been delivered to me by boat in a remote village on the Thai–Burmese border several months previously. I had been working there for a French NGO, training primary health care workers. At the time the invitation came, I was trying to grapple with all the contradictions I felt about the validity of my role as an English doctor in this remote part of Thailand. Although I had worked for the best part of eight years in Obstetrics and Gynaecology before deciding to make a major change in my career, I was totally inexperienced in tropical medicine or indeed in working in a situation with so few resources. The assumptions and expectations of being the expert , the only doctor for miles around, weighed heavily on me. I felt that I should be 'sitting at the feet' of local knowledge, but my very presence silenced that knowledge and privileged my inexperience.

It came as a relief to be approached to join a project which seemed, on the face of it, so clear-cut and unambiguous. Had I thought more clearly at that time, I should have realised that this was unlikely to be so. In fact the same questioning and anxieties were repeated many times over during my three years in Uganda. These eventually crystallised into a deep scepticism about much of the intervention made by Western organisations, governmental and non-governmental, in the lives and affairs of the so-called developing (but perhaps more accurately, dependent) countries. I present here a background to the work that we (myself and a colleague) set out to do in Uganda, a description of how the project unfolded in ways we had not anticipated, and some of the problems, doubts and contradictions which led us to formulate a critique of the widespread export of Western psychological interventions to non-Western settings.

The idea for the Uganda project had evolved from links between the Medical Foundation for the Care of Victims of Torture (a London-based charity providing assistance to refugees who had been tortured in their countries of origin) and the human rights organisation, Amnesty International. In the mid-1980s many Ugandans were escaping the brutal purges of Milton Obote, a successor to the infamous Idi Amin; possibly less well-known but no less bloody or brutal in his treatment of political opponents. His forces were responsible around this time for the horrific massacres in the Luwero Triangle. This is an area to the north-east of the capital, Kampala, in which hundreds of thousands of civilians lost their lives or 'disappeared' during counter-insurgency operations against the guerrilla movement led by Yoweri Museveni. Piles of skulls removed from mass graves, dredged from swamps or simply found in the undergrowth were arranged on trestles in the countryside in what became known as Uganda's 'killing fields', as gruesome reminders of the horrors of those years.

Obote was also involved in widespread persecution of his political opponents. Many survivors who managed to escape made their way to Nairobi in Kenya. Here, representatives of Amnesty International were asked to see some of these people who bore the scars of severe torture and ill-treatment, and, being keen to offer practical help, turned to the Medical Foundation for their assistance. A centre offering medical and psychological help, along the lines of the Medical Foundation in London, was proposed and preliminary visits were made to Nairobi by representatives of the Medical Foundation to assess the situation. However events in Uganda changed these plans when, in January 1986, Museveni's National Resistance Army (NRA) took control of Kampala and ousted Obote, who fled into exile. Museveni's new regime, the National Resistance Movement (NRM), pledged itself to the restoration of human rights, allowing the possibility of a project in Uganda itself. The new Ministry of Health was approached, the plan was accepted, and two doctors were recruited to set up the project: Pat, a psychiatrist who had been working until then in hospital-based posts in his native Ireland, and myself.

We met in London some months before we were due to go out to Uganda and found that we were well-matched in our critical approach to the work we had been doing, and were both eager to face the challenge of a different type of project. We spent the next two weeks in rounds of meetings and discussions with people known to the Medical Foundation who had lived and worked in Uganda. Although many of these encounters proved to be extremely interesting, they provided little insight into the complexities of the task we were being asked to perform: to set up a centre to provide assistance to 'victims of torture' in Uganda. The more we talked together and the more our questions were met with vague and general replies, the more misgivings we began to feel about our remit. We thought, however, that all would become clearer when we reached Uganda and met with the many people whose names and addresses we had been given. It didn't.

SETTING UP THE MEDICAL FOUNDATION (UGANDA)

As I disembarked from the plane in Entebbe, my first thoughts were about finding Pat, who had been in Uganda for about a month, arranging preliminary meetings and sorting out accommodation. Walking through the dilapidated shell that was Entebbe airport, made famous by Israeli hijackers in Amin's era, I had a taste of what was to become a familiar sight: the near complete destruction of Uganda's infrastructure by decades of war and mismanagement. The buildings had been stripped bare, even down to the last electricity socket (although these would have been of little use given the erratic electricity supply in Kampala, and its virtual non-existence outside the city). We had been given an office in Mulago Hospital, Kampala's university teaching hospital, built by the British as a parting gift after Uganda's independence was granted. Our office was a very small room in which the desk occupied almost all the available space. There was nothing else. At that time there was not even running water in the department, and conditions in the hospital itself were fairly grim. I helped out one morning a week in the department of Obstetrics and Gynaecology where the wards were full of women waiting for operations which rarely happened. It surprised me how the medical staff kept up the formalities of a teaching hospital, such as the weekly teaching ward round, when so little of the hospital was functioning. There were stories of dead bodies remaining on the wards for several days before a porter could be found to come and remove them.

People trying to work in such circumstances, in which even writing paper was difficult to come by and at a high premium, faced great difficulties. Government wages were pitiful, and people had to spend much time and effort in securing enough money to feed and clothe their families and pay for school fees. Consequently anyone working for the government had to have some form of private income. Some were lucky enough to own a shop or some other form of small business. Hospital doctors supplemented their incomes by working in private clinics. This made our task of arranging meetings a long and arduous one. We frequently bounced (a useful Ugandan term for failing to meet up with someone at the appointed time and place), and had to absorb the frustration of many wasted visits. However, worse than this was our growing sense of discomfort about what we were proposing at these meetings. The idea of setting up a centre for victims of torture was becoming increasingly problematic.

First we had to find our 'victims of torture' and to this end we visited numerous places: church organisations, government departments, hospitals, other relief organisations; in fact, virtually every group suggested to us. We explained our mandate so many times that the repetition of it became almost farcical, and each time we were met with a similar response: yes, there were many people who were victims of Obote's regime, but who exactly did we want to see? Everyone had suffered in one way or another due to the war and Obote's criminal mismanagement of the country's resources. The overriding problem was one of poverty and this was indeed a traumatic state for many. Often people said to us that the whole country had been traumatised. As well as the poverty in which people were living, hundreds of thousands had lost family members or been displaced from their homes and suffered extreme physical hardship. Many had witnessed atrocities or lived for weeks in fear of death.

It was impossible to provide criteria narrow enough to select a limited population to whom we could offer assistance. To turn people away because they hadn't suffered enough would have been bizarre. Indeed, those people who had suffered systematic torture in detention centres in Kampala had mostly either been killed or escaped the country, or simply didn't need our assistance. Very few such people found their way to see us in all the three years we were in Uganda, despite our continued efforts to publicise our availability. And perhaps, more tellingly, those whom we did see came to us for material assistance in one form or another. Some needed orthopaedic or other medical assistance and we were able to point them in the right direction to find what help they could within Uganda. We did not have the resources to finance treatment abroad, and indeed I cannot remember a single person who required it. More often though, people simply needed money to acquire the means by which they could make an income for themselves. Some even asked us for work.

The Ministry of Rehabilitation had assigned us a male social worker, and his skills were harnessed in suggesting new lines of approach in our quest for referrals. While we felt a degree of scepticism towards the project on his part, he deferred to our greater knowledge and expertise and travelled many miles on his motor bike in search of clients. Much later, when we had significantly changed the direction of the project and had acquired another larger office for ourselves, we even employed a woman to revisit the organisations we had already contacted and to find yet others, to make sure that we had explored all possible avenues. She had long experience of working for NGOs and had many contacts in Kampala. Although she came up with many victims of the war, they were all asking for material assistance in terms of money or basic medication such as antimalarial drugs or antibiotics. We could have stopped people on the street in Kampala, most of whom would have fitted these criteria. One thing that no one asked for was any form of psychological assistance.

We therefore faced a dilemma. We could not justify to our funders the setting up of a centre to care for victims of torture and trauma on the grounds of handing out simple medication and we could not offer much in the way of financial assistance. We had limited resources and a limitless demand. Moreover, a centre in Kampala would be inaccessible to those people who had suffered some of the worst of the excesses of Obote's army during the war that finally led to his deposition: the survivors in the Luwero Triangle. These people did not have the means to travel long distances to Kampala, had there been a good reason for them to do so. But there was another, far more important reason for not pursuing the establishment of a specialist centre, which gradually materialised the more we talked to the people who were referred to us, and reflected on what they had to say. We did not want to undermine the confidence of people in their own ways of dealing with misfortune and tragedy by proposing a 'better way of doing it'.

When we first arrived in Uganda we were struck by the remarkable spirit of Ugandans. The journey from the airport in Entebbe into Kampala must rank among the most beautiful airport routes in the world. It is not that the scenery is particularly spectacular, although the wide sweep of Lake Victoria is a magnificent sight, and the lush greenery and rusty brown soil of this fertile area of Uganda are striking. It's more the feeling of vibrancy of the country, which hits you after an often long and tiresome journey. Everywhere people are

working at their various tasks. Some are selling colourful produce by
the roadside, or transporting incredible loads on bicycles or on their
heads: *matoke* (green bananas, the local staple), jerry cans full of
water, or even crates of soda (fizzy soft drinks). Others are tending to
small infants or simply sitting and talking to one another. On that
first journey into Kampala, it was the buildings, rather than the
demeanour of the people that told the tale of the dreadful ravages of
the war. And this experience of the resilience of people to incredible
hardships was to be repeated to us again and again in our years in
Uganda. People coped. On top of their own suffering during the war,
they now had to spend much time and effort in securing enough
money to live on. Many had been left with children of other relatives
who had died in the war. They often had to forgo sending their own
children to school because they couldn't afford the fees. They
frequently did not have enough money to pay for medication when
their families needed treatment. But they did not come looking for
counselling or psychotherapy to help with their problems. It was not
within their frame of reference.

Now a centre in Kampala to help victims of torture, like similar
centres in Europe, must be there to provide, at some level, 'psychological therapy' in all its various manifestations and disguises. Why else
should it exist? To single out a category of 'torture victim' for
assistance is necessarily to point to some special needs of that group
over and above the wider population, be it a refugee population, or, as
in our case, a whole country. And these 'needs' are to do with finding
ways of coping with trauma on an individual basis, which inevitably
involves some form of therapy. Whether this therapy adopts a 'holistic
approach' where all the needs of the individual are supposedly
addressed, or whether it is more obviously along the lines of specific
psychological therapy, it still holds at its core the notion of treating the
'inner individual'. This notion is greatly at odds with all that we
experienced of Ugandan society. In whatever ways they managed to do
it, Ugandans were coping with the results of some of the worst
calamities imaginable, and the last thing they needed was a centre that
could only serve to show them that their ways of coping were
ultimately inferior. This would have been to commit one of the worst
crimes of which colonialism, and now neo-colonialism, has been
guilty: to undermine local knowledge and local ways of doing things in
favour of interventions of often dubious efficacy. When the West looks
back amusedly on earlier fashions located in a historical moment (be it
bottle-feeding babies or proselytising religion, or now, uncritically
exporting psychological notions and therapies to people who have very
different ways of viewing life) they also have to take responsibility for

the damage this has done to societies whose economic dependence prevents them from withstanding the onslaughts of Western aid.

We became very aware of the power and the danger inherent in our position and agreed together that whatever we did in Uganda, we wanted to be able to say that we had done no harm. We were the experts! What experts! And yet we were as well qualified for our task as many of the recruits to other aid projects whom we met in Uganda. We were both trained as specialists in our fields of medicine, we had read extensively books and articles about our subject, about Uganda, and yet we felt that we knew so little about Ugandan people and how they appeared to be coping in the aftermath of tragedy without the aid of therapist or counsellor. Feeling certain that we did not want to open a centre in Kampala, we turned to our funders to request that we make a change in the direction of the project. They were initially somewhat reluctant to change the original plans, but eventually agreed to support us.

INVESTIGATING THE EFFECTS OF THE WAR

Faced with the need to do something (we did not feel that we could just give up and come home without looking more closely at the issues we were raising), our first proposal was to visit some of the worst affected villages in the Luwero Triangle and attempt to interview as many people as we could. We wanted to determine the problems they were facing, how their lives had been affected by the events of the war, and how they were coming to terms with all that had happened to them. We also proposed that we should arrange some seminars with health-care workers to discuss the physical and psychological effects of war and trauma, alongside the work we were doing in the Luwero Triangle. The aim was to raise the awareness of people who would be working directly with survivors of the war to the current debate on trauma. We wanted to challenge the assumptions relating to Post Traumatic Stress Disorder (PTSD), that were being disseminated through the professional literature, and finding their way into curricula in Uganda.

Thus began a series of trips starting with a contact in a village called Masuulita, where Museveni had reputedly begun his campaign of resistance to Obote's government. After many introductions and discussions with members of the local Resistance Committee (the grassroots level of the NRM's system of democratic government) and other local people, we conducted a house-to-house survey of Masuulita and an adjoining village. It is hard to imagine, in the peace and beauty of this part of the Ugandan countryside, all the horrors that took place there in the 1980s. The Luwero Triangle is situated on the central African plateau, high enough above sea level so that, despite being very near to the equator, the climate is pleasant for most of the year. It seldom becomes uncomfortably hot, and even on the few occasions when it does, the shade provides easy relief. While we were in Uganda transport in the area was mostly by foot or bicycle, although many bicycles had been stolen in the war. Motor vehicles, other than those belonging to aid organisations, were uncommon except on the major roads connecting the bigger towns to Kampala. Here *matatus* (minibus 'taxis') provided often very cramped and dangerously fast transport for people travelling further afield.

At the time we visited the area, people were trying to salvage the remnants of their *shambas* (plots of cultivable land) and to make their homes habitable. Many buildings bore the scars of Obote's troops, who had gone through the area in a frenzy of terror, hacking people to death with *pangas* (machetes), looting every building for all the food and personal belongings that were worth taking. Most of the houses in this area are of mud and grass roof construction, but window frames or corrugated iron roofs were removed from any of the larger buildings that possessed them. Bullet holes and graffiti on the walls of some of the buildings were disturbing reminders of those dark days, as were a few photographs I saw taken after a massacre – one showed the corpses of an old couple lying by a photograph of themselves and their family in happier days. Other grim tokens were the piles of skulls already mentioned. During the time that we were there the process of gathering these together had begun. They were put into black plastic bags to be kept safely until a decision had been made as to how best to dispose of them. We were able to examine several which showed the damage inflicted by *pangas*.

As very few of the local people spoke English, the interviews were conducted in Luganda (the language of the people of this area, and one of the forty or so indigenous languages of Uganda) by John, the social worker. Pat and I both learnt the rudiments of Luganda, but were never able to master it sufficiently to understand the finer points of conversation. The survey consisted of a semi-structured questionnaire which assessed the experiences of people in the war by allowing them to relate their own experiences uninterruptedly, and then asking some specific questions to fill in any gaps and to standardise the interviews. We also attached two psychological instruments, that is, sets of questions relating to symptoms found in Post Traumatic Stress Disorder (see chapter 2 for a description of these). The answers can be scored, and from the score a diagnosis of PTSD can be made. These and the questionnaires were translated into Luganda by John, and were then translated back into English and checked for the accuracy of translation by several people including the head of the Department of African Languages at Makerere (Kampala's university), himself a Muganda (speaker of Luganda).

We were, and remain, deeply suspicious of the validity of translating such instruments between languages and cultures. The problems surrounding such uncritical cross-cultural transfer are complex and could form the subject of another chapter. Our justification for including them was one of interest as to what they might show; not in order to diagnose PTSD as a prelude to some treatment programme. At the end of each interview the social worker made an assessment of the social functioning of each person, as a score from 1–7 based on the Axis V scale set out in the Diagnostic and Statistical Manual of the American Psychiatric Association (DSM-III). This, again, was of limited value because of the highly subjective nature of the information it is based on. We had a notion of attempting to quantify and therefore render 'more scientific' our findings amongst the villagers. The stark and relatively uninformative nature of numbers and statistics sits most uneasily alongside the wealth of the narratives of those people and our encounters with them. However, the results did show quite clearly that there was no correlation at all between how well a person appeared to be functioning socially and the degree of symptomatology on the psychological scores.

The people in our survey were, for the most part, subsistence farmers, growing enough food for themselves and their families, and a little to sell in exchange for other necessities such as sugar and tea. Some had a few coffee bushes, the beans from which were dried and sold on to the coffee marketing board, providing the substance of Uganda's major foreign exchange earnings. Ugandans consume very little coffee. Many people had kept a few cattle prior to the war, but these had all been taken by the soldiers and I did not see a single one in any part of the Luwero Triangle during our years in Uganda. The results of the survey confirmed our experiences with people in Kampala: that, whilst many of these people had experienced terrible tragedy and witnessed horrific and brutal murders and torture, yet they were in the process of rebuilding their lives in the context of the community in which they lived. They would gladly have welcomed financial and material assistance, but they were not asking for Western therapies to mend their lives.

This was reinforced for us when we were asked to go and see several people who had testified to a commission which had been set up by the new government to look into human rights abuses committed during the war. These were all people from different parts of the Luwero Triangle who were prepared to speak out about their suffering. They had all suffered horrific injuries at the hands of Obote's soldiers and yet they were all continuing to work, with the help of family and other villagers. One had had his hands chopped off and had been operated on by a surgeon working with a foreign NGO, who fashioned the bones and muscles of his right forearm in such a way that he was able to use them in a pincer movement. He made a living by making baskets and brushes, and was able to cultivate enough land, with the help of relatives, to feed himself. He simply wanted to tell his story in the hope of some financial compensation from the government, and whilst he was happy to talk to us, he wanted nothing from us. We were also asked to see two friends who had been forced at gunpoint to bite off each other's noses and ears. They were both living with their families and working on their land but were horribly disfigured from their injuries and wanted to find out about the possibility of undergoing plastic surgery. We were able to direct them to a specialist in Kampala, but, again, there was no question of a need for any psychological intervention. This was repeated for each of the people who we were asked to see. Their needs, if any, were practical.

WORKING WITH SURVIVORS OF RAPE

A specific question asked in the survey was about the experience of rape, and very few women admitted to it. I had become friendly with the local nurse who spoke some English, and she told me that her experiences were quite at odds with this. She related that many women continued to visit her with problems that they attributed to having been raped: infertility and symptoms of pelvic infection being the most common. She did not have the medications, or the money to send them to Kampala for investigation, and requested our assistance. She was in no doubt that rape had occurred on a massive scale during the war, and that it was simply reluctance on the part of women to disclose this to a man (John) that had led to the low reporting in the survey. As this seemed to be an area in which there were inconsistencies, we decided to enquire about it in more depth. To this end we employed a Ugandan woman, Stella, who was social-work trained, and who had worked in Kampala with refugees from other parts of Uganda during the war. She proved an excellent recruit and her own background made her immediately very approachable to the women we were to interview in the villages of the Luwero Triangle.

Together, she and I spent many weeks meeting women's representatives from different village Resistance Committees. We arranged
several meetings attended by women in the area, addressed by Stella.
The strength of the taboo surrounding rape was brought home to us
when women refused to speak at one of these meetings until a man, a
local Resistance Committee member who was sitting in the doorway
of the meeting room eager to find out what was happening, had been
ejected. I sat through the meetings, understanding little of what was
being said, but inspired by the enthusiasm of the women who stood
up, one after another, to say their piece. Every now and again, Stella
would whisper to me a particular point that was being made: one of
the comments I remember was a woman with her arm in the air
saying (in Luganda), 'Who amongst us has not been raped?' and
receiving cries of approval. It felt as though a floodgate of emotion had
been opened and we were warmly welcomed and encouraged in what
we proposed to do. This was not a lot. We had suggested that rape had
been a common crime committed against the women, mostly by
Obote's soldiers during the war, and that it seemed that many women
still had physical problems as a result of it. We proposed that we
would travel to any of the villages where women were willing to talk to
us, and would interview the women in a similar vein to the survey we
had carried out in Masuulita. We offered to examine, investigate and
treat, as far as we were able, any woman in need of medical help. We
stressed that we had only basic medication and that our resources
were few, but that we wanted to try to assess the extent of the
problems ensuing from rape, and to find whether or not there were
ways in which we could facilitate help for these women.

The women's representatives informed women in their own
villages about our visits and we were surprised at the number who
came to see us. There would often be ten or so women sitting on the
ground outside the room which had been set aside for our visit at each
village, and as the day wore on more would join them. What
explanation they gave to the men of the village about our presence was
never clear, but no men came to us looking for medication, and the
women who came all had suffered rape during the war. Most came
back as many times as we revisited their villages.

At the first visit we left the women to relate as much as they
wanted to of their experiences during the war and to tell us about any
problems they were having. Each woman was then asked a series of
specific questions about the rape incident, their reactions to it,
problems ensuing from it, and whether or not they had shared their
experiences with others. I then examined each if necessary and
arranged such investigations as were appropriate and possible to

perform. The rooms we used to conduct the interviews were always very simple: a mud floor, a few benches and sometimes a table, and I often examined the women on a mat on the floor.

The interviews were all conducted in Luganda by Stella, but the fact that I was able to perform the extended greeting and say a few phrases in their language, and perhaps even more that I was heavily pregnant at the time, seemed to transcend the barrier of language and culture at some level. I really felt that I established some sort of friendship with many of these women despite the obvious difficulties. We had many laughs together. The indomitable spirit of the women made a deep impression on me and I remember the times we spent together very clearly. Stella and I were always given the warmest welcome imaginable and we were often plied with food that had been cooked specially for us: *matoke* and groundnut sauce, and chicken if one was available.

The investigations were carried out in a private laboratory in Kampala. They included high vaginal swabs for those women complaining of the relevant symptoms, and HIV testing for those who wished it to be performed. At this time in Uganda AIDS was in its ascendancy and Museveni was only beginning to implement his campaign of openness and public awareness to the ravages of the deadly virus. A group in Kampala, The Aids Support Organisation (TASO) had been established and offered advice and practical support and assistance to families and individuals afflicted with AIDS. We gave those women who proved to be HIV positive the means to travel to Kampala to receive help from TASO. Most women wanted to be tested and accepted a positive result with great fortitude. They wanted to make practical arrangements for their children. AIDS was indeed another severe blow after the devastation wrought by the war, and added another sinister dimension to the horror of rape.

Most of the stories the women told were of incomprehensible brutality. Whether in their own homes or in one of the many 'detention camps' set up by Obote's troops, ostensibly to protect the local population from the sweeping assaults against Museveni's guerrilla forces, these women had been treated with extreme cruelty. All the local population was considered to support Museveni, and Obote's army exacted its revenge in large measure. M was forty-two when the soldiers entered her village. She and her family sought shelter with some relatives in their house which was set back from the road, out of sight of the path through the village. But the soldiers searched everywhere and eventually came to the house. Despite her and her husband's pleas for mercy, several soldiers raped M and her fifteen-year-old daughter on the mud floor of the room while her husband and the rest of the family were forced to watch and clap. Afterwards, her husband's hands were tied behind his back and he was made to kneel in front of his family. One of the soldiers then shot him dead. M and her daughter had to work for the soldiers, gathering all the food from the *shambas*. The soldiers stole everything. One day, M managed to escape with her daughter and a younger child, and they stayed for two weeks in the bush, living off leaves and berries and even chewing leather for sustenance. Eventually, weak and hungry, they were spotted by relief workers and were taken to the relative safety of a hostel in Kampala. When they returned to their village after the war was over, they discovered that the rest of their relatives were dead – killed by the soldiers before they left the village. Their small mud dwelling had been ransacked and the grass roof completely burnt. Their *shamba* was overgrown and they had no tools to work with.

When we interviewed M three years later, the house had been restored and she had acquired some tools and pots with help from relief organisations and some assistance from the new government, and had partially cleared and planted the *shamba*. Life was hard and they were very poor but M talked about how 'grateful' she was that 'God had spared her' and about how they had much work to do in order to support two of her cousin's children who were orphaned during the war, as well as her own. She could not afford to send them to school. She had no male partner to help her. She complained to us of backache and vaginal discharge, which she said she had had since the time she had been raped. She had not told anyone else about the discharge, and indeed had not revealed anything of her ordeal before our meeting. She did not talk to her daughter about it, as it was a source of great shame to her. Examination and investigation revealed a trichomonal infection for which she was treated. She came back twice to see us after this initial visit and was relieved and happy that she had been treated and was 'normal' again.

G and her twelve-year-old classmate had been taken from their school by two soldiers who, laughing and joking between themselves, had slit open the girl's vaginas with their *pangas* and had raped them on the open ground outside the school. G's friend had died after her ordeal, but miraculously G survived, and was taken after several weeks, by the soldier who had raped her, to be his 'wife', when he was stationed in the north of Uganda. She had stayed there for the remainder of the war and had been forced to act as a wife: preparing food, cleaning, working on the land and having sex when it was demanded. She had a child – a little boy – during this time. He was her one source of joy, but sadly he died of measles when he was a few months old. When news reached them that Museveni had taken control of the country, the soldier fled into hiding further north, abandoning G who managed to make her way back to Kampala, and eventually her village. She discovered that all her family was dead except for her mother who had been blinded by injuries she had received during the war.

When we interviewed G, she was complaining of both faecal and urinary incontinence and lower abdominal pain. She had already had one operation to repair her wounds at Mulago Hospital in Kampala, but, as is often the case with such severe injury, the operation had not been successful, and she was awaiting further surgery. She had had her symptoms ever since her initial injuries had healed, but had been to great lengths to conceal them from everyone. She knew that there was not much that we could do about her problem (indeed the likelihood of successful surgical repair was very slim), but wondered if we could help her financially as she had little with which to support herself and her mother. We discovered on investigation that she had a urinary infection which was treated and helped her abdominal pain, and we gave her a small amount of financial assistance and suggested a few other organisations she might approach for more. Her overflowing gratitude for the little we had actually done for her left us embarrassed and humbled.

We sat and listened to tale after harrowing tale. I remembered a friend from another foreign NGO who had arrived in a village the morning after a massacre had taken place, telling us how it had taken her several months leave to come to terms with the horror she had witnessed. These women had lived the horror, and we were privileged to be talking to them when peace had been restored, and they were in the process of re-establishing their livelihoods and their communities, albeit with precious few resources. As I have already indicated, whilst many of them had lost husbands, children or other close relatives and been through some of the darkest experiences any of us could ever imagine, their spirit was inspiring.

Virtually all of the 107 women we kept records for presented with medical problems, predominantly pelvic or abdominal pain. They had been aged between six and forty-seven years when the rape incident took place. Backache and vaginal discharge were also common and many were concerned about having contracted HIV infection, syphilis or to have been rendered infertile by their experiences. In two-thirds of the women who underwent physical examination on the basis of their medical complaints there were no positive findings. Twenty-three had a simple vaginal infection, seventeen were HIV positive and three had a positive VDRL (for syphilis).

At the second visit we asked the women to answer the questions on the psychological instruments used in the earlier survey, and Stella made an estimation of social functioning as John had done previously. The results similarly showed that whilst many, on the basis of the psychological instruments, had a level of symptomatology sufficiently significant to warrant a diagnosis of PTSD, yet these were not the problems that they were presenting with and, again, did not correlate at all with the estimate of their social functioning.

And yet, here was a group of women who were asking for some degree of help because of the particular trauma that they had suffered. Their complaints were of a physical nature, which required physical solutions, even if these were simply the reassurance of good health. Whilst we had touched on the notion of counselling in our preamble about what we could offer, none of the women asked for this. They wanted advice, medication, practical and financial assistance and reassurance, some of which we were in a better position to provide than others. It is possible to couch the presentation of their complaints, many of which we did not find a physical cause for, in the language of psychology, e.g. as somatisation, or epiphenomena signifying an underlying primary psychological disorder. However, the danger of such a reduction to a Western-based way of thinking is then to assume the need for psychological solutions.

The 'mobile clinic' seemed to be very popular and we made at least three visits to each village. There usually seemed an obvious time for us to finish our work: the women were satisfied with whatever had been accomplished and it was right to move on elsewhere. In one of the villages, on what was to be our final visit, the group of women we had been seeing announced that they had decided to continue meeting together to start a basket-making project to raise money for their families and their villages. We were delighted with this development and encouraged them wholeheartedly. This project was to be the first of several. Other groups began rotating savings funds, which they used to purchase livestock such as cattle, pigs and chickens. Others helped one another to rebuild their houses by mud-block making, and women in one village also formed a cultural group to write and perform plays and songs for a wider audience. The ideas for these enterprises came entirely from the women themselves; we had simply brought together the original groups because of their shared experience of rape. It seemed to us that, almost accidentally, we had provided an impetus for the women to cement some bonds in their ravaged communities. Most of these projects were only just beginning at the time that Pat and I left Uganda.

* * *

Concurrently with the work in the Luwero Triangle, we were also involved in visiting various training institutions in and around Kampala, to share our understanding of how political, social and cultural context affects the responses to trauma, and to look at the ways in which the sequelae of trauma were dealt with in Uganda.

We found people very willing and eager to discuss different ideas and add their own insights. Although many were trained in Western medicine which has instilled a sense of shame with respect to traditional healing, and were, as virtually all Ugandans are, staunch churchgoers (either Catholic or Protestant as the historical divisions were drawn), when we had won their trust in these matters they readily discussed their own beliefs in the spirit world and forms of traditional healing. Their surprise at our interest in traditional healing underlined for me how deeply the colonial culture undermined any sense of worth in traditional ways of doing things, so much so that traditionally-held beliefs were admitted to – to a Westerner – with some embarrassment. Eventually a Ugandan primary health-care worker was employed to continue the seminars about the effects of war, torture and trauma. We wanted to promote local ways of dealing with these, and to attempt to dispel the practice of deferring to Western 'expertise'.

Pat and I made our goal the leaving of Uganda as soon as the workers there were comfortable enough with the logistics of running the office and accounts etc. without our help. A Ugandan nurse was employed (interviewed and chosen by Stella) to deal with the medical side of the project in the Luwero Triangle, and a driver. We wanted the project to be allowed to run on its own momentum with as little of our influence as possible, and if this meant that it eventually ended, then this was as it should be. The project was still funded via the Medical Foundation in London, but our vision was that ultimately it would become a locally-funded Ugandan NGO. At the last visit made by one of us in 1996, Oxfam was funding the project as a local NGO.

CONCLUSION

As I have mentioned, we were very conscious of the damage we could do in bringing more so-called expertise into Uganda at a time when the country was particularly vulnerable. This is one of the worst aspects we experienced of development work: that the governments of developing countries, faced with the desperate poverty of their people and limited economic resources, are likely to accept assistance without looking too critically at what is being offered. We saw many examples of mistakes being made and huge amounts of money being wasted whilst we were in Uganda. For example, a Ugandan clinical psychologist known to us was employed by one of the bigger aid organisations to find out why people in a series of villages did not use the boreholes sunk at considerable expense. It had not occurred to the agency to ask the villagers where the wells should be sited in the first place. The same mistakes are repeated again and again, and the benefit of the experience that ought to be gained from this seems to be lost.

Much time and money was wasted on our own project at the outset in pursuing a plan that had been hatched before we ever reached Uganda. The people in Uganda – those torture victims towards whom the project was directed, had not been consulted. Our task was simply to find them and provide a centre for them. While this plan may have met with more success in a country of exile, even as a meeting place for a defined group of people (rather than a therapy centre), it was always going to be problematic in Uganda itself. But more insidious in this kind of work than a simple waste of money and time is the gradual erosion of confidence in local knowledge by the importation of Western knowledge. The great danger in projects such as ours is that we actually leave people in a more vulnerable position than before, by leading them to believe that their ways of coping are somehow inferior to Western ones; that we have a knowledge about the effects of trauma on the individual and its treatment which supersedes their own knowledge of the ways in which healing is brought about. The lessons are clear: the perceived need which is being addressed should always be carefully investigated, with the full involvement of the people who are meant to benefit from it. This demands a respect for local priorities, which should extend to respect for local forms of healing if some kind of 'treatment' is required. Unfortunately, Ugandans who are being trained in Western institutions find themselves tutored in Western ways of approaching problems, where the importance of indigenous knowledge is not recognised. The richness and diversity of their own and other cultural approaches needs to inform the current debate about trauma.

* * *

It is possible to write the narrative of our experience in Uganda in different ways, which paint very different pictures of the work that we did there. One is a story of success. We avoided some of the more glaring mistakes: we listened to the local people and did not plunge in with our centre in Kampala when we felt it was not appropriate. (Others have felt differently, as there is exactly such a centre in Kampala now, established by another European NGO.) By patient enquiry, and allowing people to speak for themselves, we perceived a need and acted on it, which resulted in a service for Ugandans, run by Ugandans with a minimum of outside influence.

Unfortunately it has never been possible to sit back in the self-satisfied and certain knowledge of a job well done! Did we help people according to their agenda? Or rather did we try to salvage something of a project in which we felt neither confident nor comfortable, 'discovering' a need and fitting it into our own agenda of providing assistance to the traumatised? We only ever had a limited idea of the women's needs and expectations, living as we did outside the language and culture. The sight of a *musungu* (European) in the rural areas inevitably raised hopes of money or other assistance, and we were offering free medical examination and advice as well as free medication. And even if the final outcome was worthwhile, was all the expense of sending us out to Uganda, housing us there and paying our salaries justified? This forms a major part of the budget of many aid organisations. While many expatriates are being paid tax-exempted salaries into bank accounts at home as well as local allowances to pay for their keep, there are trained Ugandans, as well-qualified as their expatriate counterparts, who are unable to get work in Uganda because the government cannot afford to pay their wages.

We shall never know for certain whether or not we achieved our objective of leaving Uganda without doing any harm. We certainly learnt immeasurably from the experience, but that cannot be a measure of success. Too many projects in developing countries are justified on such a premise. My hope is that others may benefit from our experience, so that the mistakes we made do not have to be repeated over again, and that other voices, voices of some of the poorest and least powerful people on earth, may be heard as a challenge to the wisdom of the West.

7 Conflict, Poverty and Family Separation: the Problem of Institutional Care[1]

CELIA PETTY and ELIZABETH JAREG

The preoccupation with psychological trauma in work with war-affected children has resulted in a general neglect of the problem of institutionalisation. In this chapter we consider firstly, the growing problem of family separation and institutional care that contemporary conflicts have produced; secondly, psychological and social problems that are linked to this and finally, the challenge of finding viable alternatives to the institutional care of children at times of social, economic and political dislocation.

INTRODUCTION

There are no reliable statistics covering the number of children in institutional care worldwide.[2] However, we do know that in situations of conflict, the number of children in institutions rises[3] and that in all countries, insitutionalised children are exposed to multiple disadvantages and are vulnerable to both physical maltreatment and sexual abuse (Utting, 1997; Tolfree, 1995).

The global distribution of institutions reflects historical, religious and political influences as well as trends in social service provision and child development theory. But whilst recent decades have seen a reduction in the number of children in institutional care in most Western countries (Ruxton, 1996), there has been an increase in the number of institutionalised children in many of the poorest countries in Africa and elsewhere. This trend has occurred despite the traditional value placed in non-European societies on the extended family. It is a symptom of the social disruption caused by prolonged civil disturbance due to armed conflict, the increased marginalisation of the poor in countries undergoing structural adjustment, and the HIV/AIDS pandemic which has progressively eroded the resources of family networks in many countries. It is a trend that runs contrary to the norms set out in both the African Charter on the Rights and Welfare of the Child (ACRWC) and the Convention on the Rights of the Child (CRC) which has been ratified by 190 states.

SEPARATION AND SURVIVAL: CHILDREN AND FAMILIES IN CONTEMPORARY ARMED CONFLICT

The characteristics of contemporary conflict in the developing world, but particularly in Africa, have been analysed and described elsewhere (Keen, 1997; Richards, 1996; Summerfield, 1996, and chapter 1 in this volume). These include the destruction of subsistence agriculture and rural infrastructure; terrorisation of communities through random attacks; killing, rape, kidnapping and other atrocities.

In the face of these onslaughts, civilian populations have only a limited range of options, which in turn have implications for family unity and child protection and survival. Although these have not been studied systematically, there is a growing body of evidence that allows us to predict risks and potential outcomes for children. One of the most striking features of many contemporary conflicts is the increasing likelihood of separation of children from their families.

An initial classification of survival strategies and associated risks to children in recent conflicts in sub-Saharan Africa and South Asia is outlined in the table overleaf. The practical importance of this analysis is that it indicates possible entry points for action to reduce the risk of separation; this includes work in both acute emergencies and long drawn out conflict, where economic and social disruption are the major cause of breakdown in family and extended family structures.

Whilst we give prominence to problems of institutional care resulting from family separation, we do not underestimate the difficulties of preventive work in situations of conflict. Supporting children within communities requires an understanding of existing social networks and practices; without it, there is a risk that relief interventions will undermine local solutions and introduce further divisions in communities that are already under stress. It also requires an understanding of local food economies, to provide appropriate livelihood and subsistence support.

WHY INSTITUTIONS?

All conflicts increase the risk of family separation. However, the problem is most acute, and often most visible, in mass population movements. Groups of children who have become separated from their families are a common sight among the hundreds and thousands

STRATEGY	RISK
Family remains in conflict zone in their own home.	(i) Abduction of children/parents by military forces. (ii) Attack on household – parent(s) killed; home destroyed; family members wounded; crops and livestock destroyed. (iii) High level of stress due to living under continual threat; likelihood of reduced access to food/social services as conflict proceeds.
Family flees conflict zone.	(i) Accidental separation en route. (ii) Voluntary placement of child(ren) in 'centre'/institution in refugee camp to gain access to relief goods and services. (iii) Accidental separation in camps, e.g. evacuation of sick children by medical personnel without adequate documentation. (iv) Separated children may end up in places where there is no documentation/tracing programme in operation.
Child(ren) placed in institution due to: death of father/both parents; disablement; poverty; parents joining military service.	Temporary measure to safeguard child(ren) may result in long-term/permanent loss of contact with surviving family members, friends and community. Institutional placement often entails sibling separation.
Child decides/is asked to leave home due to family conflict, poverty, threat of militarisation, etc.	(i) Child becomes urban street child or rural labourer. (ii) Child joins military forces.

OUTCOME

Militarisation with the risks of death/disability/psychological stress.

Family resilience greatly reduced. Whole/part orphanhood may lead to:
– placement in institution;
– child remaining with widowed mother and low socioeconomic status or
destitition; child may drop out of school; multiple health/social risks;
– father left with small children; risk of death; abandonment.
Remarriage of surviving parent may entail a worsened situation for the
children.
Placement of children with relatives – which may or may not place them at
further risk.
Older children may leave home (see below).

Some families may adapt and cope better than others. Some may show signs
of great strain: family conflict/break-up, alcohol abuse.

All these risk factors can lead to:
Loss of knowledge of family and community identity and place of origin
(especially in small children); long-term/ permanent family separation;
multiple new separations; long-term institutionalisation.
These outcomes will of course have individual effects on children's
development and well being.

The outcome will be influenced by factors such as: age at admission, reason
for admission, type of institution, personal resilience, length of stay,
exposure to further distress or abuse in institution.
For many children, there will be degrees of developmental disturbance.
Often problems in later integration into 'normal' community life, with
difficulties in securing employment and marriage.

More positively, some children may receive a good education which opens up
new possibilities to them.

Exploitation, including sexual abuse with high risk of HIV/AIDS; discrimination and non-recognition of rights, including poor educational and employment prospects.
Disability through injury resulting in long-term poverty and soical marginalisation.

of refugees seeking safety in refugee camps, centres for internally displaced persons, or on the streets of large and small towns. Providing a safe and secure refuge for these children seems an obvious humanitarian response, but unless immediate steps are taken to trace their familes or reunify them with members of their community, there is a risk of permament severance of links with the child's family and place of origin.

Whilst the separation of children during mass refugee movements is certainly a major problem, far larger numbers of children are in fact placed in institutions due to problems arising from poverty, widowhood and rejection, which are exacerbated during conflict. Different strategies are required to prevent these separations and to reintegrate children within a family structure. But whatever the circumstances of separation, for the children themselves, removal from family, clan and community can have serious long-term consequences. Besides the developmental, psychological and child rights concerns that are associated with institutional care, in a very pratical sense, the loss of a family name and a place of origin deprives children of the links they need in many societies, to establish a foothold in the adult world.

Avoiding the Institutional Juggernaut

In spite of widespread concern about the effects of institutionalisation on normal child development, and difficulties in maintaining reasonable standards of care and protection, institutions continue to proliferate in times of conflict. This is due to both local and external factors.

Firstly, legislation and policy guidelines regulating the establishment of institutions tends to be weak or absent in poorer developing countries, and where policies are in place, the enormous pressures placed on governments to allow foreign organisations to open orphanages for war victims may block the implementation of these policies. This proved to be a serious problem in Mozambique in the early 1990s.

Secondly, in the general chaos of war, the legal protection of separated children is virtually non-existent; and although 190 countries have ratified the Convention on the Rights of the Child (CRC), which contains articles covering the rights of unaccompanied children to family reunification, few countries have integrated the articles of the Convention into national law. (The articles of the Convention relevant to children who are separated from their families are listed in Appendix I.)

Thirdly, funding for institutions is largely provided by external sources which governments managing a war or postwar economy may be unable or unwilling to restrict. This external drive to build institutions has, in recent times, been driven by a mix of genuine humanitarianism and short-term opportunism, which was well illustrated in Rwanda after the 1994 genocide. In Rwanda, many international non-government organisations (NGOs) capitalised on pathetic media images of helpless 'orphans' to raise money and profile. This was done without long-term plans for either the future of the children, or the sustainability of the institutions that were set up.

Finally, the discussion would not be complete without highlighting the part played by religious organisations in taking children into institutional care. Regardless of the culturally dominant faith, separated children have frequently been a target for Christian and Islamic organisations with the aim of religious conversion.

Thus, despite the work of some national governments, including those of Mozambique, Eritrea, Uganda and Rwanda, and the efforts of local organisations and international agencies (such as the ICRC, UNHCR, Unicef and Save the Children) to reunify children with their families, and to assist governments in developing alternatives to institutional care, there are enormous pressures working against these policies. Not least are the financial benefits to government of any new construction project, and the income generating opportunities that they offer to the owners and managers of institutions.

The implications for family tracing and reunification are far-reaching. Once the process of large-scale, unregulated intervention has started and children are placed in institutions run by many different organisations, a more detailed analysis of their actual status and coordinated efforts to return them to their communities become increasingly difficult; their fates become enmeshed with the internal economy of the institution. The task of tracing and reunification is made even more difficult where there is no national policy or government system for monitoring institutions and children in care.

Whilst international organisations such as UNHCR have produced clear guidelines on non-institutional care for separated children (UNHCR, 1994), and the UN/Graca Machel study on the Impact of Armed Conflict on Children (UN, 1996) also stressed the need for family reunification and non-institutional care, there is not yet sufficient coherence among the international funding agencies, including both religious and secular organisations, to stop the juggernaut. This remains a major advocacy challenge.

WHO ARE THE CHILDREN IN INSTITUTIONS?

Acute emergencies, generally involving mass population movements, bring with them a specific set of problems which may result in loss of identity and long term institutionalisation of large numbers of children. There is now good evidence to show that, where efforts are chanelled into rapid identification and reunification, many of these problems can be avoided.[4]

However, many other factors, also linked to conflict, are responsible for the separation of children from their families in less dramatic circumstances (see table). These relate to poverty, disability, widowhood and the general wearing away of a family's ability to provide protection and care for its children. For example, in many countries the rights of widows to inherit their husband's land and other property may not be assured, and the lack of means of subsistence and shelter often leads the family into new separations, destitution or prostitution. Remarriage may mean that the new husband is unwilling to take on the role of father and provider to the widow's children. In these situations, widowed mothers, either through their own initiative or through pressure from their extended family, seek admission for all or some of their children into an institution.

The placement of children can also become part of the coping behaviours people use to tackle the insecurity and deprivations brought about by conflict. Throughout the armed conflict in Sri Lanka, a survival strategy for many young widows from the north and east has been to take employment in middle-eastern countries such as Kuwait and Saudi Arabia. The terms of employment do not allow them to bring their children with them, and the duration of contracts is often very long, at times up to ten years. The solution for many of these mothers has been to place their children in an institution, thus embarking on a long-term separation and possible permanent estrangement from them.

During conflict, other groups of 'children in difficult circumstances' at risk of institutionalisation are: children with disabilities caused by war injuries, babies born as a result of rape or liaisons between civilian and military/peace-keeping personnel, babies and small children left with widowed fathers, and children who have been demobilised from the military. The use by the military of women who are mothers can also result in the institutionalisation of children during wartime. For example, during the late 1980s, Eritrean troops were comprised of about 30 per cent females, many of whom had children; a high proportion of these children were cared for in large institutions such as the Solumona orphanage.

Circumstances like this explain the fact that the number of children in institutions who have lost both parents is generally smaller than might be expected. The proportion is likely to rise where genocide has occurred (for example in Rwanda, Burundi and Bosnia) or where women have been recruited into the armed services. However, projects offering services to 'separated' children during conflict usually draw in many non-separated, non-orphaned children, who may have parents and siblings living nearby. Poverty remains the major block to the reintegration of these children, and of others who were institutionalised due to genuine separation; disabled children remain the hardest to reunify. This reinforces the importance of reviewing the circumstances of each child who is being placed in an institution (Petty et al., 1998).

SOCIAL AND PSYCHOLOGICAL ASPECTS OF INSTITUTIONAL CARE: THE RIGHTS AND NEEDS OF SEPARATED CHILDREN

The Problem with Institutions

In the absence of other, community-based options, institutions can fulfil an important humanitarian role, providing temporary care and protection for children whose families are being traced. However, we have seen that the establishment of institutions often by-passes a critical analysis of childrens' needs and rights. This in turn gives rise to situations where the needs and interests of the institution and donors override the needs and rights of the children who are in their care. The present and future well-being of separated children can be jeopardised by the persistent lack of such an analysis.

From a child development perspective, the care and upbringing of children in large, impersonal institutions always gives rise to concern. The risks to child development, both during institutionalisation and in the long term (i.e. substantially increased adult psychopathology and difficulties in integrating into mainstream society) have been well-documented in institutionalised children in Western countries, although much less so in developing countries (Tizard and Rees, 1975; Tizard and Hodges, 1978; Rutter et al., 1994; Wijetunge et al., 1992).

Given the range of factors that contribute to the outcome for an individual child, studies into the effects of institutionalisation on development will always be open to interpretation. Some of the main determinants of the well-being and development of children raised in institutions operate in many different cultural settings, although the specific effects on child development remains a subject for further study. Relevant factors include: the quality of the child's family environment before admission, and the type of crisis or reason(s) which led to admission; the handling of the actual admission procedure; the level of training in child care and development of the management and staff, and their attitudes to the children. The possibility for children to receive personalised attention and re-establish attachment to one or a few persons (staff–children ratio) and the general environment within the institution are also crucial. This will depend on whether routines are centred around children's real needs or those of adults; whether or not efforts are made to keep up contact with family, friends and the child's original environment; the quality of care and interaction between children and staff, and the degree to which they are protected from further abuse and exploitation. Finally, the extent to which children are accepted and integrated in the local community, the quality of education offered to children, and not least, the preparation for leaving and follow-up of children once they have left the institution, will all have a major impact on their successful transition to adult life.

As well as these contextual factors, the personal characteristics and resources of the individual child cannot be disregarded. The degree of resilience a child has and his or her ability to adapt to the institutional environment, the child's age and length of admission, whether alone or with siblings are all relevant factors. The child's own interpretation of the reason he or she was admitted to the institution may also have significant effects on behaviour and adaptation (Jareg, 1992; Jareg, 1989a; Wijetunge, 1992).

Special Concerns Relating to the Psychological and Social Development of Children in Armed Conflict

Many of the concerns about children admitted to institutions due to war are common to all institutionalised children. However, there are some issues that are specific to war. An overriding concern is the lack of knowledge and insight into factors affecting the well-being and development of children who have gone through extreme or traumatic experiences related to armed conflict.

During armed conflict, children admitted to institutions have very often been through horrific experiences, which may include witnessing the death of close family members due to military attack, or the torture, rape, and/or murder of parents, siblings and friends. Children may themselves have participated in acts of violence. It is crucial that children who have been exposed to severely distressing experiences of this kind should be protected from further avoidable distress, since it is the accumulative and interactive effect of these which undermines the normal development process, and greatly increases the suffering of children.

In our experience, very few institutions have staff who are adequately equipped to deal with children who have suffered in this way and who are manifesting grief reactions and disturbances in development, function and behaviour, as is typically seen in children following such events. This is not an argument for Western-style therapy or counselling. On the contrary, it is an argument for better trained local staff who can provide consistent care and support in a safe and secure environment, while children are awaiting reunification with family members. To do this, they need to have some awareness of the personal histories of the children. As well as lack of training, the number of children and the sheer physical size of some institutions, combined with the demands of domestic and administrative routines, do not allow for the continuous, close personal support and comfort that children who have suffered separation in war need to regenerate their development, self-esteem and hope.

Disturbances in behaviour caused by the child's grief and other reactions to his or her experiences may be understood as 'naughty' and in need of punishment, since the behaviour may interfere with the routines to which children are expected to adhere. Too easily, a cycle of unmatched communication between child and caregiver can arise, and vital opportunities to help the child may be lost as he or she retreats behind a wall of isolation or unmanageable aggressive behaviour. Although it is possible to find many people working in institutions who are genuinely interested in and fond of children, and who give their support to individual children, the sheer numbers of children, the lack of sufficient staff and the compelling demands of institutional routines, often prevent those with natural empathy and skills in communicating with children, from using their talents.

Sometimes, caregivers may consciously avoid becoming emotionally involved with children, as this example from Eritrea indicates.

Several members of the caregiving staff working in Solumona orphanage (between 500–700 children) were interviewed about their relationships towards the children. They all maintained that they actively avoided holding, cuddling or trying to enter into a conversation with individual children since these actions caused such aggressive expression of jealousy among the other children, who immediately clamoured for special attention. The caregivers felt they would be totally overwhelmed (which they would be) if they opened up for close contact with the children. (Jareg, 1988)

The following example from Sri Lanka describes what many war-affected children will be struggling with when admitted to an institution:

Nirosha and her younger sister were brought to the home after her father and older brother were killed by the terrorists. Nirosha dreams of her father often and once she dreamt that he came and took them home. The following day she cried constantly and was feverish. Nirosha pines for her mother as well and particularly at night she and her sister miss their mother for they used to sleep on either side of her at home. (Wijetunge, 1992)

Some children have also experienced direct physical as well as psychological trauma and have to face life-long disablement, for example due to landmine injuries. These children may be at special risk of long-term institutionalisation and suffer further disadvantage if special efforts are not made to integrate them into school. However, some institutions do give specialised help and training to children with disabilities and may also co-operate with community-based rehabilitation programmes (for example the institution for blind children in Beira, Mozambique). These are important considerations that need to be investigated before children with physical or mental disability are admitted to institutions, since parents and relatives may not be aware of alternative means of assistance.

Lack of Preparation of Children for Separation from Parents and Admission to the Institutional Environment

Admission into an institution may bring about new severely distressing experiences for children, as when a widowed mother feels compelled to place her child (or one of her children – thus causing even more distress) in an institution. Usually, the admission procedures do not take account of what children may be feeling or thinking. The examples given below are from Eritrea and Sri Lanka.

Many children told us they were brought to the Home not knowing what was going to happen. These children spoke of how painful it was for them at the beginning, how angry they felt at being deceived. (Jareg, 1988)

Shani's mother brought her to the home and slept the night with her. She was then three years old. In the meanwhile, her mother and the warden hatched a plan that the mother would leave in the morning while Shani was still asleep. Next morning while the mother crept away to dress, Shani woke up and started howling for her mother. In the midst of her pitiful screaming, her mother had to leave. According to the warden, she kept up crying and lamenting for the mother to come back for two days on end. She ran all over the compound calling for her and could not be contained. (Wijetunge, 1992)

Exposure to Further Traumas and Distressing Experiences

One common finding is the use in institutions of harsh disciplinary measures for often relatively small misdeeds, often reflecting the cultural and traditional attitudes to disciplining children. The danger for war-affected children is that their sometimes difficult behaviour can be interpreted as 'naughtiness' and punished, for example by caning, isolation and insulting verbal reprimands. Again, these are all factors which hinder the healing of psychological wounds.

A child's place in the institution's informal social hierarchy will have implications for a wide range of factors which relate to his or her well-being; for example, access to food can be affected unless staff are fully aware of, or concerned about, the effects of such mechanisms. This can be especially difficult for children who have been through extreme and distressing experiences. Children may face a struggle to find a place in the hierarchy where they can 'survive', and this may dominate their experience of childhood in the institution.

I was able to observe the children having their main meal. Groups of about 8–10 children were placed round a table, and a large platter of *injera* (a large pancake) and *wot* (sauce) was placed in the middle of the table. The group of children was comprised of older and younger, and the young children had difficulty in reaching the food since their small arms could not stretch as far, and they were not able to eat quickly enough. None of the older children helped them, they were too busy trying to get as much of their share as possible. There appeared to be no supervision which picked up on this, and no attempt to organise feeding of the small children at a table for themselves. It was a free-for-all, and the biggest won the day. (Jareg, 1989b)

Children develop their own strategies in order to satisfy their need for contact and recognition. Those with natural attributes such as an attractive physical appearance and a friendly nature, those who are well-behaved and clever, may become the favourites of the staff. Children suffering in the aftermath of disastrous events are often not able to compete. However, children often develop strong attachments with each other, and this can be of considerable help to them.

All children in institutional settings, and especially young girls who have been raped, are exposed to the risk of further sexual abuse, whether by staff members, older children or even visitors. Staff may not be aware of these traumas in the child's previous life, and thus will not be alerted to the risk. It is now widely recognised that sexual abuse is very difficult to uncover and deal with (Utting, 1997; *Guardian*, 1997). Obviously, children are at their most vulnerable in an institution since they have nowhere else to go, and may be threatened with expulsion if they expose the perpetrator.

Interviews with institutionalised children also reveal that they are often exposed to discrimination and hostility when they come into contact with the surrounding community.

> 17-year-old Hemapala, an orphaned boy, was very conscious of being belittled by other children in school, for being in the Home. He felt that teachers scolded children from the Home more than the others in the class, for similar misbehaviours. (Wijetunge, 1992)

At times, hostility is a problem between local populations and children's homes established by groups taking refuge in the country:

> A big problem here is that if the children try to go outside and play, they are attacked by the local people – both adults and children attack them. Even if the children go outside with the caregivers, these are also threatened. Therefore we just have to stay inside all the time. (Jareg, 1989b)

Maintaining Contact with the Family

During armed conflict, keeping up contact between institutionalised children and their family members is an even greater challenge than in peacetime. However, this contact is crucial if children are to maintain a sense of who they are and where they come from – in other words, their sense of identity. Widowed mothers and other family members often cannot afford transport for the journey if the institution is far away. It is frequently unsafe, especially for women, to move about in conflict areas. Families may have to flee from the area without being able to inform the institution, and post or telephone services are often disrupted or not functioning. There are also documented instances where the father or mother has been killed after the child's admission, and the child is not informed about the event due to a misplaced wish to protect the child from further distress. Explanations then have to be found as to why the parent/s no longer visit the child.

Yet another highly distressing feature of institutionalisation, especially for children whose parents have been killed, is their further separation from their siblings, since many institutions operate separate facilities for boys and girls. Siblings may be placed in homes far from each other, and there may be no attempt to maintain contact between them. The need for contact with surviving family members is crucial if children are to develop a sense of their cultural roots and identity. It also lessens the loneliness and estrangement of large, impersonal institutions.

Children in Institutions – at Special Risk of Recruitment

Although difficult to quantify, institutions appear to have been widely used in some conflicts, for the forced recruitment of children into military units (Brett and McCallin, 1996; Africa Watch, 1991; Human Rights Watch/Africa, 1995). Countries where this has been documented include Ethiopia, Mozambique (where an attack by Renamo on the orphanage in Chimoio resulted in the abduction of over fifty children), Northern Uganda, Sri Lanka, Burma, Peru, Angola and Liberia. Various factors contribute to the particular vulnerability of children in institutions. Firstly, having no parental protection, these are children who, in the eyes of recruiters, do not need to be accounted for. Secondly, it is possible to recruit many children in a single raid on an institution. Finally, it is unusual for institutions to be adequately protected, and many are situated in fairly isolated locations. Institutions may also have resources such as vehicles, and stores of food, medical equipment and blankets that are useful to impoverished armies, and increase the likelihood of attack.

In the middle '80s, the provincial orphanage in Manica, just outside the town of Chimoio, was attacked by Renamo forces. All the children (over fifty) were taken prisoner and abducted to the Renamo bases. Information about their further destiny is fragmentary, but many of them underwent military training. (Provincial Office of the Ministry of Social Action, Chimoio, Manica Province, Mozambique)

In Ethiopia during the war with Eritrea, also in the early '80s, the military demanded that an institution for parentless children hand over thirty boys between twelve and fifteen. These boys were sent, after a very short training, to the war front. When the personnel protested in writing, the head of the institution was deported to another province, and the boys were taken. None came back. Several of the personnel left the institution in protest. (Personal communication)

In addition to these specific vulnerabilities, the institutuionalisation of children has also been used to advance ethnic policies and various forms of political indoctrination. There is very little documentation of this particular violation of rights. However, one of the most overt examples occurred in Ethiopia in the 1970s and 1980s, under Mengistu, when Amharic parents were forced to separate and settle in 'enemy' territory, and their children were taken to orphanages in Eritrea. According to anecdotal reports, about 1,000 families suffered this fate.

During the assessment made of the situation of separated children in Eritrea in 1992 by Redd Barna and Rädda Barnen, the investigators were told that about 750 victims of the assimilation policy had been sent back to Ethiopia from orphanages in Eritrea as part of the postwar agreements. On visiting an orphanage where many of these children had lived, the investigators were informed that there was virtually no documentation on the background of these children. On their return to Ethiopia, the children were apparently sent to orphanages in different parts of the country. (Personal Communication)

There are also instances where institutions have been established to further political ideologies, as well as providing a future source of very young military personnel. This method has been used by the Liberation Tigers of Tamil Eelam (LTTE) in Sri Lanka. International donors may be unaware of the implications of supporting such enterprises. During ongoing civil war, there is always a possibility that institutions may also be used to procure funds which are partly used for military purposes.

Leaving 'Home' – With Nowhere To Go

The question of where and to whom one belongs becomes crucial during adolescence and takes on very real perspectives as the young person realises that he or she will have to leave the institution. This can be especially difficult when the country is in the throes of civil war.

> Many children were in the predicament of having no place to go after the maximum age limit for remaining in the institution ... Sriyani has been informed by the warden that her period of stay in the Home will soon be up. Her mother is a domestic servant and has no place to take her. Sriyani has been told that they will summon her mother by telegram if she does not come to take her. She is devastated at her plight and was unsure whether her mother would come for her. 'My whole being is now a problem' she said. (Wijetunge, 1992)

Although some institutions do make attempts to prepare young people for leaving, usually at the age of seventeen to eighteen, but sometimes sixteen years, by giving them vocational training or obtaining school places, very few have the resources to energetically follow up those who leave. Sometimes, the problem is solved by children staying on at the institution, and themselves becoming staff, perhaps also marrying other children who have grown up in the same place. Institutions for girls may try to select husbands for them, with the intention of securing their protection and respectability.

The combination of leaving an institution in the context of civil war, with little experience of coping with ordinary life, and no support from social or community networks, can be disastrous for the young people concerned. The options open to them are extremely limited and they are likely to find their only means of survival on the streets and in the informal economy. The likelihood of involvement in crime or commercial sex is extremely high.

These are some of the most common factors that threaten children's well-being and development when they are institutionalised during war, and which relate specifically to the fact of warfare. Whilst some of these issues can be addressed by improving the quality of institutional care, many are an integral part of the structure of institutional life, and are therefore less amenable to change. The fact that institutions may themselves become targets for recruitment or attack during wartime underlines the need for special measures to find alternative forms of care.

Institutionalisation of Children and the Convention on the Rights of the Child

The almost worldwide ratification of the Convention on the Rights of the Child means that in most countries children are now recognised as persons with defined social and civil rights; these are rights that states are obliged to implement and monitor to the best of their ability. However, the Convention is still a long way from influencing the fate of separated children during and following armed conflict. The articles that are of particular relevance to children in institutions include: the right to maintain parental contact; the right to protection against all forms of physical or mental violence; the right of children placed under the care of authorities to regular assessment of their treatment and care; the right to participate in decisions concerning oneself; the right to privacy; the right to feedom of expression; and the right to freedom of religion, thought and conscience (see Appendix I).

Children growing up in institutions, especially under conditions of civil war, are dependent on them to such a degree that the risk of expulsion, if they took the initiative to exercise some or any of these rights, would be too great for most children to contemplate. This is not generally the case for their contemporaries growing up in families. The dependence of institutionalised children and the very uneven balance of power between children and adults demand a high degree of awareness of the basic rights of children on the part of management, staff and children. Raising awareness that children are beings with rights accorded them by the State through its ratification of the Convention on the Rights of the Child, is a significant challenge. If acted on, this would have far-reaching implications for the way in which institutions are staffed and run, and also for the placement of children in institutions.

What are the Alternatives? Developing and Adapting the Roles of Institutions in Armed Conflict and Postwar Reconstruction

The question of increasing the safety and promoting the rights of children during armed conflict is under constant discussion among humanitarian agencies. This was the subject of a major UN study led by Graca Machel, which reported in 1996 (UN, 1996) and of meetings and studies organised by the Organisation of African Unity (OAU) and African non-government organisations such as ANPPCAN, since the late 1980s.

Prevention of separation is the immediate priority in conflict zones, followed by *ongoing action to identify, document and trace separated children*. This should not overlook the importance of work to reunite displaced and refugee street children, children held in prisons or rehabilitation centres and demobilised child soldiers. In many countries (for example Angola and Mozambique) large numbers of displaced children sought refuge in the main provincial cities and remain permanently separated from their communities of origin.

Fostering

In the case of children separated from their families in war zones, access to *safe interim care* is a priority. However, in view of the social, psychological and developmental problems associated with insititutional care, the tendency now is to look for families that are willing to *foster* children while efforts are made to trace their families. Although this is preferable to admitting children to large impersonal institutions, the practice does have its own problems. For example, in some areas, it is very difficult to find foster carers, either due to the fact that people are on the move, exhausted, afraid, have already taken in non-related children spontaneously and/or it is not culturally acceptable to care for non-related children. Where there is no social work infrastructure to monitor or follow up children placed in non-related foster families, there may also be concerns about the protection of children in these situations (Charnley et al., 1993; Petty et al., 1998).

Community-based Care Arrangements

In situations where fostering is problematic there are already some examples of *institutions adapting to fulfil different functions*. This may involve support to foster families providing interim care, provision of day care or acting as a focal point for tracing and reunification. In Rwanda, for example, some institutions that provided places of safety for large numbers of children separated during the conflict, have developed smaller family-like arrangements for children whose families have not been traced (SCF, 1998). This has given rise to opportunities to train staff as protectors and promoters of the rights of children in their care, as well as supporting their basic needs. In Burundi, Liberia and elsewhere, a number of well-established institutions have also redirected funds from large centres to community-based care.

In Angola, where SCF (UK) has promoted an active programme of family tracing for children in large government-run institutions, *small family group homes* linked to these institutions are now being supported. This has enabled disabled widows (for example women who have been injured in land-mine accidents) to continue to care for their children in a home environment. The sustainability of the units has been promoted by the allocation of plots of land.

For children requiring long-term care, for whom no relatives can be found, *community-based foster homes* may be a solution. These have been tried out on a small scale in Ethiopia, Rwanda and Uganda. Although not without problems, some of the results have been encouraging in terms of integrating children into the local community.

The basic design in a programme run by Redd Barna in Ethiopia is that a mature, respected, widowed mother whose own children have begun their independent lives agrees to take on the permanent care of a small group of children for whom no relatives can be traced. Support from an outside agency or social welfare department is given for a period of two to three years with the specific aim of helping the family to become self-sufficient. The community is encouraged to assist the children in taking part in community activities and children are encouraged to go to school; some may and some may not, as with other children in the particular community. Agreements regulating the arrangement are signed by the widow and the community, and these are also made known to the children. The foster mother may receive some remuneration during the first three years until the income-generating inputs start to take effect. The family lives in the widow's original home, or alternatively a home in keeping with the style and standard of the community may be built. Community-based foster homes require regular monitoring, but do seem to overcome the problem of reintegration and estrangement often connected with upbringing in large institutions.

Home Construction Programmes for Adolescents

Finally, for adolescents whose community of origin is unknown, or who are unable to return for reasons of their own security, 'home construction' programmes have been successfully undertaken in Angola, and are underway in Liberia and Rwanda. This involves basic skills training, support in negotiation to secure land rights and, in some instances, assistance in establishing income-generating activities. Follow-up and long-term evaluation of these projects will provide important insights into the transition from institutional care to independent living.

CONCLUSIONS

Institutions give rise to a specific set of problems for children that have long-term economic, developmental and social implications. The causes and effects of these are even more complex in the context of armed conflict. We have argued that the solution is not to provide better regulated, more accountable institutions. Even if this were possible or desirable, such institutions could only ever support a small minority of children whose families and communities have been ravaged by war. A more relevant approach is one that promotes reunification with surviving family members, and where this is not possible, supports a range of non-institutional alternatives.

These objectives cannot be achieved in isolation: communities recovering from the chaos and economic disruption of war have only a limited capacity to absorb additional welfare demands. A non-institutional response therefore requires simultaneous investment in local economic and social infrastructure across the community as a whole. None of the community-based alternatives that have been outlined are likely to be sustainable without this broader investment in the reconstruction of livelihoods and the social fabric.

This requires, firstly, a far better understanding of changes in rural economy and social structures brought about by war, than is presently available in most agencies, and secondly, a far greater emphasis on social policy coherence among governments, donors and non-government organisations involved in postwar reconstruction. In particular, reconstruction efforts need to be sensitive to demographic changes and 'new' household formations such as extended households headed by widowed mothers, aunts and grandparents; adolescent- and sibling-headed households etc. Where appropriate policies are implemented to support these households (which may range from changing the rules governing access to credit, to reform of inheritance laws), the risks of further disruption in the lives of children resettled into these households are likely to be greatly reduced.

Work at this level seems a long way from the trauma of rape, militarisation and violent bereavement. However, social and economic security are the mainstays of the future development of all children whose lives have been affected by conflict. Without it, whole generations will continue to suffer the consequences of war, and those who have already lost family, homes and friends, will risk further abandonment and social marginalisation. The consequences for the children themselves, and for the governments and international community that has failed them, are immeasurable.

APPENDIX I

Summary of Articles of the Convention on the Rights of the Child Relevant to Children in Institutional Care

Article 3
The best interests of the child: this article also refers to the rights of children in institutions.

Article 9, para. 3
A child separated from his parents has the right to maintain a personal communication with both parents on a regular basis, unless this is against the best interests of the child.

Article 12
The child's right to freely express his or her viewpoint in matters of concern to the child, and that, according to the child's age and maturity, those opinions must be taken into account in decisions made about the child.

Article 13
The child's right to freedom of expression etc.

Article 14
The child's right to freedom of religion, thought and conscience.

Article 15
The child's right to participate in peaceful assemblies, and to join organisations of his or her choice.

Article 16
The child's right to a private life.

Article 19
The child's right to be protected against all forms of physical or mental violence, harm or abuse.

Article 20
Concerning the rights of children removed from their family environment.

Article 23
Concerning the rights of children with mental and physical handicap.

Article 24
The child's right of access to health services of the highest possible quality.

Article 25
The right of children placed under the care of authorities to have regular assessment made of their treatment and care, as well as all other circumstances of importance for the child's placement.

Article 27
The child's right to a standard of living compatible with the child's development.

Article 28
The child's right to education.

Article 30
Of relevance for children who belong to ethnic minorities placed in institutions (in some countries they are over-represented among institutionalised children).

Article 31
The child's right to rest and recreation and to participation in cultural activities.

Article 34
The child's right to protection from all forms of sexual abuse.

Article 38
The child's right not to participate in armed conflict while under the age of fifteen.

Article 39
The child's right to rehabilitation.

Notes

1. The term 'institution' is used in this paper to refer to orphanages and other centres that are the child's only home. It does not refer to boarding schools from which children return home for holidays.
2. In 1985, Defence of Children International (DCI) estimated that there was a total of 6–8 million children in institutions worldwide. However, figures of this kind are extremely difficult to verify.
3. Figures are available from countries where SCF (UK) has been working to reunify children separated from their families. For example, in Rwanda, prior to the genocide of 1994, there were twenty children's homes. This figure rose to seventy centres housing 12,000 children in 1995. Following intensive efforts to reunify children, by November 1997 there were fifty centres accommodating 6,353 children. Similarly, in Uganda there were about thirty children's homes prior to the 1979 war. In the early 1990s, prior to a programme of reunification, there were seventy-five homes housing 3,000 children; by 1997, the number had fallen to forty-four homes with 1,200 children. Ongoing poverty and insecurity in Burundi is linked to the number of children in institutions more than doubling, from 900 to 2,000 children, in the period 1995–96 (Unicef figures). Finally, a study carried out by SCF (UK) in Liberia in 1995 found that there were twenty 'orphanages' functioning in Monrovia alone, with a population of 1,484 children. Less than 15 per cent of these children were either genuinely orphaned or had no knowledge of their parents' whereabouts. Prior to the war, there were only five child welfare institutions in Monrovia, all of which catered for relatively small groups of children.
4. During the mass repatriation of refugees from Zaire to Rwanda in November 1996, only 1 per cent of children became separated from their families (see Brodie, 1997, *Zaire and Tanzania Repatriations: Report of National Tracing Coordinator*, SCF (UK)).

References

Africa Watch (1991). *Angola Civilians Devastated by Fifteen Years War*. New York: Africa Watch.

Brett, R. and McCallin, M. (1996). *Children: the Invisible Soldiers*. Stockholm: Radda Barnen.

Brodie, D. (1997). Zaire and Tanzania repatriations: report of National Tracing Coordinator. Unpublished document. London: Save the Children Fund (UK).

Charnley, H., Mausse, M. and Sitoi, M. (1993). *The Role of the Subsititute Family in Mozambique*. Case study No. 2 for Roots and Roofs project. London: Save the Children Fund (UK).

Guardian (1997). *Society Supplement*: 24 September 1997. London: *Guardian*.

Human Rights Watch/Africa (1995). *Children of Sudan*. New York: Human Rights Watch.

Jareg, E. (1988). *Report on an Assessment of Solumona Orphanage, Eritrea*. Oslo: Redd Barna.

Jareg, E. (1989a). *Four Reports on Unaccompanied Children, Ethiopia.* Oslo: Redd Barna.

Jareg, E. (1989b). *Observations on a Visit to a Home for Eritrean Children in Sudan.* Oslo: Redd Barna.

Jareg, E. (1992). *Report on a Consultancy Visit to Eritrea.* Oslo: Redd Barna.

Keen, D. (1997). A rational kind of madness. *Oxford Development Studies* 25, 1, 67–75.

Machel, G. (1996). *Impact of Armed Conflict on Children.* Report of the expert of the Secretary General pursuant to General Assembly resolution 48/157. New York: United Nations.

Petty, C. with Tamplin M., Uppard, S. and Brown, M. (1998). *Keeping Children with Families in Emergencies.* Report of an inter-agency conference. London: Save the Children Fund (UK)

Richards, P. (1996). *Fighting for the Rain Forest.* Oxford: James Currey.

Rutter, M., Taylor, E. and Hersov, L. (1994). *Child and Adolescent Psychiatry: Modern Approaches* (3rd edition) Oxford: Blackwell Scientific Publications.

Ruxton, S. (1996). *Children in Europe.* London: NCH action for children.

Save the Children Fund (UK) (1998). *Keeping Children with Families in Emergencies.* Presentations and background papers from an inter-agency meeting. London: Save the Children Fund (UK).

Summerfield, D. (1996). *The Impact of War and Atrocity on Civilian Populations.* Relief and Rebilitation Network London: ODI.

Tizard, B. and Hodges, J. (1978). The effect of early institutional rearing on the development of eight-year-old children. *Journal of Child Psychology and Psychiatry* 19, 99–118.

Tizard, B. and Rees, J. (1975). The effect of early institutional rearing on behavioural problems and affective relationships of four-year-old children. *Journal of Child Psychology and Psychiatry* 16, 61–74.

Tolfree, D. (1995). *Roofs and Roots: The Care of Separated Children in the Developing World.* Aldershot: Arena.

UNHCR (1994). *Refugee Children Guidelines on Prevention and Care.* Geneva: UNHCR.

Utting, W. (1997). *People Like Us: Review of the Safeguards for Children Living Away From Home* London: Department of Health, Welsh Office.

Wijetunge, S. et al. (1992). *A Study of Children's Homes in Sri Lanka.* Colombo: University of Colombo.

8 Looking Before and After: Refugees and Asylum Seekers in the West

NAOMI RICHMAN

The experiences of asylum seekers in the West are in many ways different from those of refugees or the locally displaced, who remain with their compatriots and in a more or less familiar culture. The former face unique issues of loss, confrontation with an alien culture, and challenges to identity.

Assistance to refugees in the West must take into account their need to make sense of their sudden exposure to a new culture and the often serious obstacles to settlement that exist. As well as dealing with the events that took place before leaving their country of origin, events occurring once they have arrived in the country of refuge may in themselves be so distressing that they seriously affect the asylum seeker's emotional state.

This chapter discusses two aspects of the process of adaptation: factors that affect integration with the host culture, and the relevance of support offered to refugees.

THE PROCESS OF ADAPTATION

'Loss is a magical preservative. Time stops at the point of severance. Nostalgia ... crystallises around ... images [of the past] like amber. The largest presence within me is the welling up of absence, of what I have lost.' Thus Elsa Hoffman in her book *Lost in Translation* (Hoffman, 1989 p. 115) describes her efforts to come to terms with being a migrant to Canada after leaving Poland with her family at the age of thirteen. Her family had not suffered the extremes of political oppression that disrupt family and normal life, but she expresses the complexity of emotions that face so many refugee children and adults. Their struggles to comprehend and deal with these emotions should not be seen as pathological but rather as an inevitable response to a challenging situation.

Hoffman confronts 'the ... dangers of both forgetfulness and clinging to the past' and finds that 'I can't afford to look back and I can't figure out how to look forward ... I am stuck and time is stuck within me' (p. 116). 'Now time has no dimension, no extension backward or forward. I can't throw a bridge between the present and the past, and therefore I can't make time move' (p. 117).

Her task was to integrate the past and present so that time could move on, and the book charts her convoluted journey, her hesitations and doubts. She quotes Theodor Adorno, who 'once warned his fellow refugees that if they lost their alienation, they'd lose their souls. But how does one bend towards another culture without falling over?' (p. 209) and writes 'I have to make a shift in the innermost ways. I have to translate myself. But if I'm to achieve this without becoming assimilated – that is, absorbed – by my new world, the translation has to be careful, the turns of the psyche unforced' (p. 211).

This process can be particularly complex for children who have to deal with both growing up, and growing into, an understanding of their new society. Over many years Hoffman reached a sense of integration. 'Perhaps I've had to gather enough knowledge of my new world to trust it, and enough affection for it to breathe life into it, ... once time uncoils and regains its forward dimension, the present moment becomes a fulcrum on which I can stand more lightly, balanced between the past and the future, balanced in time'· (p. 280). 'From now on, I'll be made, like a mosaic, of fragments – and my consciousness of them. It is only in that observing consciousness that I remain, after all, an immigrant' (p. 164).

Each family and individual travels their own journey. The process depends on many factors: on age, experiences before and after exile, family situation, religious and political factors, opportunities in the host country, motivation to stay or return, possibilities of return. Those who are uncertain about whether they can or will be forced to return, or ambivalent about whether they want to return, find themselves in an intense predicament. Unlike Hoffman, many asylum seekers and refugees also have to come to terms with an oppressive and cruel past which has disrupted their family and their lives.

Efforts to facilitate a satisfactory integration must acknowledge the complexity of this process. The journey cannot be seen as a linear progression; rather the analogy could be life experienced as a fugue in which themes related to loss, culture, identity and the search for understanding recur and modulate throughout life.

The following sections of the chapter consider some of the crucial influences that affect integration.

INFLUENCE OF THE HOST ENVIRONMENT

Asylum Issues

In this chapter the term refugee is used to refer to those who are applying for asylum or appealing against refusal, as well as those who have been granted asylum or permission to stay on humanitarian grounds (Exceptional Leave to Remain or ELR).

Currently, a major source of distress for many refugees is the difficulty in gaining refugee status. Although less than 5 per cent of the world's refugees are in Europe, they increasingly encounter, in what has come to be called 'fortress Europe', a culture of disbelief that they are genuine asylum seekers, and diminishing support for settlement or welfare. A prolonged asylum process with little assurance of success, the uncertainty of their situation and the fear of deportation, cause enormous anxiety, and obstruct the process of looking forward. For some detention, often arbitrary, is an added distressing affliction.

As an example, in the UK the number of refugees who are granted full asylum status is decreasing. Out of 17,490 decisions on asylum processed in the first six months of 1996 only 1,080 (6 per cent) were granted refugee status, with a further 2,195 (13 per cent) receiving humanitarian status (ELR). The latter gives less security, reduced entitlements to benefit and education, and fewer rights e.g. to family reunification. By comparison, ten years earlier, in 1986, 82 per cent of applicants were given leave to remain in the UK, either with refugee status or ELR (Refugee Council 1997).

Littlewood and Lipsedge (1989) suggest that an important factor for migrant well-being is the degree of dissonance between their expectations of life in the new country and the gradual awareness that initial aspirations are not going to be met. Experiences of refugees vary, but many are dismayed by the prevailing culture of disbelief facing asylum claimants, and the discrimination and racism they encounter.

It might be expected that refugees become more settled with time, but some, affected by such factors as poor English, undetermined asylum status, absence of family support and lack of work, remain in a state of tension and uncertainty for years. A sense of unease may therefore increase over time as refugees discover the blocks to integration. Liebkind (1983) studied over 150 Vietnamese young people between fourteen and twenty-four years of age and their carers. Symptoms of depression and anxiety increased in both generations over time but were higher in carers than in children.

Carey-Wood et al. (1995) interviewed 263 adults in the UK who had refugee status or ELR. Their concerns centred on lack of employment, problems with English (especially for women), accommodation, and health. Half had experienced racial discrimination, and 13 per cent had been physically attacked. Although more than two-thirds felt part of their local community, less than half wanted to settle permanently in Britain. Many had a high level of education and skills but usually could not find work commensurate with their experience.

In my study of sixty refugee children and their mothers from a London borough I found that for women problems in learning English, housing, unemployment, and health were major issues (Richman, 1996). Of thirty mothers interviewed, fourteen had experienced threat, violence or robbery. Nineteen reported feeling lonely and only four were speaking and reading English fluently.

Out of thirty-three children in the same study, nineteen reported bullying at school and eleven had been attacked or seriously threatened in the neighbourhood. Six children had changed or were about to change school because of bullying. In every focused group discussion with refugee children and youth, experiences of bullying were mentioned spontaneously (Richman, 1996).

Communities

Refugees bring with them rich social experiences of family, clan, and neighbourhood, of work and political and religious life. But they have lost this social network, and are faced with constructing new social ties from their own community as well as the host community. Loizos (1981) noted the loss of the customary daily rhythms in Greek Cypriots fleeing from the north of Cyprus, and especially of the 'dense' social life of communal living.

Eastmond (1989) has described the ways in which the Chilean community in exile in the US struggled to cope with their situation and maintain their identity through political commitment, affirmation of their culture, and mutual support. She recounts how the refugees tried to make sense of what had happened to them, and to construct a personal 'narrative' that helped them to understand the events that led to flight and the reality of their current situation. An initial period of relief at gaining safety was followed by a prolonged process of mourning the loss of homeland, possessions and status: a process of 'cultural bereavement' (Eisenbruch, 1991; Munoz, 1980).

As with many other refugee groups, they expected to stay in exile only a short time, and even learning English was not necessarily a priority. Gradually they had to evolve longer-term goals as the possibility of return receded (Eastmond, 1989). This view of exile as temporary is common and may be protracted and interfere with efforts to settle in the new country, and to learn the language.

Being part of a community helps to validate political, religious and other values, and to maintain a sense of continuity and self-worth. The community provides a supportive network to replace the loss of family and neighbourhood. However, as time passes, individuals and families often take on some of the individualism of the host community, and communal action and group cohesion may become less prominent (Eastmond, 1989). Communities inevitably change over time as younger people, more integrated into the new society, begin to assert themselves and no longer defer to elders or to older traditions.

Refugees need contact with others who reflect their values, prize their culture, and share common experiences. Studies suggest that when they are living within a vigorous community of compatriots, this support plays an important role in preventing mental distress (Valtonen, 1994). However, communities are not homogenous, and within them, groups are distinguished by their language, geographical origin, religion, or political affiliation. Intricate religious, political and social characteristics influence the structures of community networks and available support. Religious and political distinctions take on more salience as individuals strive to reaffirm their identity. Thus, individuals do not necessarily feel supported by their community.

The Political Dimension of Being an Asylum Seeker

The political dimension has more or less significance in the life of refugees depending on the level of their political involvement. Not all refugees have been activists. Bosnians fled from unexpected violence, and many refugees are caught between various factions in violent confrontations which they cannot control, as in Columbia at the present time.

The politically involved, the fighters for justice and human rights, may have suffered from detention, torture and disruption of family life. Their beliefs and commitment give a meaning to this suffering, and a context in which they can go on struggling. Political activity is central to their identity and daily life. The importance of political life to activists who feel doubly bereft after losing their political role as well as their country must always be recognised (Gorst-Unsworth, 1992; Gorst-Unsworth and Goldenberg, 1998; Hauff and Vaglum, 1995).

Families

Changes in family life are inevitable for the refugee, and family members are affected differently by their situation. New models of behaviour for children, women, and for married couples, confront the family.

Parents are also faced with new social rules about child rearing; transgression may even lead to intervention by social workers or the courts. Roles shift as men lose their function as breadwinners, women become single parents and children take on new responsibilities, for example as interpreters. The capacity of the family to support children may be strained because of the parents' own difficulties in adjustment and sorrowing about their losses. Separation from family members, who are perhaps living in danger, and with no possibility of reunification, is a potent source of distress (Woodcock, 1994).

Marriages may be affected because of differing views about exile, for example one partner may not have been as politically active as the other, and is therefore resentful about having to seek asylum. Torture, especially when it has involved sexual abuse of one or other partner, can seriously interfere with the relationship (Munoz, 1980; Barudy, 1989; Woodcock, 1995). As well as migrating to a new country, some refugees also face the strains of sudden urbanisation.

Women are struggling with changes of role and responsibility, and yet lack the support they used to have. 'The process of relocation is one in which the emotional needs of individuals increase markedly, while their social support network is severely disrupted' (Sluzki, 1989). They are often not linked into the networks of their own community, and time and travel costs prevent them from meeting friends, especially if they have children. Fear of violence on the streets and difficulties of communication limit contacts with neighbours. This lack of contact restricts information about norms of child care, and also limits neighbourly support: in an emergency they may have no one to call upon. Thus there is a low affiliation to the neighbourhood and a sense of isolation and anomie.

The lack of safety in their neighbourhoods adds to their sense of living in a dangerous environment in which they have no support, and which is risky for their children. Poor English skills affect advice seeking, health care, and contacting children's teachers. Progress in learning the host language is hindered because of time constraints, inaccessibility of classes, or lack of confidence.

For children, learning English and school work are often sources of anxiety (Richman, 1996). Education is particularly vital for refugee children because of its role in social integration, language development, and access to services and employment. A study of refugees' educational experience describes difficulties in finding a school place, and lack of adequate assessment and guidance which led to inappropriate courses. Only a quarter were satisfied with the language and learning support they had received (McDonald, 1995). Lack of financial and other resources in the educational system add to difficulties (Power et al., 1995).

Generational Strain

Different perceptions of what is suitable behaviour can lead to friction within families (Nguyen and Williams, 1989). Generational issues about ways of life and values cause uncertainty in both children and parents. Changes in attitudes and behaviour are observed by parents with dismay as Hoffman discovered: 'My mother says I'm becoming English ... she means I'm becoming cold ... I learn restraint from [my friends], my teacher tells me to "sit on my hands [so as not to gesticulate] and then try talking"' (Hoffman, 1989 p. 146).

Styles of dress, use of make-up, times of going out and returning home, religious observance and so on, can lead to disruptive conflict within the family, as parents try to maintain the family's original cohesion and values, which they see as threatened by individualism and consumerism. Liebkind (1993) suggests that the reason girls had higher symptom scores than boys in her study is because of the extremely different notions of female gender roles in Vietnamese and Finnish cultures.

Children's views about their future may also differ from that of parents. Young people usually have more contact with the receiving society through school and friends, and generally feel more comfortable with the values and behaviours of the host society than their elders. Their home culture may seem distant or be viewed as oppressive and violent. In some cases, first language skills are not maintained and contact with community groups is limited, so that there are diminishing links with their own community, although this might change in later adolescence.

MENTAL HEALTH

Based on screening questionnaires, high rates of symptoms of distress are reported in refugees in the West, ranging from 26–45 per cent in a sample of South Americans in Toronto (Allodi and Rojas, 1985), to 52–56 per cent in a sample of Vietnamese in the US (Lin et al., 1982).

An estimated 30 per cent of refugees in the Netherlands ask for help for psychological problems (Boekhoorn, 1987).

Mollica et al. (1987) describe high rates of major depression and PTSD in a *clinic* sample of fifty-two Southeast Asian refugees in Boston. They also noted the difficulties encountered by their patients with language (92 per cent), employment (62 per cent), and housing (54 per cent), and the inhibitions of refugee women in talking about their experiences of rape.

In general, studies tend to look only at the effects of events occurring before arrival in the host country, but a review of the literature suggested that post-exile aspects are also influential. The following factors appeared to increase the risk of psychological morbidity:

- separated from family
- isolated from own community
- either an adolescent or of senior age group
- unable to speak the host language
- loss of socio-economic status
- prolonged or severe suffering prior to exile
- an unfriendly host community

(Canadian Task Force on Mental Health Issues Affecting Immigrants and Refugees 1988)

Hauff and Vaglum (1995) found that morbidity in a group of Vietnamese in Norway was predicted by negative life events following the initial traumatic situation, including separation from close family, absence of a confidante, severe previous trauma, education, younger age and gender.

Gorst-Unsworth and Goldenberg (1998) interviewed 150 Iraqui males who were consecutive referrals to the Medical Foundation for the Care of Victims of Torture in London. Difficulties experienced by individuals in their social and personal lives in exile were associated with distress. Separation from children, low confidant support, low number of social activities, lack of contact with political organisations in exile and a low level of affective support, were all associated with psychological morbidity. Lack of political involvement and lack of emotional support were particularly important. Interestingly, the level of trauma suffered prior to exile did not appear to influence the scores relating to psychological distress.

Similar risk factors are highlighted as sources of strain by respondents in many different studies (Carey-Wood et al., 1995; Valtonen, 1994; Richman, 1996).

Children

The long-term effects on personality and relationships of living under a repressive regime and the complexity of the forces acting on individual children are highlighted in clinical case studies (Melzak, 1992). Possibilities for normal development may have been severely restricted for the children for months or years before their arrival in exile, for example Vietnamese children living in Hong Kong camps. They may have experienced deprivation, harassment and threat, destruction of normal social life, terrifying experiences in flight, and difficulties in reunification with their family. Loss or separations from carers or disappearances of relatives have the most serious impact on their development. Even if parents survive and the family is eventually reunited, relations may be strained and difficult after years of separation (Arroyo and Eth, 1985).

For children, their family situation and the nature of the care they receive are usually the major factors in their subsequent adjustment. Living with parents, or if unaccompanied, maintaining contact with their culture and community of origin, appear to be important protective factors (Kinzie et al., 1986; Sack et al., 1986; Eisenbruch, 1991). Issues of identity and loyalty can cause considerable distress in children, especially in adolescence (van der Veer, 1992). When they became targets of violence, Muslim Bosnian young people had to reconsider the meaning of being a Muslim. Those who had fled Bosnia were often torn between wanting to make a new life in the country of exile, and wanting to support their parents who wished to return to Bosnia.

Unaccompanied children are most at risk psychologically, and their future depends to a large extent on the adequacy of their care and social support, which is often difficult to organise. Keilson (1992) was involved in the assessment and placement of Jewish children in the Netherlands after the end of World War II. Most of the children had survived the war in the care of non-Jewish foster parents; a few had been in camps; none had surviving parents. Some children remained with their foster parents whilst others were placed in Jewish children's homes or with relatives. Keilson followed up this group of Dutch child survivors and considered that the decisions on placement were crucial to later adjustment. Over twenty years later he was able to see how issues of loyalty, identity and mourning affected the adaptation of these children in adulthood.

In my study of refugee children and their families in London, children presented with behavioural or emotional problems in schools or clinics most commonly because of family tensions or because of inadequate care. This latter could be related to being an unaccompanied child, or to the death of, or separation from, the main carer. Some were living with siblings, or other relatives, barely older than themselves and unable to respond fully to their emotional needs (Richman, 1996).

Mental health problems in youth are also related to school problems. Bullying and racism, and difficulties with school work and with English are sources of tension (Richman, 1996).

APPROACHES TO SUPPORTING REFUGEES IN THE WEST

The above brief review indicates that, just as in non-refugee populations, a wide range of factors affect refugee mental health. A variety of current stressors are at least as important as past experiences of violence and torture in causing distress. These include loss, bereavement and separation from family members, and current difficulties related to asylum, poverty, housing and obstacles to integration. For many, the existential dilemmas of exile and identity are crucial issues (Turner and Gorst-Unsworth, 1990; Gorst-Unsworth et al., 1993; Eisenbruch, 1991; van der Veer, 1992).

Most refugees are not in a 'post-traumatic' situation, since they continue to endure a variety of distressing experiences. Nor can assumptions be made about which factors are most painful for them to deal with: the experiences of detention and torture may have less salience for individuals than other experiences such as loss and bereavement, inability to be at their parents' funerals, separation from children or other relatives, death of comrades, the political situation in their country of origin, and the impunity of their oppressors (Summerfield, 1995).

Thus, supporting refugees is not simply a question of 'treating their trauma'. It requires an understanding of the complexity of their situation and of the adaptations they must make. Initially, many avoid feeling overwhelmed by devoting their energy to the most urgent practical considerations. Emotions about loss and separation are controlled in order to manage what is most pressing. This is not denial, but a way of avoiding being submerged by the obstacles faced.

A conviction that mental illness, especially PTSD, is usually present in refugees is unhelpful. It is not uncommon for 'experts' to find that their offers of help are unacceptable because their approach is based on the premise that a high proportion need therapy, and that this needs to be focused on their past traumas (personal interviews). Refugees feel patronised and undermined when they are told they are traumatised, and need treatment, especially as in many cultures psychological treatment is only for the 'mad'. Instead of being able to decide their priorities for themselves they may be faced with a predetermined programme of therapy (Richman, 1993; Bracken et al., 1995).

This does not mean that support cannot be helpful. A mutually comprehensible communication between refugees and their would-be helpers has to be developed, and the support offered must be acceptable and comprehensible to people who are not accustomed to 'psychological' discourse (Reichelt and Sveass, 1994). Western assumptions about what is helpful must be looked at historically and socially in order to understand the role of therapy in our culture and its relevance to other cultures. Cultural differences in dealing with emotion and distress must be appraised and valued (Kleinman 1980; Davis, 1992; Bracken, 1993).

How should we understand the remarkable growth of counselling in Western countries over the past few decades, especially in Britain and the US? Hoffman tries to explain to Polish friends why so many Americans go to psychiatrists:

> It's a problem of identity. Many of my friends don't have enough of it. They often feel worthless, or they don't know how they feel. Identity is the number-one problem here. There seems to be a shortage of it in the land, a dearth of self hood amidst other plenty – maybe because there are so many individual egos trying to outdo each other and enlarge themselves. (Hoffman, 1989 p. 262)

Various influences are suggested to explain the search for therapy and the kind of therapy proffered, related to current Western expectations and perceptions of the individual.

High expectations of a 'good life', health and affluence, are increasingly confronting economic and political uncertainty about how this might be achieved. When these aspirations of well-being are frustrated and something goes wrong, someone must be to blame, rather than chance or destiny or God's will. Rising rates of litigation are but one facet of this trend of distrust and blame. Füredi (1997) suggests that increasing individuation, a lack of social cohesion, and diminishing moral convictions based on religion or political beliefs, impair our ability to deal with the strains of life.

At the same time, in spite of the fact that standards of living and life expectation are higher than they have ever been, life is perceived as increasingly risky. Threats lurk in everyday things like food, which is no longer assumed to be wholesome; global warming threatens the very existence of earth; strangers are seen as potentially violent. Increasingly, legislation such as that related to the use of seat belts and crash helmets, or smoking, is enacted to lower risk. But this seems to increase the sense of risk rather than diminishing it. Media exaggeration adds to distrust and misgivings about the world. It is suggested that all these factors undermine our sense of competence and our capacity to cope with difficulties (Füredi, 1997).

Western responses based in psychology and psychiatry have developed, and are developing, in a particular historical and social context. Comparing attitudes about the relationship of the individual to the group in India and the US, Schweder and Bourne conclude that the '"sociocentric" solution [of the former] subordinates individual interests to the good of the collectivity, while in the "egocentric" solution [of the latter], society becomes the servant of the individual, i.e. *society is imagined to have been created to serve the interests of some idealised autonomous, abstract individual existing free of society yet living in society'*. (Schweder and Bourne, 1984 p. 190) (my italics). These issues are also discussed in chapter 2.

Mental Health Approaches

A mental health approach that has arisen in the 'egocentric' context that has been described may not, therefore, be relevant in the 'sociocentric' context. An approach that 'turns experiences into symptoms' and ignores the collective aspect of political violence will not be appropriate. Therapeutic approaches become decontextualised when they focus on the individual and his or her symptoms, and do not encompass the social setting. Firstly, that is because social factors in the exile situation leading to 'loss of status, the gradual erosion of self esteem and ongoing negative life events [are often] more powerful factors in ... difficulties in recovery than the original traumatic event', such as torture (Gorst-Unsworth, 1992); secondly, because it was their membership of a political or social grouping that caused people to be targeted for violence; thirdly, because the mechanisms of oppression purposely disrupt culture and social cohesion and create distrust and isolation, and it is through a collective endeavour that people can best make sense of their experiences and become active participants in their own advancement.

Through practical experience, a number of workers have concluded that community projects are the most effective means of providing support to refugee communities. This is in part because of the large numbers involved but also because this approach is meaningful and acceptable, and emphasises the importance of collective identity.

These projects have usually entailed similar elements, beginning with the belief that they must be developed in conjunction with members of the community, if they are to be successful and have the right priorities. The elements include responding to the practical needs of daily life (housing, welfare, advice on asylum, education and training, language classes); 'breaking the silence' through providing opportunities to talk about their experiences and difficulties in small groups; facilitating recreation and other activities; promoting education and work opportunities; making links with the host community; and encouraging self-advocacy.

The following examples illustrate this preventive mental health approach, which links emotional and practical needs, aiming to restore autonomy and self-respect, and acting as a link between the refugee world and the unknown world of the receiving country. Helping people to feel safe is a crucial first step, although difficult to achieve when asylum is not assured.

The need to have a broad approach is described in a manual produced by the Canadian Centre for Victims of Torture (Price, 1994), which cites the setting-up of a group for Somali women. Preliminary discussions showed that the priority for the participants was not the past trauma they had experienced before arrival (often rape or other violence), but current difficulties such as family separation, asylum procedures, cultural barriers, social isolation, housing and welfare issues, and anxieties about children becoming acculturated to Canadian mores.

As well as the regular group meetings, participants were assisted with welfare, housing and immigration claims, language classes and job training. The group was considered to be successful in that the members used each other for support, developed more self-confidence, and were able to act successfully as advocates for themselves and their community, in particular for better housing access. This group work has been extended to other refugee women's groups and to men.

The success of the programme was thought to be related to the non-threatening, culturally sensitive approach, and the practical emphasis: education about how to access resources, a self-defence course and a parenting course; the formation of enduring bonds between group members who formed a new family for each other; and community development aspects which enabled members to act as advocates. A few women were referred for individual counselling (Blakeney et al., 1994).

A project supporting Bosnian refugees in a Swiss canton aimed to promote identity through collective and cultural activities; attending to welfare needs; supporting the work of Bosnian healers; and providing occupation (Loncarevic, 1996).

This evidence suggests that a preventive approach should deal with practical support, assuring a rapid and just resolution to asylum seeking; dealing with issues such as housing, benefits, language courses, education and training; helping with family reunification; and ensuring access to advice on legal, housing, welfare, educational and health matters. It would also try to avoid isolation through befriending schemes, accessible language lessons, and the availability of well-trained advocates, interpreters and bicultural workers.

Many school initiatives have been developed with the aim of providing a milieu that promotes safety, belonging, and learning for refugee children. These include developing a whole school policy that responds to both social and educational needs of refugees, and that provides peer support; anti-racist and anti-bullying policies; befriending schemes; homework clubs; recreation and youth clubs; and activities that allow expression of feelings and exploration of the refugee dilemma such as drama, poetry, writing, making videos and oral history projects (Rutter, 1994; Brown et al., 1991).

Counselling and therapies for refugees whose distress is persistent and disabling must, in the same way, take into account cultural factors and current stressors (van der Veer, 1992). Ideally, such work should be undertaken in collaboration with people from the refugee communities trained as therapists or counsellors, as well as involving bicultural workers to act as cultural mediators and advocates.

At the Medical Foundation for the Care of Victims of Torture in London, besides more conventional approaches like individual, marital or family work, there is group work in a variety of forms such as the storytelling group, art therapy, a craft and textile group, a gardening project, physiotherapy, movement therapy and work based on the Alexander technique. Support does not have to be based on words: symbolic and non-verbal activities can be equally relevant and acceptable.

CONCLUSION

Work that seeks to support refugees must encompass cultural sensitivity. This implies sensitivity to features of Western culture including our understanding of the person, of autonomy and the personality, and the influence this has had on concepts of emotional disturbance and of psychological treatments. It also implies understanding the concepts and cosmology of the refugee communities. This sensitivity only comes about through collaboration, dialogue, developing trust, and working together to determine what is helpful.

The problems faced by refugees are complex; practical issues are as important as issues about past trauma and must be tackled simultaneously. There can never be a single type of treatment or support that incorporates all these concerns and an eclectic approach is indispensable. Promoting family reunification, or enabling someone to find work, may have a far greater impact on psychological well-being than individual counselling.

References

Arroyo, W. and Eth, S. (1985). Children traumatised by Central American warfare. In R. Pynoos and S. Eth (eds) *Postraumatic Stress Disorder in Children*. Washington, DC.: American Psychiatric Association.

Barudy, J. (1989). A programme of mental health for political refugees: dealing with the political pain of exile. *Social Science and Medicine* 28 ,715–27.

Blakeney, J., Fadumo, J.D. and Macrae, M.A. (1994). Empowering traumatized Somali women. A support group model for helping survivors to cope. In K. Price (ed.) *Community Support for Survivors of Torture: A manual*. Toronto: Canadian Centre for Victims of Torture, pp. 74–9.

Boekhorn, P. (1987). Quoted by G. van der Veer (1992). *Counselling and Therapy with Refugees. Psychological Problems of Victims of War, Torture and Repression*. Chichester: Wiley, p. 12.

Bracken, P.J. (1993). Post-empiricism and psychiatry: meaning and methodology in cross-cultural research. *Social Science and Medicine* 36, 265–72.

Bracken, P.J., Giller, J.E. and Summerfield, D. (1995). Psychological responses to war and atrocity: the limitations of current concepts. *Social Science and Medicine* 40 1073–82.

Brown, C., Barnfield, J. and Stone, M. (1991). *Spanner in the Works. Education for Racial Equality and Social Justice in White Schools*. Stoke on Trent: Trentham Books.

Canadian Task Force on Mental Health Issues Affecting Immigrants and Refugees (1988). Review of the literature on migrant mental health. Health and Welfare Canada: Minister of Supply and Services, Canada. (Quoted in Liebkind, K. (1983) op. cit.)

Carey-Wood, J., Duke, K., Karn, V. and Marshall, T. (1995). *The Settlement of Refugees in Britain*. London: HMSO.

Davis, J. (1992). The anthropology of suffering. *Journal of Refugee Studies* 5, 149–61.

Eastmond, M. (1989). The Dilemmas of Exile. Chilean Refugees in the USA. PhD. University of Gothenburg.

Eisenbruch, M. (1991). From post traumatic stress disorder to cultural bereavement: diagnosis of Southeast Asian refugees. *Social Science and Medicine* 30, 673–80.

Füredi, F. (1997). *Culture of Fear. Risk-taking and the Morality of Low Expectation*. London: Cassell.

Gorst-Unsworth, C. (1992). Adaptation after torture: some thoughts on the long-term effects of surviving a repressive regime. *Medicine and War* 8, 164–8.

Gorst-Unsworth, C., van Velsen, C. and Turner, S.W. (1993). Prospective pilot study of torture and organised violence – examining the essential dilemma. *Journal of Nervous and Mental Disease* 181, 263–4.

Gorst-Unsworth, C. and Goldenberg, E. (1998). Psychological sequelae of torture and organised violence suffered by refugees from Iraq. *British Journal of Psychiatry* 172, 90–4.

Hauff, E. and Vaglum, P. (1995). Organised violence and the stress of exile. Predictors of mental health in a community cohort of Vietnamese refugees three years after resettlement. *British Journal of Psychiatry* 166, 360–7.

Hoffman, E. (1989). *Lost in Translation.* London: Minerva.

Keilson, H. (1992). *Sequential Traumatization in Children.* Jerusalem: Magnes Press.

Kinzie, J.D. et al. (1986). The psychiatric effects of massive trauma on Cambodian children; 1. The children. *Journal of American Academy of Child Psychiatry* 25, 370–6.

Kleinman, A. (1980). *Patients and Healers in the Context of Culture.* Berkeley, CA: University of California Press.

Liebkind, K. (1983). Self-reported ethnic identity, depression and anxiety among young Vietnamese refugees and their parents. *Journal of Refugee Studies* 6, 25–39.

Lin, K-M., Masuda, M. and Tazuma, L. (1982). Problems of Vietnamese refugees in the US. In R.C. Nann (ed.) *Uprooting and Surviving.* Dordrecht: Reidel.

Littlewood, R. and Lipsedge, M. (1989). *Aliens and Alienists. Ethnic Minorities and Psychiatry.* London: Unwin Hyman.

Loizos, P. (1981). *The Heart Grown Bitter. A Chronicle of Cypriot War Refugees.* Cambridge: Cambridge University Press.

Loncarevic, M. (1996). 'MIR' socio-cultural integration project for Bosnian refugees. In G. Perren-Klingler (ed.) *From Individual Helplessness to Group Resources.* Berne: Haupt.

McDonald, J. (1995). *Entitled to Learn?* A report on young refugees' experiences of access and progression in the UK Education System. World University Service.

Melzak, S. (1992). Secrecy, privacy, survival, repressive regimes and growing up. *Bulletin of the Anna Freud Centre* 15, 205.

Mollica, R.F. et al. (1987). The psychosocial impact of war trauma and torture on Southeast Asian refugees. *American Journal of Psychiatry* 144, 1567–72.

Munoz, L. (1980). Exile as bereavement: socio-psychological manifestations of Chilean exiles in Great Britain. *British Journal of Medical Psychology* 53, 227–32.

Nguyen, A.N. and Williams, H.L. (1989). Transition from East to West: Vietnamese adolescents and their parents. *Journal of the American Academy of Child and Adolescent Psychiatry* 28, 505–15.

Power, S., Whitty, G. and Youdell, D. (1995). *No place to learn. Homelessness and Education.* London: Shelter.

Price, K. (ed.) (1994), *Community Support for Survivors of Torture: a Manual.* Toronto: Canadian Centre for Victims of Torture.

Refugee Council (1997). *Asylum Statistics 1986–1996.* London: Refugee Council.

Reichelt, S. and Sveass, N. (1994). Developing meaningful conversations with families in exile. *Journal of Refugee Studies* 7 125–43.

Richman, N. (1993). Annotation: children in situations of political violence. *Journal of Child Psychology and Psychiatry* 34, 1286–1302.

Richman, N. (1996). *They Don't Recognise our Dignity. A Study of the Psychosocial Needs of Refugee Children and Families in Hackney.* London: City and Hackney Community Services NHS Trust. Child and Adolescent Services.

Rutter, J. (1994). *Refugee Children in the Classroom.* Stoke on Trent: Trentham Books.

Sack, W.H. et al. (1986). The psychiatric effects of massive trauma on Cambodian children; 11, The Family, the home and the school. *Journal of the American Academy of Child Psychiatry* 25, 3377–83.

Shweder, R.A. and Bourne, E.J. (1984). Does the concept of the person vary cross-culturally? In R.A. Shweder and R.A. LeVine (eds) *Culture Theory. Essays on Mind, Self, and Emotion.* Cambridge: Cambridge University Press.

Sluzki, C.E. (1989). Network disruption and network reconstruction in the process of migration/relocation. In F.E. Atkinson (ed.) *Treatment of Torture, Readings and References.* Ottawa.

Summerfield, D. (1995). Raising the dead: war, reparation, and the politics of memory. *British Medical Journal* 311, 495–7.

Turner, S. and Gorst-Unsworth, C. (1990). Psychological sequelae of torture. A descriptive model. *British Journal of Psychiatry* 157, 475–80.

Valtonen, K. (1994). Adaptation of Vietnamese refugees in Finland. *Journal of Refugee Studies* 7, 63–78.

van der Veer, G. (1992). *Counselling and Therapy with Refugees. Psychological Problems of Victims of War, Torture and Repression.* Chichester: Wiley.

Woodcock, J. (1994). The cruelty of waiting. Clinical work with refugee families who have suffered atrocity and separation. Dissertation: Advanced Clinical Training in Family Therapy.

Woodcock, J. (1995). Family therapy with refugees and political exiles. In *Context. Ethnicity, Culture, Race and Family Therapy.* Association for Family Therapy. Basingstoke, Hants: Basingstoke Press.

Conclusion

The critique of trauma programmes developed in this book has already drawn a sharp response. Protagonists of trauma work generally concede that local idioms of distress do exist, but argue that there is, nevertheless, a central 'non-culturally determined' and universal reaction to terrifying events which is captured by the PTSD model. This provides the rationale for using Western psychotherapeutic techniques alongside social interventions and more traditional local healing approaches. This position depends on a particular understanding of the relationship between individuals and the culture in which they live. It assumes that there are core psychological processes in the individual which are independent of culture. According to this view, culture is like the 'icing on the cake': it adds colour and decoration to basically similar individual psychologies. It assumes that culture has a relatively 'shallow' effect in determining the ways in which individuals respond to terrifying, often life threatening, events. Furthermore, it assumes that Western psychiatry and psychology, because they are scientific enterprises, have direct access to this non-cultural core and so their technologies are universally relevant, albeit in need of adjusting to fit different local situations.

An example of this approach is the call by the psychologist Alastair Ager for a 'phased response to psychosocial needs'. Ager suggests that Western agencies should look first to facilitating the work of local supportive structures that help victims in war-affected populations. However, when there are remaining 'unmet needs', he argues, there is a place for 'targeted therapeutic interventions' which are based on Western concepts and approaches

> The delivery of such clinical interventions must clearly take due account of prevailing cultural norms: but ... it is necessarily and fundamentally driven by external technical understandings of psychological process and function. (Ager, 1997)

This position incorporates the traditional model used in cross-cultural psychiatry, in which the individual 'represents a basic psychological or physiological core, surrounded by a series of envelopes, awaiting unpacking by a cultural psychiatrist' (Littlewood, 1986). In the past twenty years this position has been convincingly challenged, both from philosophical and anthropological sources. It has become clear that human emotional experiences, understandings of self and others and approaches to healing are cultural through and through. In their introduction to a volume entitled *Culture and Depression. Studies in the Anthropology and Cross-Cultural Psychiatry of Affect and Disorder*, Arthur Kleinman and Byron Good write:

> So dramatic are the differences in the cultural worlds in which people live that translation of emotional terms requires much more than finding semantic equivalents. Describing how it feels to be grieved or melancholy in another society leads straightway into analysis of different ways of being a person in radically different worlds. (Kleinman and Good, 1985)

Psychotherapy, as conceived and practised along Western lines, is alien to most peoples of the world. Its focus on detached introspection is at odds with the healing practices of most cultures. As White and Marsella indicate:

> the use of 'talk therapy' aimed at altering individual behaviour through the individual's 'insight' into his or her own personality is firmly rooted in a conception of the person as a distinct and independent individual, capable of self-transformation in relative isolation from particular social contexts. (White and Marsella, 1982)

Very different approaches to the issue of personhood and social connectedness exist in many non-Western societies (see chapter 2, this volume). The argument put forward by Ager, and others, that some form of Western psychotherapeutic intervention should be directed at those who suffer most, and are most alienated from those around them, makes no sense. In fact, such people are perhaps the most vulnerable to the negative effects of outside interventions. They need, more than anything else, to be helped to feel a part of their community and to share their grief and suffering with others from that community. The prescription of Western-based interventions can have the effect of increasing alienation.

Another objection, similar in its general thrust, is that our critique somehow denies the anguish and suffering brought about by war for people in the developing world. The suggestion that it is not a good idea to export Western therapeutic techniques to situations of warfare and disaster in developing countries is taken to imply that we do not recognise the suffering involved, or that we are, in some ways, attempting to minimise this suffering. Nothing could be further from the truth. Our critique is based upon a strong desire to avoid further suffering, confusion and alienation for victims of violence. Psychiatric and psychological universalism is premised on an approach which assumes the superiority of Western understandings of suffering and Western approaches to healing. Our central challenge is to this assumption of superiority.

LOOKING TO THE FUTURE: A NEW RESEARCH AGENDA

There is clearly a need for further research in this area. However, studies carried out from *within* the currently dominant framework are inadequate to assess its validity and interrogate the issues raised in this book. For example, studies that have already been undertaken in conjunction with trauma projects have used questionnaires based on the concept of PTSD to estimate the number of 'traumatised' people in a given population. Typically, these provide a reference point for reports to donors which assess project impact in terms of the number of people 'trained' and the number of people 'treated'. (These activities can be carried out in the short time-frame of a typical emergency programme, i.e. nine to twelve months, and therefore make a trauma project an attractive 'emergency package'; as discussed in the introduction, access to donor funds has been relatively easy.) But although such assessments may satisfy the demands of donor accountablility, they clearly do not amount to critical evaluation.

Studies that attempt to make a more serious analysis of the effectiveness of trauma programmes are rare. The assumption that providing counselling, or 'debriefing', is a good thing and the sooner it is offered to victims the better, has, until quite recently, been left unchallenged. However there is a growing literature which questions this assumption. Several reviews of studies on the effectiveness of psychological debriefing have been carried out in Western populations (for example, see Bisson and Deahl, 1994). The results are inconclusive. Indeed, Raphael et al. (1995) cite evidence that some people actually fare worse after receiving this kind of therapy.

When it comes to the export of post-traumatic counselling to non-Western communities there are questions which cannot be answered by quantitative, questionnaire studies alone. The contributors to this book argue that the paradigm at the heart of the current trauma discourse is 'culture bound' and that, as a result, the application of this discourse in non-Western settings is misguided. One of their central concerns is with the potential damage that can be done to local healing and supportive social systems by this application. Questionnaires based on symptom checklists, developed in Western centres, simply cannot encompass these concerns.

We propose that there is now an urgent need for properly organised, multi-disciplinary research and assessment exercises which would look critically at the wider impact of trauma projects. Such work would require a degree of cultural awareness and conceptual sophistication not currently apparent in these projects. In addition, and crucially, such work would require substantial efforts to hear the voice of local people: their priorities, their agendas, their ways of healing and their ways of organising social support.

LOOKING TO THE FUTURE: THE IMPORTANCE OF SOCIAL ASPECTS OF RECOVERY

While the contributors to this book vary greatly in their professional backgrounds and their experiences of the effects of warfare, they all emphasise the social aspects of suffering and healing. They wish to replace the current narrow focus on the intrapsychic with an orientation towards the social and cultural contexts in which people recover from violence. Rethinking the trauma of war means a shift away from projects targeted at individuals, or specific groups of victims such as 'child soldiers' or 'victims of rape'. It involves a concern to help rebuild, or invent anew, the social structures through which lives are lived and found to have a meaning. Normalisation and recovery, from this perspective, touches all aspects of social and economic survival; for children, it involves the context in which development and learning takes place, and for all people, it involves notions of justice, reconciliation and breaking cycles of impunity.

Evidence presented in these chapters suggests that the goals of peace, reconciliation and socio-economic recovery cannot be secured by ad hoc interventions aimed at 'trauma victims' or other groups defined as having special needs. The underlying problems require strategic policy and funding decisions across a range of sectors (including agriculture, finance and credit, health, education and justice) which may in turn involve dialogue with international donors and financial institutions, as well as national and local authorities. Structural adjustment policies that keep children out of school and prevent poor families from accessing health care, and credit policies that hit poor subsistence farmers work against efforts to rebuild safe and secure communities, where the bonds of mutual support have already been weakened. Programmes working with survivors of conflict at community level need to be based on an understanding of how these policies affect people's attempts to rebuild their lives, and where necessary, to use this knowledge to promote their needs and interests through rigorous documentation and advocacy.

We have emphasised the need for interventions such as family tracing and reunification, rebuilding local economic and social infrastructures, and policy analysis and advocacy. But whilst these may be preconditions for social reintegration and reconstruction, the lesson of recent conflicts is that peace and security cannot be consolidated without also breaking the cycle of impunity. Communities recovering from war are increasingly faced by unresolved problems caused by the absence of justice. Establishing a sense of justice within society is a multi-layered task. Crucially, it means that the victims' voices are heard, that their suffering is recognised and that perpetrators are publicly held accountable. But it also extends beyond internal judicial processes to a far broader range of issues such as the burden of debt, the arms trade and inequities in trading relationships between the world's richest and poorest states. This requires a far greater sense of 'social justice' and accountability on the part of the international community than currently exists.

Although the emphasis will vary, questions of justice, reparation and impunity have a direct bearing on consolidating peace at community level, and allowing survivors of conflict to enjoy a perspective on the future that is not coloured by the real or perceived wrongs of the past. We have highlighted the problems caused by Western agencies that impose their own priorities on communities devastated by conflict, and indicated the role that constructive advocacy can play in promoting social and economic rehabilitation. This is familiar territory. However, UN and non-government development agencies are increasingly working in the context of wars fought on the back of civilian abuses. This creates new challenges and dilemmas and will demand new ways of working. Not least, agencies will need to gain a better understanding of the motives and priorities of people of all ages. And whilst there is some experience of dialogue with adults who have suffered injustice and abuse (see chapters 1 and 8), in the case of children, little is understood of the way they deal with their sense of injustice and loss, or indeed how a deep sense of wrongs done to themselves or their families affects their social and emotional development. Perhaps this is because they are rarely asked. However, the words of an eleven-year-old Rwandan boy, whose only surviving relative is a five-year-old sister, found among the bodies of their parents and other family members, leave no room for doubt:

I will hunt the killers to the end of the world. If the government doesn't arrest them, I will kill their children when I grow up. I know the killers, even seventy years from now I will remember how they and their children look. No escape. (Quoted by Mary Kateysi Blewitt)

This is a plea, not for therapy, but for justice. It is a plea that the international community, UN agencies and non-government organisations may well ignore, but at enormous cost.

References

Ager, A. (1997). Tensions in the psychosocial discourse: implications for the planning of interventions with war-affected populations. *Development in Practice* 7 402–7.

Bisson, J.I. and Deahl, M. (1994). Psychological debriefing and prevention of post-traumatic stress. *British Journal of Psychiatry* 165 717–20.

Kleinman, A. and Good, B. (1985). *Culture and Depresion. Studies in the Anthropology and Cross-Cultural Psychiatry of Affect and Disorder.* Berkeley, CA: University of California Press.

Littlewood, R. (1986). Russian dolls and Chinese boxes: an anthropological approach to the implicit models of comparative psychiatry. In J. Cox (ed.) *Transcultural Psychiatry*. London: Croom Helm.

Raphael, B., Meldrum, L. and McFarlane, A.C. (1995). Does debriefing after psychological trauma work? Time for randomised trials. *British Medical Journal* 310 1479–80.

White, G.M. and Marsella, A.J. (1982). Introduction. In A.J. Marsella and G.M. White (eds) *Cultural Conceptions of Mental Health and Therapy*. Dordrecht: Reidal Publishing Company.

Index

Admira 122, 124
Adorno, Theodor 171
Africa Watch 159
African Rights 13
Ager, Alastair 187, 188
Agger, I. 28
aid agencies 34, 56, 58, 144
Aideed, General 14
AIDS 19, 139, 141, 146
Allen, T. 19
Allodi, F. 176
Al Rasheed, M. 21
American Psychiatric Association (APA) 38
Amin, Idi 129
Amnesty International 129
Angola 159, 164–5
Argentina 16, 25, 27
Armed Forces Revolutionary Council, Sierra Leone (AFRC) 80
Arroyo, W. 178
artificial intelligence 44, 51
Ashir, Dr Farooq Ahmed 14
Asia Watch 14
asylum seekers/refugees 20, 21, 170–84
  children 173, 175–6, 178, 183
  and community/family life 34, 173–4, 175–6, 181–2
  language 175–6
  and mental health 176–7, 179–83
  support programmes 179–84

Autonomous Women's Centre Against Sexual Violence 122, 124
avoidance/denial 38, 45, 46

Ba'athist regime, Iraq 26
Bangaladesh 12
Barudy, J. 175
Basoglu, M. 20
behaviourism 44
Ben-Hirsch, Capt. 83, 84
Berry, J. 31
Biko, Steve 57
Bio, Capt. Julius Maada 79
Bisson, J.I. 189
Black Consciousness Movement (South Africa) 57
Blakeney, J. 182
Boekhoorn, P. 177
Boer War 22
Bolton, D. 48
Bosnia
  and disappearances 27
  refugees 174, 178, 183
  separated children 153
  and trauma programmes 28, 32, 112
Bosnian Serbs
  atrocities 10, 11, 14, 16, 24
  rape 12, 122
Bourne, E.J. 54, 181, 188
Boyden, J. 29, 32
Bracewell, W. 123
Bracken, P. 40–1, 41, 180

Index compiled by Sue Carlton

Also published by Free Association Books

MAKING AND BREAKING FAMILIES
Jill Curtis

Making and Breaking Families looks at the many new combinations which have come to constitute a family at the end of the twentieth century: families where the grandparents have become parents of their children's children; families where one or both parents are gay or lesbian, with custody of a child from a previous relationship; 'double' families where perhaps a father shares his time behveen two families.

Society no longer frowns upon divorce, but it does not offer solutions to the problems caused by splitting and merging. This book tries to address some of the issues and questions arising from this quite profound social change. For much of the book the issues are addressed through the words of the many women and men to whom the author talked, as they describe what happened when their marriages broke, and how their new families emerged, sometimes through great difficulties. Often these new families do not at all resemble what used to be generally perceived as A Family, but such families can and do offer the kind of closeness, love and support which we have traditionally associated with family life. The book closes with guidance to the many professionals who might find themselves counselling or giving guidance to families as they go through a demanding period of transition.

JOHN BOWLBY: HIS EARLY LIFE
A Biographical Journey into the Roots of Attatchment Theory
Suzan van Dijken

This insightful treatment of the early years of John Bowlby's life and work sheds light on a number of events that are very much linked to the eventual creation of Attachment Theory but have not been known about or published to date. It also provides much new information about topics that Bowlby was quite reluctant to discuss in detail and yet are clearly connected to Bowlby's later life and theoretical pursuits.

This is a biographical portrait that covers in great depth Bowlby's family of origin, his upbringing, schooling and later education, his little-known work with Cyril Burt, his introduction to psychoanalysis, and his involvement in some of the major events in that world, including the Controversial Discussions between Anna Freud and Melanie Klein.

THE BUTTERFLY AND THE SERPENT
Essays in Psychiatry, Race and Religion

Roland Littlewood

In the last twenty years cultural psychiatry and medical anthropology have become firmly established as academic and clinical disciplines in the UK and North America. Through his research and his writings, Roland Littlewood has emerged as one of the leading and most distinguished contributors to the field of cultural psychiatry. This collection ranges across culture, history, language, religion, and gender and presentmaterial from several continents. All of it provides clear theoretical positions through accessible narrative accounts. For students, teachers and researchers in psychiatry, medicine, social anthropology, ethnic and racial studies, and medical sociology, this provides an outstanding and original overview of this fascinating and rapidly developing area.

PILLAR OF SALT
Gender, Memory, and the Perils of Looking Back

Janice Haaken

The transformation of childhood abuse from distant, forgotten events to salient, remembered experience has prompted much controversy. For some, recovered memories are accurate images of actual events that have been repressed; for others, these are fictions or false memory syndrome. For Janice Haaken, neither position satisfactorily captures the power, the place, and the role of memory for women. Her book shows how women's stories reveal layers of gendered and ambiguous meanings, spanning a wide historical, cultural, literary, and clinical landscape. In making use of the concept of hidden knowledge, clinicians in the 1980s and early 1990s become mediums of a spellbinding genre of tales about the past, from father/daughter incest to Gothic stories of familial barbarism and sadistic orgiastic encounters. She explains how these narratives dramatize more mundane forms of distress in women's lives and how they precipitated rebellious currents within the mental health field. Haaken provides an alternative reading of clinical material, showing how sexual storytelling traverses the symbolic and the 'real' and how the cultural repression of desire remains as problematic for women as does the psychological legacy of trauma.